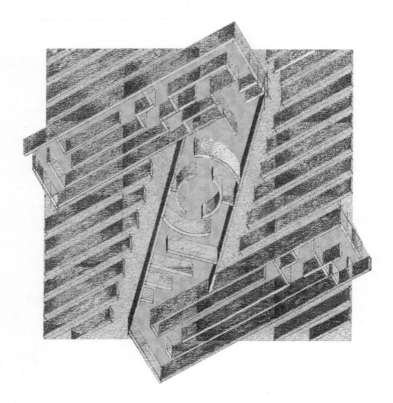

Formal Specification
Using Z
A Modelling Approach

Formal Specification
Using Z
A Modelling Approach

Leonardo Bottaci
John Jones

INTERNATIONAL THOMSON PUBLISHING

I(T)P An International Thomson Publishing Company

London • Bonn • Boston • Madrid • Melbourne • Mexico City • New York • Paris • Singapore
Tokyo • Toronto • Albany, NY • Belmont, CA • Cincinnati, OH • Detroit, MI

Formal Specification Using Z
A Modelling Approach

Commissioning Editor: Samantha Whittaker
Editorial Assistant: Jonathan Simpson

I(T)P   A division of International Thomson Publishing Inc.
        The ITP logo is a trademark under licence

Made in Logotechnics C.P.C. Ltd., Sheffield
    Project Management: Sandra M. Potestà
    Production: Hans-Dieter Rauschner + Team
    Artistic Direction: Stefano E. Potestà
    Cover Illustration: William Smith

First printed 1995

International Thomson Publishing
Berkshire House
168–173 High Holborn
London WC1V 7AA

ISBN   1-850-32109-4

British Library Cataloguing-in-Publication Data
A catalogue record for this book is available from the British Library

Contents

Calogero, Vittoria and Jane

Carole, Margaret and Mog

Preface

This book is about the use of mathematically based techniques for specifying software and hardware systems. The level of formal mathematics required to profit from this book is not very high and indeed there is more to the application of the techniques than formal mathematics. We feel it is important to make a clear distinction between the process of constructing a mathematical model and the translation of that model into a formal notation such as Z or VDM. The use of a formal notation is, of course, challenging and many texts are aimed directly at teaching this activity. Often, however, the most difficult aspect of specifying a system is not the formality of the mathematics involved but the construction of a suitable mathematical model. We use the term 'model' in the sense of applied mathematics rather than its more technical meaning from set-theoretic semantics.

Our experience in teaching formal methods is that students experience significant problems in the initial construction of a suitable mathematical model. It is quite common to encounter the student who can prove, for example, that set union is commutative but who cannot decide if it is appropriate to use a set rather than a function for a particular part of a specification.

Given that the model can have a profound influence on the ease with which a formal specification can be constructed and used for reasoning, it is important to get the model right. Consequently, this book emphasizes equally both model building and the use of a formal notation, in our case Z. As such, it is very much a first course on the use of formal methods and the Z specification language in particular. Much of the material in this book has been given as a one-semester course to second-year undergraduates at the University of Hull.

Structure of the book

The book is in four parts. In the first part we argue the need for formal specification, discuss the general issue of modelling, and give a first example of the development of a model and the subsequent presentation of a specification.

In the second part of the book we present a selection of the basic mathematical tools which are included in Z either as primitives or through the mathematical library. The topics of these chapters are logic, sets, relations, functions, sequences and bags. Each chapter in this part of the book begins with a practical modelling example which requires a specific mathematical object or theory. At the end of the chapter we return to the modelling example, or one very similar, and apply the newly introduced material.

The third part of the book covers extended examples. These are presented to consolidate the material of earlier chapters. In the final part of the book we place formal specification in the context of formal methods and introduce the notion of refinement and proof.

In writing this book we have attempted to accommodate readers with different aptitudes for mathematics. Readers who have undertaken a course on discrete mathematics will find that they can progress rapidly through the early chapters and that they can gain much from Chapter 6, which deals in more depth with the Z notation, on a first reading. The extended examples are each divided into two parts, the second being more challenging than the first.

Standardization of Z

There is, as yet, no definitive version of Z, although it is currently being standardized[4]. For some time [20], and an earlier version of it, has acted as a *de facto* standard. We have attempted to adhere to the draft standard. We have also attempted to adhere to broadly accepted conventions about the presentation of Z specifications.

Examples and exercises

Examples are provided throughout the text to illustrate and reinforce the concepts and definitions presented. Exercises play a similar role and it is for this reason that the exercises are not all collected at the end of each chapter but placed at the point where the reader will profit from taking time out from reading to do some thinking.

We have included three kinds of exercise and these are distinguished in the text by a number of stars. An unstarred exercise is a very routine exercise which closely resembles an example already covered in the text. On the whole these are relatively short exercises which should take at most a few minutes to complete. Complete solutions are provided for all of these exercises.

A one-star exercise is less routine. It typically requires some insight into the material covered so far in the chapter and may well involve the use of the material in a manner that has not yet been explicitly covered. Readers who encounter difficulties with these exercises may find that they can make progress once the chapter has been completed. Complete solutions are provided for all of these exercises.

A two-star exercise is more substantial again. Typically these will be open-ended questions and for this reason it is not practical to give complete solutions to these exercises. They may, for example, be used for tutorial discussion or projects. In some cases we have one or two specific points in mind in setting the exercise, in which case a sketch solution may be included.

Acknowledgements

We would like to thank Mike Spivey for making his LaTeX Z macros for the Z notation available, Xiaoping Jia for the type checker ZTC, and Kurt Dowson for the drawing of the dog used in Chapter 1. We would also like to thank Fethi Rabhi for reviewing a full draft of this book.

I owe a great deal to my father who, before I was old enough to go to school, persuaded me to fill an exercise book by writing successive natural numbers.

lb

I would like to thank Carole for her patience and understanding.

jgj

Shortly after the completion of the manuscript for this book, John Jones died in a climbing accident in the Peruvian Andes. To survive is to live always with the death of your companion.

lb

Chapter 1

Models and Model Building

1.1 Models

A large part of this book is about building mathematical models and since mathematical models have much in common with models in general we begin by discussing these. We, presumably, all have a reasonably good common-sense notion of what a model is. In general, one might say that it is an artefact constructed to represent something. But what do we mean by represent? This is actually quite a profound and difficult question which we will not attempt to answer. Given the aims of this book, we view models from a different perspective. We choose to emphasize the purpose of a model. A model is constructed for a specific purpose and the design of the model will consequently reflect that purpose. The following examples of familiar models illustrate how model and purpose are closely related.

A model is not necessarily a poor substitute for the real thing.

Example 1.1 Model railway: Suppose, for example, that my young daughter has become very interested in trains. She has read all the 'Thomas the Tank Engine' books and now she daydreams about being a station manager and would dearly love to manage a rail network. Even though I may be rich enough to buy her a section of the national rail network, my daughter does not want to manage a real rail network with all the problems of old rolling stock, increasingly strict safety regulations, industrial disputes and lack of investment. She is not interested in passengers and has no patience for the requirements of a national timetable. What my daughter actually wants is to watch a train (of some description) moving along a track and be able to stop and start it and control its journey at will. If she misdirects a train she wants to be able to pick it up and place it on the correct track. A model railway is specifically designed so that my daughter can do all of these things.   □

A model is often used to communicate ideas.

Example 1.2 Architect's model: An architect may use a model to describe a proposed building and hopefully impress a client who will pay for it. The model needs to be constructed with this purpose in mind. This will mean that the model will be to scale and reproduce in detail any architectural features that make the building look distinctive. If the client is concerned about how the proposed building will blend in with the surrounding buildings, these will also be modelled.   □

Our intention in presenting these two examples of very conventional models is to emphasize the similarities between conventional models and mathematical models which we discuss next.

1.2   Mathematical models

A mathematical model is simply a model constructed from mathematical objects such as numbers and sets. Let us continue looking at how an architect uses models.

An architect is concerned not only with the appearance of a building but also has a responsibility, for example, to ensure that the building does not sway too far in gale force winds. The model that shows off the architectural features to clients is clearly not suitable for this purpose. Even if the model could be tested in a wind tunnel, the result would be revealing about the strength of the model rather than the strength of the proposed building.

One solution the architect could adopt is to measure the amount of sway in an identical building. This identical building would essentially be a model as far as the architect is concerned. The problem with this approach, however, is that there may not be an identical building, not to mention the need to wait for gale force winds.

Let us assume that the architect finds a building which is reasonably similar in design, the main difference being that the proposed building is taller. The architect therefore proceeds as follows. The sway in the existing building is measured while moderately strong winds are blowing. This is found to be 100 millimetres, see Figure 1.1. The architect decides that a taller building will be more exposed to the wind and assumes that the degree of movement is proportional to the height of the building. The architect thus also measures the height of the existing building; this is 100 metres. The architect can now calculate that in a strong wind the building sways one millimetre for every metre in height and can produce the formula:

$$sway = height/1000$$

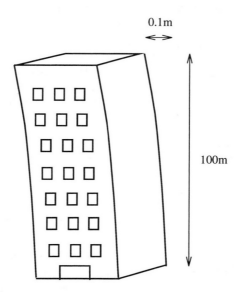

0.1m

100m

Figure 1.1: The movement of a building in a strong wind

The sway also depends on the strength of the wind, so the wind speed is measured and found to be $40km/hr$. Since gale force winds are twice as fast as this the architect assumes the sway will be twice as large, so the complete formula is:

$$sway = 2 \times height/1000$$

This formula is a simple mathematical model of the building. The value of the variable *height* represents the height of the building, and the value of the variable *sway* represents the movement of the building in a gale.[1]

For a variety of reasons, it may seem strange to regard a formula as a model. Let us consider what is probably the most obvious objection. The formula is not made from familiar modelling materials such as cardboard and glue. This boils down to the objection that the model is not tangible or physical. But given the variety of purposes for which models are built, we must surely allow ourselves flexibility in the materials we use; and if a model serves its purpose, does it matter what it is made of?

Another possible objection is that it is not the formula that is the model but rather the existing building. Indeed, had the building been the same height as the proposed building, we would not have needed the formula at all. We cannot, however, always rely on the presence of a suitable physical model. The following example illustrates this.

---

[1] We do not want to suggest that this simple-minded approach is realistic; it is not. Even so, the point of the example does not depend on the detail of the formula.

Example 1.3 Fish population: Fish stocks are declining and we wish to discover how long we can fish the sea given that we have a fixed catch per year. We could attempt to construct a physical model to answer this question. A lake could be stocked with trout, one trout standing for a million fish currently in the sea. Friends would be invited for a fishing weekend and told to catch a certain number of trout per hour, the number of trout representing the number of fish caught in the sea in a year. The number of hours of fishing required to catch all the trout would then correspond to the number of years that we can continue fishing the sea before it is exhausted.   □

Admittedly, the above example caricatures the empirical approach to problem solving but it does highlight the obvious disadvantages of performing an experiment using a physical model of this kind. The model cannot represent, for example, the fact that fish in the sea will reproduce. The lake may contain several hungry pike that will consume a good proportion of the trout. All in all, the outcome of the experiment is likely to be very misleading.

The sort of model we require is a model that specifies the relationships between numbers of fish in the sea in successive years. We are led to consider a mathematical model because the problem we wish to solve is a problem about quantities and how quantities change. The problem is not essentially about fish because we would have a similar problem if we were hunting seals or in fact any species. Let us build a mathematical model involving the quantities of interest to us.

We use variables to represent unknown quantities. Let the fish population at the start of some year t be represented by pop_t. From this number we must subtract the number caught during the year and add the number of fish hatched during the year. This will give us the number of fish remaining at the start of the next year. We have assumed that the number of fish caught each year does not vary. The number hatched, however, is likely to depend on the number of fish available to breed. If we use the variable *birthRate* to represent the rate at which fish reproduce in a year then:

$$birthRate * pop_t$$

is the number of fish that hatch in year t. The population at the start of the next year is thus:

$$pop_{t+1} = pop_t - catch + (birthRate * pop_t)$$

Our model is simply an equation that specifies the relationships between the quantities of interest to us. For example, if the value of the variable *catch* goes up, the value of the variable pop_{t+1} goes down by the same amount. Having constructed our model we are in a position to use it to answer our question about the number of years that we can continue fishing the sea at a given rate. We need to know the current population of fish, the number caught in a year and the birth rate. We can substitute these numbers in the above equation to obtain the population at the start of the next year. We can repeat the process using this new population value to obtain the population in the following year, and so on until we obtain a zero population.

The two previous examples of mathematical models have both involved quantitative concepts, namely height and population, which we have modelled using numbers. Moreover, these numbers were used to represent tangible quantities in the real world. Mathematical models do not always involve numbers, however, and the things that mathematical models model need not be tangible. The following example illustrates this.

Example 1.4 Deductive reasoning: Consider the sort of reasoning made famous by the detective Sherlock Holmes.

> If Jane swam across the river then she would be wet.
> Jane is dry so she did not swim across the river.

At first sight the above deduction (also known as a logical argument) seems correct, but can we be absolutely certain? What sort of model could we use to test the argument? It is not clear that asking someone to swim across a river will prove anything. In order to act out the situation described we require the person representing Jane to be dry. Anyway, we want to test the reasoning in the argument, not the real world.

The correctness of the argument can be justified as follows. Assume Jane swam across the river. We do not know that she did and we may well be wrong, in which case we will retract the assumption, but for now let us assume that she did indeed swim across the river. If she swam across the river then she would be wet. We know, however, that Jane is dry. Something is wrong. We anticipated this problem earlier when we made the assumption that Jane swam across the river. It seems we were wrong to assume she swam across the river and so we must retract this assumption. Now Jane either swam across the river or she did not but whenever we assume she did, we get a contradiction. We must conclude that Jane did not swim across the river. □

In spite of the justification given above, some readers may still refuse to accept the argument because Jane might have worn a dry suit or been provided with a towel immediately on climbing out of the water. These objections are sensible and justified if we are concerned with real people actually swimming across rivers. We are concerned, however, with the correctness of a logical argument, that is, a collection of statements which may or may not be consistent with each other, not a real-life situation. If we set ourselves the task of determining whether a collection of statements is consistent, we must take the statements at face value. If we do not accept the statements as given, where do we stop? It might be possible to argue that the water in the river is polluted in such a way that it has a very high surface tension, so much so that it loses the property of being wet. The consequence of refusing to accept the statements at face value is that they become meaningless and consequently the question of correctness is rendered meaningless.

This is a point that many students find troublesome, so to let us make the same point using another example. Consider the statements:

> Lanky is twice as tall as Shorty.
> Lanky is 2m tall.

It would be reasonable to conclude that Shorty is 1m tall. In this situation, we would not be persuaded by anyone who claimed that Shorty is in fact 1.5m tall because the statement that Lanky is twice as tall as Shorty is, for example, an exaggeration.

To return to the original argument, an examination of the justification we used to show its correctness will reveal that this justification does not depend on the meaning of the statements in the argument. This is clear when we consider that the same justification could be used to show the correctness of a superficially different argument.

> If Jane eats meat then she is not a vegetarian.
> Jane is a vegetarian so she does not eat meat.

Because this second argument has the same structure as the first one, we can justify it with essentially the same justification. The required model should thus be sensitive only to the structure of the argument and not to the meanings of the statements it contains. Such a model can be constructed by using logic. Let P stand for a statement such as 'Jane swam the river' or 'Jane eats meat' and let Q stand for 'Jane is wet' and 'Jane is not a vegetarian'; then we can model both arguments using a more general argument:

if we accept the statement:

> *the truth of P implies the truth of Q*

and the statement:

> *Q is not true*

we are logically obliged to accept the statement:

> *P is not true*

1.3   The role of mathematical models

In many situations the advantages of mathematical models are obvious. The example of the lake stocked with trout illustrates how mathematical models put the modeller in complete control of the model. The intangibility of mathematical models makes them immune from the complexities and uncertainties of the real world.

We would not want to suggest, however, that mathematical models are always superior to physical models. In many situations, we do not understand enough about a problem to rely entirely on mathematical models. In the design of an aircraft, for example, complex mathematical models of the aerodynamics of the aircraft are used to ensure that a proposed aircraft will actually fly when it is built. It is rare, however, that the first aircraft built from the design is the aircraft delivered to the customer. The testing performed by a test pilot will lead to many improvements which could not have been achieved through mathematical models.

Mathematical models are typically used early in the problem solving process to ensure that the solution is basically sound. Problems of detail are often tackled with a prototype or by experimentation with the real problem situation. The place of mathematical models in the problem solving process is shown in Figure 1.2. The arrows pointing down the page indicate the ideal progression

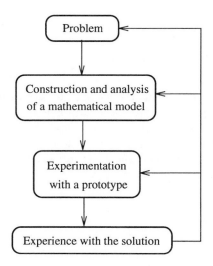

Figure 1.2: The place of mathematical models in the problem solving process

of the various stages of the problem solving process. The other arrows indicate that results from the later stages of the process can sometimes require changes or additions to what has been done in the earlier stages.

1.4 The modelling process: constructing a good model

An illustration of the relationship between a subject and a model of that subject is shown in Figure 1.3. The modelling process starts with the subject we wish to model. The subject may be a real-world object or situation or something hypothetical. The purpose of our model will dictate which aspects of the

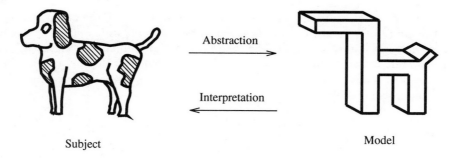

Figure 1.3: The relationship between a subject and a model

subject are required in the model and which can be ignored. This process of selecting relevant aspects is known as abstraction. To abstract is to select what is relevant and to ignore what is irrelevant. Through abstraction we can arrive at a model that suits our purpose and typically one that is much simpler and more manageable than the corresponding subject.

A mathematical model will at some stage be used to produce a result which must be related to the real world. For example, if $pop_8 = 0$ in the fish population model, this is taken to mean that in 8 years the population of fish will be exhausted. This is an interpretation of a result in the model. Interpretation is the inverse process to abstraction. Clearly, abstraction and interpretation must be consistent with each other.

Validity of the model

The abstraction process is of vital importance. The consequences of getting it wrong are that although we may have built a model, that model will not accurately represent what was intended. Figure 1.4 is an illustration of the idea of an inaccurate model. To consider a concrete example, we return to the fish population model where fish reproduction was modelled by assuming that the number of fish hatched in a year is proportional to the population in that year. This would be incorrect if the offspring are not hatched until two years after conception,[2] that is, the fish hatched in any one year are the offspring of fish that were alive two years before. In this respect, the model is clearly wrong since it assumes that the contribution to the population in the next year is proportional to the population in the current year. The model can be corrected by ensuring that the birth rate is multiplied by the population in the appropriate year. The new model is:

$$pop_{t+1} = pop_t - catch + (birthRate * pop_{t-1})$$

---

[2]Fish eggs are fertilized outside the body of the female.

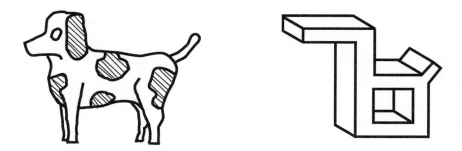

Figure 1.4: An invalid model

The process of checking that we have abstracted correctly and built the right model for our purpose is known as validation. To validate a model it is necessary to compare the model with reality. This typically requires specialist real-world or domain knowledge in addition to the mathematical knowledge required to build a mathematical model.

Consistency of the model

Sometimes it is obvious that there is something wrong with a model without any specialist knowledge of the thing being modelled. Figure 1.5 illustrates

Figure 1.5: An inconsistent model

the idea of an intrinsically flawed model. For a concrete example, let us return once more to fish populations. We modelled the fish caught in a year by a constant number that does not depend on the population. This is unrealistic because it makes no allowance for the fact that there might not be sufficient fish to allow the fishermen to catch that number. We can illustrate this problem in the model by substituting the following values:

$$pop_0 = 10000 \quad pop_1 = 10000 \quad catch = 30000 \quad birthRate = 1$$

The resulting expression for pop_2 is:

$$10000 - 30000 + 10000$$

which is a negative number and clearly nonsense. Implicit in the population model is the fact that:

$$pop_t \geq 0$$

for all t.

We thus have a contradiction between the condition that $pop_t \geq 0$ for all t and $pop_2 = -10000$. A model that is flawed in this way is said to be inconsistent. An inconsistent model is a special case of an invalid model. An invalid model does not model what is intended. It may, however, model some other subject. In contrast, an inconsistent model does not model any possible subject. An inconsistent mathematical model can be thought of as an empty model because there are no mathematical objects (in this case, numbers) that satisfy the conditions of the model.

Exercise 1.1 * We can improve the fish population model by assuming that the number of fish caught in a year is proportional to the population except that it does not exceed a fixed quota. Modify the population model to represent this assumption.   □

Simplicity of the model

Poor use of abstraction can lead to the inclusion of features that are irrelevant to the model's purpose although they are present in the subject. Figure 1.6 is an illustration of this.

Figure 1.6: An overly complex model

As an example of a model that is more complex than its purpose demands, consider the following model of a system used for controlling access to a car park. The car park is barrier controlled and the barrier does not open to let a car into the car park unless there is room. The car park has a fixed capacity of 500 spaces. The purpose of the model is to specify exactly when the barrier should open and when it should not. We can imagine that the specification will be used to commission the design and construction of a real barrier system.

Each space in the car park is either vacant or occupied. For our purpose, we can therefore model a space by a variable which has one of two values. We model each of the 500 spaces in this way with the result that our model consists of 500 variables. When the car park is empty, every variable should have the value that represents a vacant space. When a car enters the car park and occupies a space, one of the variables representing a vacant space must take a value representing an occupied space. If there is no such variable in the model, the barrier should not open.

Exercise 1.2 * Simplify the above model by drastically reducing the number of variables. □

Exercise 1.3 * Develop a model to control bank account deposits and withdrawals. Any amount of money can be deposited but a withdrawal must not allow the account to go overdrawn. Hint: develop the model constructed as an answer to the previous exercise. □

A model that contains irrelevant features is undesirable. Models are often constructed for explaining or teaching something and the presence of inessential features will make the model more complex than it need be. In addition, there will be a need to explain which parts of the model are essential and which are not.

1.5 State-based models

The remainder of this book concerns the construction of mathematical models based around the concept of state. These models have three main characteristics: inputs, outputs and state. Each part is described in terms of mathematical objects. The following example illustrates the idea of a state-based model.

Example 1.5 Consider a model of a bank cash machine, also known as an automated teller machine. The inputs to the machine consist of a bank card, a personal identification number (PIN) and one or more options from a menu. The outputs of the machine are various messages, hopefully some cash and a previously inserted card.

Now let us suppose that we attempt to specify the behaviour of the cash machine by relating specific inputs to specific outputs. On a certain day, I may insert my card, my PIN number and a request for £200, and the machine duly outputs £200 and my card. We might assume that we have identified a small part of the machine's input/output behaviour but this is not so. On another day, I may enter precisely the same inputs to the machine without receiving the same outputs, because, for example the machine has insufficient money. This means that we cannot properly specify the behaviour of the machine without introducing the notion of the state of the machine. We are forced to specify the output of the machine in terms of the input and the machine state rather than the input alone.   □

Figure 1.7: The behaviour of the machine depends on its state as well as the input

Many kinds of machine or system require the use of the notion of state in order to accurately describe their behaviour. A question arises as to how we pick the states to use in a model. There are no hard and fast rules for doing this. If we are producing a model of a system then we should identify the states that suit the purpose of the model and ignore states that are not relevant. For example, when the cash machine is taken out of service it will be in a state in which it accepts no inputs. If, however, we are constructing a model of the normal behaviour of a cash machine then this state can be ignored. A state in the model may correspond to a group of states in the system. This is a good modelling strategy when the system has many states and the differences between some states are not relevant to the purpose of the model.

We can illustrate this strategy by returning to the cash machine example. Suppose we wish to construct a model of the cash machine with the purpose of describing its behaviour from the point of view of a potential user of the machine. We might construct such a model to analyse the user friendliness of the cash machine. A simple user-oriented state-based model of a cash machine

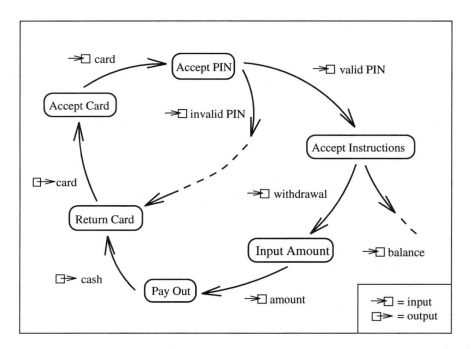

Figure 1.8: A simple user-oriented state-based model of a cash dispensing machine

is illustrated in Figure 1.8. The machine is initially in a state in which it will accept only one kind of input, a bank card. Customers are alerted to the fact that the machine is in this state by a message inviting customers to insert a card. Once a card has been inserted, the machine will not accept another card until that card is removed; it has changed state. In this new state, the machine expects the customer to enter a personal identification number. If the number entered is valid, the customer may proceed to withdraw some cash. Once a transaction is over, the machine returns the card and normally returns to a state in which it expects a card to be inserted.

In the model illustrated in Figure 1.8, we have identified a number of states, each corresponding to a group of similar states in the machine. We stress that the states in a single group are similar from our point of view only; we might choose to group states differently if we were producing a different model. An important point to bear in mind is that states are chosen to provide a convenient means of relating inputs to outputs.

Operations

It is useful to think of the behaviour of a state-based model in terms of operations. An operation is a part of the behaviour that cannot be broken down into smaller parts. If an operation is performed then it is performed in its entirety. Inserting a card into the cash machine is an operation in our model and so is the input of the pin number, even though in reality it may involve several key presses. In the diagram of the cash machine model (Figure 1.8), the arrows indicate operations.

In general, an operation has input, produces output and causes a state change, but not all operations have all three features. For example, there might be no state change in our model when we ask the machine for a bank balance. Similarly, an operation might not produce an output or require input. In Figure 1.8 operations are labelled with an input or an output. If an operation is labelled with an input, it indicates that the operation occurs only if that input is received. If an operation is labelled with an output, that is the output associated with that operation.

Modelling the inputs and outputs of the cash machine

To construct a model of the cash machine we must model the inputs and outputs. Let us start with the bank card. There is no ready-made mathematical object that can be obviously used to model the bank card. We might initially consider modelling each card with a number; we might even consider using the customer's account number. This would not, however, be a wise choice. For example, a bank might wish to issue two cards for the same account. Even if we could ensure that the numbers used were unique, numbers have many properties that bank cards do not. For example, two numbers can be added together to produce a third; clearly this operation is meaningless for bank cards.

We are in a similar situation with the personal identification number (PIN) which a customer must enter to verify the card. Since it is a number, it seems obvious that it should be modelled using a number. But again, this is not a wise choice. The personal identification number is essentially a password and there is nothing intrinsically numeric about it, which means that in the future the bank may decide to issue customers with a personal identification code consisting of numbers and letters, or even require a signature for verification.

To model the output of the machine we must model cash. Again, the use of numbers comes to mind but after our consideration of bank cards and personal identification numbers, we would be wary of using numbers without some thought. The complications surrounding cash include: different currencies, the fact that 100 pennies are equivalent to one pound, the fact that there is no seven-pound note, and so on.[3] These complications, however, are not of the

---

[3] The biggest problem with cash is, of course, getting enough of it.

same kind as those associated with the use of a number to model a bank card or a personal identification number. These complications are really to do with the details of cash which is itself a representation of money. It is possible to abstract away from all these complications and model the concept of monetary value. This is a quantity, something that can be counted, and therefore suitable for modelling as a number.

This is probably a good place to stress a general point about the use of numbers in mathematical models. Less experienced modellers have a tendency to overuse numbers, probably because they are familiar objects. In fact, numbers should be used only in situations where their numerical properties and operations are relevant. A useful design heuristic for model building is: 'numbers should be used only for counting and ordering'.

To model bank cards and personal identification numbers it is best to use objects that have no operations defined on them other than those pertaining to bank cards and personal identification numbers. The techniques for doing this are the subject of a good part of this book and so we will not say very much about it here. Let us assume for the moment that we have a set of unique values:

$$\{ bankCard1,\ bankCard2,\ bankCard3, \ldots \}$$

to represent bank cards, and an analogous set:

$$\{ pin1,\ pin2,\ pin3, \ldots \}$$

to represent personal identification numbers. It is important to appreciate that elements such as *bankCard*1 are values and not names of values. When we say 'let $x = 3$', for example, x is a name and 3 is a value.

Modelling states

The construction of suitable state descriptions is an important part of model building and can be seen in terms of making relevant observations. For example, we might observe that the machine expects different kinds of inputs in different states. We might also observe that the cash held in the machine will change with some state changes. We might thus take these two particular observations:

- the kind of input the machine is expecting, and

- the amount of cash held,

as the basis for describing the required states.

We typically model the possible values of each observation as a set of values. A set of values to model the possible kinds of input might be:

$$\{ anyBankCard,\ anyPin,\ anyInstruction,\ noInput, \ldots \}$$

If we use a number to model the monetary value of the cash held then the following two values:

> *anyBankCard* 800

represent a possible state of the cash machine. The machine is expecting a card to be inserted and holds £800 in cash. The following two values:

> *anyPin* 800

represent a cash machine which is waiting for a PIN number to be input. The machine also holds £800 in cash. If we assume that £20 has been withdrawn and the card returned, then the state of the machine is represented by the two values:

> *anyBankCard* 780

Recall the earlier discussion concerning the modelling process and in particular the relationship between the model and the subject modelled (§1.4). We said that an invalid model does not represent what is intended. If we consider the two values:

> *anyBankCard* 0

we notice that these should not be a state in our model. The cash machine will not accept a bank card when it has run out of cash and so it is not a state that we ever want to represent. If we were to allow these two values to constitute one of the states of our model then the model would be invalid.

The exclusion of invalid states is a crucial part of building state-based models. In order to exclude invalid states we impose conditions or restrictions on the values of the observations. Often these conditions are expressed in terms of the values of other observations. For example:

> $expectedInput = anyBankCard$ implies $cashHeld > 0$

Notice that to make it convenient to express this condition, we have given names to the two values of the observations of the state, *expectedInput* and *cashHeld*.

Let us spell out exactly what the above condition means. If the *expectedInput* is *anyBankCard* then the value *cashHeld* must be greater than zero. That seems simple enough, but what if the value *expectedInput* is not *anyBankCard*? In this case, the condition above, because of the meaning of 'implies'[4], imposes no restriction on the value *cashHeld*. The reader may not be entirely happy with the idea that when *expectedInput* is not *anyBankCard*, *cashHeld* can be any

---

[4]Strictly speaking, it is the meaning of the word 'implies' used in its logical sense. We devote Chapter 3 to logic.

value and may in fact be negative. A negative value is clearly not acceptable for the amount of money held in the machine.

If we wish to disallow negative values for *cashHeld*, we can do so by adding another condition:

$$cashHeld \geq 0$$

This condition makes no reference to any other state observation and so it is applicable irrespective of the values of other observations.

The set of states that we want to include in our model is called the *state space*. An important part of defining the model is specifying the rules or conditions that specify which combinations of values constitute a state in the state space and which combinations of values should never occur. These conditions are called the *state invariant*.

Modelling the changes of state

Once we have included sufficient conditions in the state invariant and thereby specified the state space, we can begin to specify the state changes. To model a change of state we describe two states, the state before the change (known as the before-state) and the state after the change (known as the after-state). In this way we avoid modelling, or abstract away from, how the change is to be achieved. The skill in building a model is to ensure that the states and state changes are chosen to suit the purpose of the model and in such a way that the details of how a state change takes place are not relevant to that purpose. An example state change is illustrated in Figure 1.9.

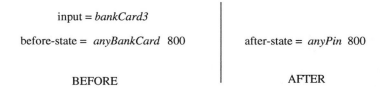

input = *bankCard3*

before-state = *anyBankCard* 800   after-state = *anyPin* 800

BEFORE   AFTER

Figure 1.9: Modelling an operation using 'before' and 'after' states

In practice, it is convenient to specify a group of similar state changes in a single description. We do this by using variables. For example:

input is a bank card, and
before-state = (*anyBankCard, cashHeld*) where *cashHeld* > 0, and
after-state = (*anyPin, cashHeld*)

Notice that by using the variable *cashHeld* to represent a number that is not precisely determined, we can specify that the before-state is any one of a number of states that conforms to the given condition. One useful thing about using a variable like this is that we do not need to specify a value for the amount of cash in the machine in order to specify the state change. We can see from the description that the value of the *cashHeld* observation does not change during this operation.

In general terms, therefore, a description of an operation has the following form:

> conditions on the input, and
> conditions on the before-state, and
> conditions on the after-state, and
> conditions on the output

If we specify that the before and after states are equal then we have a description of an operation in which the state does not change.

To summarize, the construction of a state-based model requires the following steps:

1. Identify the operations.

2. Model the inputs and outputs.

3. Model the states by identifying the observations of the state and specifying the values that each observation may take. We do this using conditions that we call the state invariant. The set of allowable states is called the state space.

4. Operations are specified in terms of conditions on inputs, outputs and before and after states.

Exercise 1.4 ** Draw a diagram similar to Figure 1.8 to model a drinks dispensing machine. Assume that the machine can provide both tea and coffee, each with or without milk and sugar. It does not provide a drink if any of the ingredients are exhausted. Tea costs 15p and coffee costs 20p. The machine accepts 5p, 10p and 20p coins and gives change if available.   □

This section has presented an overview of how to construct a state-based mathematical model. The overview has concentrated on the concepts involved and used very little mathematics. In the rest of the book we introduce the mathematics necessary to construct a formal mathematical state-based model.

1.6   Applicability of state-based models

Let us stand back a bit and review what has been said so far in this chapter. We have argued for mathematical models, described some desirable properties for them and looked in some detail at one kind of model, a state-based model. So far so good, but what if the subject we wish to model does not resemble a cash machine in the sense that it does not obviously fit the state-based model stereotype?

There are two issues that are important here. Firstly, the state-based model is clearly suited to modelling subjects with attributes that take discrete values. For the most part, computer hardware and software systems fall into this category and such systems are rapidly becoming ubiquitous. Secondly, subjects with attributes that take continuous values may still be usefully modelled using a state-based approach. For example, as I write this paragraph I look out onto my window ledge and notice that the snow is 20mm deep. When I first came into my office, bright and early this morning, I noted that the snow was only 10mm deep. If I model the depth of snow using an integer then the falling of the snow can be viewed as a state change and modelled using two integers; one integer is the depth before the state change and the other is the depth after.

Admittedly, this seems to be a crude way of describing the steadily increasing depth of snow. We describe the situation before the change and the situation after, but not the process by which the change takes place. The reader might well feel that we are not modelling what is really happening. Suppose, for the sake of argument, that the 10mm increase in the depth of the snow was caused by a fall of 5mm and the wind blowing an additional 5mm. Our 'net change' description completely ignores this detail. How can we be sure, one might argue, that this detail is not important in a model?

The answer is, of course, that if the distinction between the snow that falls and the snow that is blown is important then we must model that distinction, and it follows that our simple state change description, a single 10mm increase in the depth of snow, is indeed inadequate. The remedy, however, is simply to introduce additional states and describe the overall change as consisting of two changes, each, of course, defined in terms of the net change. We describe a state change in which the depth of snow increases by 5mm due to the fall of snow and another state change in which the depth of snow increases by 5mm due to the wind. In many situations, we can model more and more detail about the way in which a change takes place without having to use any mechanism other than describing the net change between two states. We simply choose the states in such a way that they are sufficiently discriminating.

1.7   Models and software development

Developing software is a difficult and time-consuming activity. Part of the reason for this is that programming languages require the programmer to specify in considerable detail how a problem will be solved. The consequence of having to work in this way is that while the programmer is concentrating on the detail of the solution, he or she is unable to think adequately about the overall problem.

Readers without experience of developing a substantial piece of software may not have personally experienced this difficulty. The difficulty, however, is not limited to the realm of software development. Indeed, it is a problem common to all practical and especially engineering activities. Suppose, for example, that you are building a house and that you are currently laying the bricks for the bathroom wall. Imagine, further, that you are concentrating on laying a straight line of bricks and, at the same time, you are laying the bricks briskly in order to finish the wall before the cement dries. You would not, at this stage, want to have to make a decision about how many doors the bathroom should have. Obviously, plans for the whole house should have been prepared before construction began. In general, a task should be specified before it is implemented and software development is no different in this respect.

Software specifications can be written in a natural language such as English and indeed many are. A natural language has the advantage that it is well known, it is very expressive and requires no special training to use. Often diagrams are used; many kinds are possible, ranging from informal sketches to carefully drawn diagrams that adhere to strict rules. Diagrams, certainly the informal kind, possess much the same advantages as natural language.

A disadvantage of natural languages and informal diagrams is that they lack precision. We have all had someone read something that we have written and understand it in a very different way from what was intended. Here is an example of an ambiguous specification.

> The high-pressure signal must be sent when the pressure exceeds the safety limit and the low-pressure signal must be sent when the pressure falls to the low-pressure value.

Problems with this statement include:

- If we send the high-pressure signal whatever the pressure then we will be satisfying the condition to send the signal when the pressure exceeds the safety limit. Is this an acceptable reading of the specification? The same problem arises with the low-pressure signal.

- Suppose the pressure is lower than the low-pressure value and subsequently rises (rather than falls) to the low-pressure value. Should the low-pressure signal be sent in this situation?

- Is it acceptable to assume that the signals are mutually exclusive or is it possible, for example, that the high-pressure value is lower than the low-pressure value?

No matter how careful we are in using a natural language, we cannot entirely control the way in which a reader interprets what is written. Unless we can completely control the interpretation, there is always the risk of ambiguity.

Mathematical models provide a solution to this problem because they can be expressed unambiguously. This is because mathematical objects, numbers, sets, functions and so on, the basic components of mathematical models, each have a precise meaning. The user of a mathematical model thus has essentially no choice in the way in which he or she interprets that model. Because mathematical models are precise they can be used for rigorous logical reasoning. For example, from a suitable mathematical specification of how the high and low-pressure signals described above should be generated we could answer questions such as whether both signals may ever be sent at the same time.

Having said that the user of a mathematical model has no choice in the way in which it is interpreted, we lose this advantage if we express the model in an informal language such as English. For example, a set of numbers could be described in English as:

the set of numbers from 3 to 7

but this description is not precise because it is not clear, for example, whether the set of numbers should contain only whole numbers, nor is it clear whether the limits 3 and 7 are to be included in the set. Such problems do not arise with the use of a formal mathematical notation such as $\{3, 4, 5, 6, 7\}$ or $\{x : \mathbb{Z} \mid 3 \leq x \leq 7\}$.

To produce an unambiguous model or specification we must express that model in a formal mathematical notation. The notation we will use in this book is known as Z. It is important to bear in mind that although a mathematical model is not precisely described until it is expressed in a formal notation, the creation of the model and its expression in a formal notation are two logically distinct activities.

1.8 Summary

- This chapter has introduced the basic ideas of model building, concentrating on mathematical models. We have argued that a mathematical model is simply a model constructed from abstract mathematical objects.

- The purpose of the model is a crucial concept in model building. Almost every aspect of a model can be justified by appeal to its purpose. If our purpose is to model the appearance of an object, it may be appropriate to build a model using cardboard and glue. If our purpose is to model its behaviour, a mathematical model may be more appropriate.

- The relationship between a subject and a model can be one of several kinds. An invalid model models some subject (perhaps hypothetical) that is not the subject intended. An inconsistent model cannot model any subject. Above all, a model should be as simple as its purpose allows.

- Mathematical models may contain objects other than numbers, and in fact we can create objects as required. Numbers should be used only for counting.

- We have characterized a particular kind of model by describing the concepts of input, output and state. These concepts are important since they provide a framework around which an important class of model can be based.

- Mathematical state-based models can be used to specify software systems.

Chapter 2

A First Example of Modelling and Specification in Z

In this chapter we develop a simple specification in Z for part of a system controlling access to a car park. We begin by identifying the purpose of the specification. Then, we explore the appropriate modelling techniques and develop an informal description of the model. Finally, this model is used as the basis of a complete specification in Z.

The formal specification of a system occurs ideally after requirements capture and analysis has been performed. In this ideal situation, the requirements are accepted uncritically. In practice, it is possible that a lack of precision or inconsistencies in the requirements are uncovered during the process of specifying the system. This is not surprising given the attention to detail that is necessary in order to produce a formal specification, and it can be argued that this is one of the benefits of producing a formal specification. Given that the purpose of this book is to teach formal modelling and specification rather than requirements analysis, we will simply state requirements with little or no analysis or justification.

2.1 Car park: first description

In many car parks, entry is controlled by an automatic barrier, so that a customer may enter the car park only if there is space. Some car parks also make provision for pass holders who have reserved spaces. At the entrance there is a special machine which validates season passes. The entrance barrier will lift

23

on the presentation of a valid pass, and the pass is returned. At the exit, they again present their pass.

A car park clearly has a maximum capacity, so to ensure that pass holders may always enter, spaces are reserved for them. Ordinary customers, however, must compete for spaces, and they may not always be able to enter the car park. Thus, when we refer to the capacity of the car park we are referring to the limit on the number of ordinary cars that may be in the car park.

In this chapter we shall construct a model of the control system for the barriers of the car park. The model we identify will ensure that:

- an ordinary customer is admitted if there is a space available, and is refused entry if there is not;

- a pass holder may always park in the car park.

The specific mechanisms for entry and exit and the physical organization of the car park need not concern us, nor will we address payment.

It is clear that a state-based model is required for our purpose. The distinct operations the model must include are suggested naturally by events that take place at the barriers:

- ordinary customer arriving

- ordinary customer departing

- pass holder arriving

- pass holder departing.

Let us consider what implications these operations have for the state space.

Identifying the state space

To identify an appropriate state space for the model, we must first identify the observations of the state we wish to make. Let us begin with ordinary customers, who do not have a pass. Whether an ordinary customer arriving at the entrance barrier is admitted depends on whether there is a space, which in turn depends on the number of ordinary cars in the car park and the capacity of the car park. The number of ordinary cars in the car park is therefore one of the observations we shall make. Clearly, the values of this observation may not be arbitrary. We have already noted that the number of ordinary cars present must not exceed the capacity of the car park. In addition, it obviously cannot be less than zero. These restrictions will be part of the state invariant.

Now let us consider pass holders. We shall assume that there is a space reserved for every pass holder. It might then seem that the role of a pass is simply to distinguish a pass holder from an ordinary customer. It is not quite that simple, however. This viewpoint is only appropriate if, in any given state of the car park, each pass car (a car admitted by use of a pass) is accounted for by a different pass. Unfortunately, we cannot guarantee this. For example, it would be possible for an unscrupulous pass holder to take a car in with his pass, walk out, and later take in a different car using the same pass. To avoid this possibility, we have to be able to determine whether a pass already accounts for a car in the car park; let us say such a pass is 'in use'. Thus, the model must record those passes that are in use. An appropriate modelling technique is to define a set of passes in use. There is no need for the specification to say anything about what a pass is, or how it may be represented. This means that the members of the set of passes in use may be any objects we can tell apart. We shall thus assume a set of values for passes.

Thus, we may make two observations of the state of the car park in the model:

- a number that represents the number of ordinary cars in the car park, and

- a set of passes that represents the passes in use in the car park.

The state invariant includes the conditions:

- The number of ordinary cars in the car park cannot be less than zero.

- The number of ordinary cars in the car park must be less than or equal to the capacity of the car park.

In addition, we note that the capacity of the car park cannot be less than zero, otherwise our model would be inconsistent.

The model of the car park with the car park in a particular state is illustrated in Figure 2.1.[1] Figures 2.2–2.4 show some illegal states of the car park, that is, states which are not in the state space.

Exercise 2.1 * Why are the states illustrated in Figures 2.2–2.4 illegal?   □

The operations of the system

We know from Chapter 1 that an operation of the system will be described in terms of inputs, outputs and the effect it has on the state of the system. An operation can have more than one outcome. For example, an ordinary customer arriving at the entrance may be either admitted, or refused entry

---

[1] In order to be able to depict the passes we have had to invent some values, $p0, \ldots, p3$, but we will not use these in the specification.

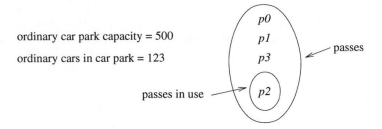

Figure 2.1: The car park in a legal state

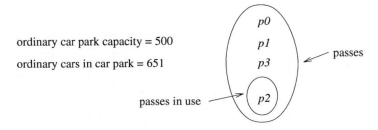

Figure 2.2: The car park in an illegal state

because the car park is full. In this example, every operation will have an output which we interpret as a report on the outcome of the operation. The expected outcome will yield the report 'success'. Other outcomes will yield a value that explains the outcome. You may, if you like, think of these latter reports as error messages.

A report is an object in the model, so we must have a set of values from which those objects may be selected. We shall want to state specific reports for the various operations, so for this set we shall need to say what its members are.

Arrival of an ordinary customer

Let us consider an ordinary customer arriving at the entrance barrier. The outcome will depend on the state of the car park, so let us consider the various possibilities. If there is a space available the barrier opens and the number of ordinary cars in the car park increases by one. On the other hand, if there are no spaces available for ordinary customers, the barrier remains closed, and the number of ordinary cars in the car park remains the same. We shall refer to

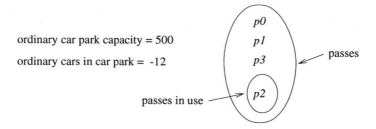

Figure 2.3: The car park in an illegal state

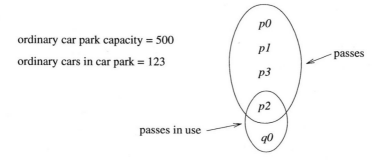

Figure 2.4: The car park in an illegal state

these possibilities as *subcases*, and call the criteria that identify a particular subcase a *subcase property*. Which of these subcases applies depends only on the state of the car park, so this operation will have no inputs.

The subcase in which an ordinary customer may be admitted is identified by the property:

- The number of ordinary cars in the car park is less than the car park capacity.

The state change that takes place in this subcase is such that the after-state is like the before-state except that the count of ordinary cars increases by one. This state transition is illustrated for the car park of Figure 2.1 in Figure 2.5. The report in this subcase is simply that the operation was successful.

The subcase in which the ordinary customer is refused entry is identified by the subcase property:

- The number of ordinary cars in the car park equals the car park capacity.

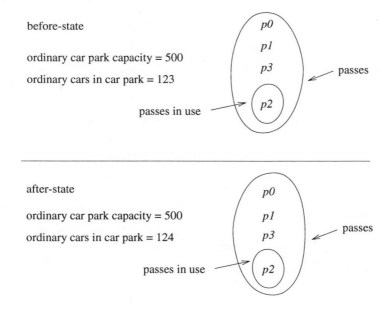

before-state

ordinary car park capacity = 500

ordinary cars in car park = 123

passes in use

p0
p1
p3
p2

passes

after-state

ordinary car park capacity = 500

ordinary cars in car park = 124

passes in use

p0
p1
p3
p2

passes

Figure 2.5: State transition for an ordinary customer entering the car park

In this case, the after-state is the same as the before-state, and the report is that the ordinary car park is full.

We have described two subcases for the arrival operation, each dealing with a group of states. Are there any other groups of states that we have not considered? The answer is no, because either the car park is full or it is not full. We may thus be confident that we have not forgotten some special case for this operation.

Departure of an ordinary customer

When an ordinary customer leaves, we must reduce the count of ordinary cars in the car park by one. This is possible only if the number of ordinary cars in the car park is greater than zero. Thus, there are also two subcases for this operation. The outcome depends only on the state of the car park, so the operation has no inputs.

The subcase in which the ordinary customer leaves the car park is identified by the subcase property:

- The number of ordinary cars in the car park is greater than zero.

In the after-state the number of ordinary cars is one less than in the before-state. The report is that the operation is successful. The other subcase of this operation is identified by the subcase property:

- The number of ordinary cars in the car park is equal to zero.

In this case, the after-state is the same as the before-state, and the report is that there are no ordinary cars in the car park.

In a similar manner to the argument given above for the arrival operation, it is fairly clear that we have taken all possibilities into account for this operation.

Exercise 2.2 * Comment on the following argument.

> In a real car park, the operation for an ordinary customer wanting to leave could be invoked only if there actually was an ordinary customer wanting to leave. That is, this operation can happen only when it is appropriate. Thus, its description needs only one case and there need be no subcase property.

$\square$

Arrival of a pass holder

We have already argued that this operation will depend on the identity of the pass, so that this must be given as an input, and we have to check whether the pass is in use. The subcase in which the pass holder is admitted is defined by the subcase property:

- The pass is not in the set of passes in use.

The state transition is such that in the after-state the set of passes in use comprises all those in use in the before-state, with the addition of the pass just proffered. Figure 2.6 illustrates this change of state for the car park state illustrated in Figure 2.1. The report is that this subcase of the operation is successful.

The subcase in which the pass holder is refused entry is defined by the subcase property:

- The pass is in the set of passes in use.

In this case the after-state is the same as the before-state, and the report is that the pass is in use.

In states, in which the pass that is offered is not in use, this operation will model the entry of the pass holder. In states, in which the pass offered is already in use, the operation models the refusal to admit the pass holder. Since either a pass is in use or it is not, we have clearly considered all cases.

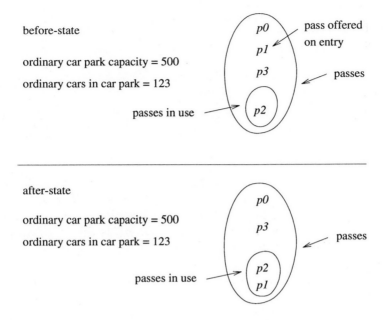

Figure 2.6: State transition for pass holder entering the car park

Departure of a pass holder

A pass holder must show his or her pass on leaving, so this operation will have a pass as input. To ensure that the record of the passes currently in use remains accurate, this pass must be taken out of the set of passes in use. This is only possible if it is a member of that set. Thus, this operation has two subcases. The first subcase is characterized by the property:

- The pass is in the set of passes in use.

In this case the state transition is such that in the after-state the set of passes in use comprises all those in use in the before-state, with the exception of the pass just proffered. The report is that this subcase of the operation is successful.

The second subcase is characterized by the property:

- The pass is not in the set of passes in use.

In this case the after-state is the same as the before-state, and the report is that the pass is not in use.

As with the arrival of a pass holder, it is clear that for this operation we have considered all cases.

Table of operations

It is helpful to summarize our decisions about the operations in a table. We have done this in Table 2.1.

Operation	Input	Subcase property	State change	Report
Ordinary arrival	*None*	Ordinary cars less than maximum	One more ordinary car	Success
		Ordinary cars equals maximum	*None*	Ordinary car park full
Ordinary departure	*None*	Ordinary cars greater than zero	One less ordinary car	Success
		Ordinary cars equals zero	*None*	No ordinary cars present
Pass arrival	Pass	Pass not in use	Pass now in use	Success
		Pass in use	*None*	Pass in use
Pass departure	Pass	Pass in use	Pass no longer in use	Success
		Pass not in use	*None*	Pass not in use

Table 2.1: The operations required for the car park

We will use a number of such tables throughout the book, so it is worth explaining their structure. There are a number of rows in the table for each operation the system is required to provide. In this case there are four operations. The division of the table into operations is most apparent in the first two columns, which describe the operations and inputs, if any. The remaining columns of the table are divided according to the various subcases. They give the subcase properties, state change and report for each subcase of an operation. In cases where there is no change of state, for example, that fact is noted explicitly rather than leaving an entry in the table blank.

The reader might imagine that we do not need to consider all of the subcases listed in Table 2.1. For example, it seems plausible that in a real system, the operation for an ordinary car leaving the car park could be invoked only if there actually was an ordinary customer wanting to leave. If that is the case, perhaps there is no point in considering the other subcase in which the car park contains no ordinary cars. We should not, however, rely on how the operations are used to ensure the integrity of the model. In a Z specification we specify operations but not how they are used. In addition, such an approach makes no allowance for faults in the system.

The initial state

Clearly, the conditions of the state invariant should not be so restrictive that
there are no states that satisfy them, and we should always show that there
is at least one state in the state space. We do this by identifying a particular
state, which we call the *initial state*. In this example we identify the state in
which there are no ordinary cars in the car park and no passes in use.

2.2   Car park: second description

It would be possible to proceed directly from the description of the model
we have given to a specification in Z. Indeed, in later chapters of this book,
that is what we shall do. In this first example, however, we shall include
an intermediate step in which we use only the bare minimum of Z notation.
We do this so that the formalization is not obscured by the as yet unfamiliar
notation employed in a Z specification and the further formalities that must be
considered when a complete specification is presented.

The capacity of the car park

The specification must refer to the capacity of the car park, that is, the limit
on the number of ordinary cars that may be in the car park. In order to do
this we shall introduce a variable *carParkCapacity*, which is a name for this
number. We know that:

$$carParkCapacity \geq 0$$

although we do not know the precise value of *carParkCapacity*. A condition
such as this is called a *predicate* in Z.

The state space

To describe the state space it is convenient to have names for the values of
the two observations. Let *ordinaryCars* be the name of the number of ordinary
cars in the car park, and let *passesInUse* be the name of the set of passes in use.
The state invariant may be formalized in terms of these variables by means of
the following predicates:

$$ordinaryCars \leq carParkCapacity$$
$$ordinaryCars \geq 0$$

Describing an operation

The description of a state involves two variables. Since the description of an operation involves the before-state and the after-state, the description will involve four variables in all. In describing the state above, we introduced variables for the values of the observations, and it is conventional in Z to use the same names when we are referring to a before-state in the description of an operation. Thus, a before-state of the car park will be characterized by the values of the variables *ordinaryCars* and *passesInUse*. For the after-state we require two further variables, and we shall use *ordinaryCars'* and *passesInUse'*. As you can see, the names of these two variables are the same as those for the before-state except for the presence of the primes. This similarity in names is one of the conventions in Z that help to emphasize the role of the various components in a specification. The names *passesInUse* and *passesInUse'* are different, and they denote different values. The obvious similarity in name is an indication to the reader regarding the interpretation of these two variables.

When we described a state above, we included the state invariant. It is inherent in the Z style of specification that when an operation is specified the before- and after-states satisfy the state invariant. That is, whenever an operation of the car park is being defined we know that:

$$ordinaryCars \leq carParkCapacity$$
$$ordinaryCars \geq 0$$
$$ordinaryCars' \leq carParkCapacity$$
$$ordinaryCars' \geq 0$$

Exercise 2.3 Why did we write $ordinaryCars' \leq carParkCapacity$, rather than $ordinaryCars' \leq carParkCapacity'$? □

The specification of each operation will require the formulation of conditions in addition to the state invariant. We now consider each operation in turn.

The operations

Ordinary customer arriving

The relevant part of Table 2.1 is:

Operation	Input	Subcase property	State change	Report
Ordinary arrival	*None*	Ordinary cars less than maximum	One more ordinary car	Success
		Ordinary cars equals maximum	*None*	Ordinary car park full

In the first subcase for this operation, the number of ordinary cars in the car park after the operation is one more than it was before the operation, while the set of passes in use does not change. This relationship may be formalized by means of the predicates:

$$ordinaryCars' - ordinaryCars = 1$$
$$passesInUse' = passesInUse$$

Since the after-state must always satisfy the state invariant we know that:

$$ordinaryCars' \leq carParkCapacity$$

Using the first of the above equalities we see that:

$$ordinaryCars + 1 \leq carParkCapacity$$

That is, it follows logically that $ordinaryCars < carParkCapacity$. Thus, perhaps contrary to your expectation, the appropriate subcase property is inherent in the description we have given of the state change. There is no mystery here; it is simply a consequence of the fact that the two states being related satisfy the state invariant.

Let us consider the implications of this. If the subcase property is inherent in the state change description, we need not include it explicitly in the specification. Omitting it would have the advantage that the description is shorter, and we may avoid a potential bias towards a particular conception of the operation, and hence a potential bias towards a particular implementation[2]. However, there are other considerations. For example, the specification is intended to communicate to the designer, and although the logical deduction of the subcase property involves only a few steps, perhaps it would be helpful to draw particular attention to the conclusion by including it explicitly.

We do not believe that a uniform stance on this issue is possible. For example, it is not clear that including the subcase condition under such circumstances will always be an improvement in understandability. Indeed, as we have suggested, it may be misleading. Thus, we shall not give a ruling on the matter. In this chapter we shall omit the subcase property in this case so as to draw attention to the role of the state invariant in the specification. We shall, of course, draw attention to this omission when presenting the specification. We return to this issue in Chapter 6.

This operation makes a report on the success or otherwise of the operation. Let the name of the report be $r!$. The ! indicates that the variable denotes an output. In this subcase we shall define:

$$r! = success$$

---

[2]Those readers familiar with a logic programming language, such as Prolog, should recognize that an implementation of this subcase in such a programming language would not require the subcase property to be expressed explicitly.

In the second subcase of this operation, the after-state is the same as the before-state. This relationship is easily specified by the following predicates:

$$ordinaryCars' = ordinaryCars$$
$$passesInUse' = passesInUse$$

The state invariant tells us:

$$ordinaryCars \leq carParkCapacity$$
$$ordinaryCars' \leq carParkCapacity$$

Unlike the previous subcase, the subcase property we identified is not a logical consequence of these four predicates. Thus, it must be stated explicitly:

$$ordinaryCars = carParkCapacity$$

and directly associated with the two equalities given above.

The difference between this subcase and the previous one is that the relationship between the observations of the before- and after-states in this case, namely equality, could logically apply to any before-state. This includes states where the car park is not full, and the result would be that customers are excluded when it is not necessary.

In this subcase the operation is not successful, and the report is defined as:

$$r! = ordinaryCarParkFull$$

Ordinary customer departing

The relevant part of Table 2.1 is:

Operation	Input	Subcase property	State change	Report
Ordinary departure	*None*	Ordinary cars greater than zero	One less ordinary car	Success
		Ordinary cars equals zero	*None*	No ordinary cars present

In the first subcase, the change of state may be specified:

$$ordinaryCars - ordinaryCars' = 1$$
$$passesInUse' = passesInUse$$

Since we know from the state invariant that:

$$ordinaryCars' \geq 0$$

it follows that *ordinaryCars* > 0 and so there is no need to express the subcase property explicitly.

This subcase is successful:

$r! = success$

For the second subcase, there is no change of state, and this is written exactly as it was for the previous operation. In this case, the subcase property must be expressed explicitly:

$ordinaryCars = 0$

The appropriate report is:

$r! = ordinaryCarParkEmpty$

Pass holder arriving

The relevant part of Table 2.1 is:

Operation	Input	Subcase property	State change	Report
Pass arrival	Pass	Pass not in use	Pass now in use	Success
		Pass in use	*None*	Pass in use

This operation has an input, in the form of a pass. Let us suppose this is *arrivee?*. The ? indicates that this variable denotes an input.

As far as the new state is concerned, *passesInUse'* comprises all the members of *passesInUse* with the addition of the new pass *arrivee?*. In Z this is written using the set union function $\cup$:

$passesInUse' = passesInUse \cup \{arrivee?\}$

Set union is a function which defines a new set in terms of two existing sets. This is why *arrivee?* is presented in this predicate as a set, $\{arrivee?\}$, with one member.

The number of ordinary cars in the car park does not change, so that:

$ordinaryCars' = ordinaryCars$

The subcase property for the first subcase is that *arrivee?* is not a member of the set *passesInUse*. This does not follow from what has already been specified, even with the addition of the state invariant, so we must express it explicitly. In Z this is written using non-membership, $\notin$, as follows:

$arrivee? \notin passesInUse$

Non-membership is a relation between an element and a set. The report is:

$r! = success$

In the second subcase, there is no change of state, which we denote as before. The subcase property does not follow from what has already been expressed. It is written using set membership, $\in$, as follows:

$arrivee? \in passesInUse$

The report is:

$r! = passInUse$

The details of membership, non-membership and union, as well as other aspects of sets, are covered in Chapter 4.

Pass holder departing

The relevant part of Table 2.1 is:

Operation	Input	Subcase property	State change	Report
Pass departure	Pass	Pass in use	Pass no longer in use	Success
		Pass not in use	*None*	Pass not in use

Let us suppose that the pass presented as input to this operation is *departee?*. The set of passes in use after this operation comprises all those in use before the operation, with the exception of *departee?*. In Z this is written using the set difference function, $\setminus$, and so the new state is given by:

$passesInUse' = passesInUse \setminus \{departee?\}$
$ordinaryCars' = ordinaryCars$

The subcase property is not a logical consequence of these equalities and the state invariant, so we express it explicitly:

$departee? \in passesInUse$

The report is:

$r! = success$

In the second subcase, there is no change of state, which we denote as before. The subcase property requires stating explicitly:

$departee? \notin passesInUse$

The report is:

$r! = passNotInUse$

The initial state

It is conventional in Z that the initial state of the system is described as if it is the after-state of some operation. Thus we need to define suitable values for *ordinaryCars'* and *passesInUse'* that satisfy the after-state invariant. We may take:

$$ordinaryCars' = 0$$
$$passesInUse' = \varnothing$$

In this example, the symbol $\varnothing$ denotes the empty set of passes, that is, a set of passes with no members.

2.3   The Z specification

In this section we present the complete specification of the barrier-control system in Z. A Z specification comprises both mathematics and natural language commentary. The presence of the mathematics is essential if the specification is to have the properties we desire of it, namely that it is precise, concise and amenable to formal reasoning. The commentary is included in the specification by way of explanation of the mathematics. In this chapter, we have already explained the model and some of the mathematics concerned. Thus in these special circumstances it only remains for us to introduce the formal notation. Accordingly, what commentary we do include will be by way of explanation of the various Z constructs employed in the specification.

There are several reasons for a special notation. Although in our second description of the model we have begun to use mathematics, we have done so only for the main parts of the specification of the operations. There are many other details to be tackled. What we have done so far would be worthless if these loose ends allowed ambiguity to enter the specification.

Secondly, you may have noticed that there is considerable repetition and similarity in structure in the presentation of the operations. For example, the same variable names are used again and again, and each operation includes subcases where there is no change of state. Such repetition is unavoidable, since it is bound up with completely describing the operations. However, the specification will be easier to read and understand if the impact of that repetition is minimized and the similarity is exploited. One of the advantages of Z is that it provides a number of constructs and conventions to achieve these ends.

Since we shall be presenting a complete Z specification, we must necessarily employ a range of concepts and techniques from Z with which you are not familiar. Since the rest of the book explains them at some length, we shall only give a brief explanation at this stage. In this chapter it is sufficient for you to see the general nature of the specification, and to see its relationship to the model.

Basic types

Our first description of the model identified some sets of values that we require in order to build the model. These sets are known as *basic types*. In this section we see how basic types may be introduced into the specification.

The variable *ordinaryCars* takes integer values, so its type is integer. This type is included in the Z library, a collection of definitions that are frequently required in specifications, and there is no need for us to introduce it explicitly into our specification. The type integer is denoted $\mathbb{Z}$[3].

We also need a basic type for passes. We do not need to say anything about the members of this type; we simply want to name the type. In Z we would do this as follows:

$$[PASS]$$

This is called a *given set* declaration. In this example we are assuming that the type $PASS$[4] has a member for each pass that has been issued, and no others.

We finally need to give the type of the reports. Unlike *PASS*, we wish to state the specific values of this type. This is achieved in Z as follows:

$$
\begin{aligned}
REPORT ::= \ &success \\
| \ &ordinaryCarParkFull \\
| \ &ordinaryCarParkEmpty \\
| \ &passInUse \\
| \ &passNotInUse
\end{aligned}
$$

The declaration of *REPORT* is called a *free type* definition.

The names of these types may be used anywhere in the remainder of the specification.

Global variables

The maximum number of ordinary cars allowed in the car park is the value of *carParkCapacity*. We need to introduce this variable into the specification, give its type, and associate the restriction with it. This is written in Z as follows:

$$
\begin{array}{|l}
carParkCapacity : \mathbb{Z} \\
\hline
carParkCapacity \geq 0
\end{array}
$$

This is called an *axiomatic definition* or description. The part above the centre line, known as the *declaration* part, includes the declaration of the variable

---

[3] There is no relationship between Z and $\mathbb{Z}$.

[4] It is conventional in Z that the name of a given set is in upper case. It is also conventional that the names of given sets are singular.

carParkCapacity, which introduces the name and associates it with the required type, namely integer. The part of the axiomatic definition below the centre line, the *predicate part*, gives the restriction on the value of *carParkCapacity*. In this example the predicate part comprises a single predicate, although in general there may be many. This definition does not fix a specific value for *carParkCapacity*.

Exercise 2.4 Modify the definition of *carParkCapacity* so that the maximum value it may take is 500.   □

An object introduced into a specification by means of an axiomatic definition is a global variable and thus it may be referred to anywhere in the remainder of the specification. A variable always denotes a specific object or value although the specification may not always specify exactly what that value is. In the case of *carParkCapacity*, we have specified that the value must be a number greater than or equal to zero. See Chapter 6 (§6.2, §6.7) for a more detailed discussion of variables.

The state

The states in the model are defined by two variables whose values are restricted by the state invariant. Every time we describe an operation we shall need to refer to the state description, so there is a mechanism in Z, called a *schema*, whereby we may introduce a name for the state description. We may then refer to the state description by name, rather than explicitly listing it in full.

When we name a state description we must declare each variable involved and include the state invariant. For the car park, we shall name the state description *CarPark* and its definition is written in Z as follows:

$$
\begin{array}{|l}
\_\,CarPark \,_____ \\
ordinaryCars : \mathbb{Z} \\
passesInUse : \mathbb{P}\,PASS \\
\hline
ordinaryCars \geq 0 \\
ordinaryCars \leq carParkCapacity \\
\end{array}
$$

The declaration part, above the centre line, gives the declarations of the state variables. These will be referred to as *components* of the schema. The variable *ordinaryCars* is of type integer. In the declaration *passesInUse* : $\mathbb{P}\,PASS$, $\mathbb{P}\,PASS$ is pronounced 'set of pass', and it indicates that the value of *passesInUse* is a set of passes, rather than an individual pass. The predicate part, below the centre line, lists the state invariant. Observe that the name of the state description is included as part of the top line of its definition.

A schema is used to group elements together and to give that group a name. Schemas are very important constructs in Z for structuring the specification. They will also be used in the specification of operations of the system.

The initial state

As we have already observed, it is a convention in Z that the initial state is described as an after-state, and in this case it is as follows:

```
┌─ InitialCarPark ────────────────────────────────
│ CarPark'
├──────────────────────────────────────────────────
│ ordinaryCars' = 0
│ passesInUse' = ∅
└──────────────────────────────────────────────────
```

The inclusion of *CarPark'* in the declaration part of this schema indicates that the predicate part will involve the variables *ordinaryCars'* and *passesInUse'* and the predicates $ordinaryCars' \leq carParkCapacity$ and $ordinaryCars' \geq 0$.

This definition of the initial state gives explicit values for *ordinaryCars'* and *passesInUse'*. In order for this schema to specify a state the system can occupy, we have to be sure that these values satisfy the state invariant, namely that $ordinaryCars' \geq 0$ and $ordinaryCars' \leq carParkCapacity$. These are clearly satisfied by the specific values given so the initial state is in the state space.

The operations

Ordinary customer arriving

Each subcase of this operation will be defined by means of a schema, which groups together the four variables needed for the description: *ordinaryCars*, *ordinaryCars'*, *passesInUse* and *passesInUse'*. For the first subcase, in which the ordinary customer is admitted, there is a change of state, and the schema to describe this is written:

```
┌─ OrdinaryEntryOK ────────────────────────────────
│ ΔCarPark
│ r! : REPORT
├──────────────────────────────────────────────────
│ ordinaryCars' − ordinaryCars = 1
│ passesInUse' = passesInUse
│ r! = success
└──────────────────────────────────────────────────
```

The name of this schema is *OrdinaryEntryOK*. The $\Delta CarPark$[5] in the declaration part indicates that this schema describes a change of state of the car park. The inclusion of $\Delta CarPark$ introduces all the appropriate variables and the before- and after-state invariants. The declaration *r! : REPORT* introduces the variable required to describe the report. The predicate part of the

---

[5] Δ is the fourth letter of the Greek alphabet, in upper case, and is suggestive of change. $\Delta CarPark$ is pronounced 'delta car park'.

schema includes all of the predicates required to relate the before-state and the after-state, and the definition of the report, in the form we presented them earlier. Recall that the subcase property, $ordinaryCars < carParkCapacity$, is a logical consequence of the predicates included in this schema.

In the second subcase for this operation the after-state is the same as the before-state. To avoid specifying this explicitly in the schema, we include $\Xi CarPark$[6] rather than $\Delta CarPark$. We may then omit the definition of the after-state; $\Xi CarPark$ tells us it is the same as the before-state. The schema is thus:

$$
\begin{array}{l}
\underline{\quad OrdinaryCarParkFull\underline{\qquad\qquad\qquad\qquad\qquad\qquad}} \\
\Xi CarPark \\
r! : REPORT \\
\hline
ordinaryCars = carParkCapacity \\
r! = ordinaryCarParkFull \\
\end{array}
$$

Unlike the previous subcase, in this subcase we do need to include the subcase condition.

Having dealt with the two subcases, we may now specify the operation for ordinary arrivals described in the table of operations, Table 2.1. In Z this is written:

$$OrdinaryEntry \,\hat{=}\, OrdinaryEntryOK \lor OrdinaryCarParkFull$$

This is a *schema definition*. The symbol $\hat{=}$ is pronounced 'is defined to be', and the *schema disjunction*, $\lor$, is pronounced 'or'. The effect of this definition is that an operation is introduced for which the effect on a given state is defined by either the schema $OrdinaryEntryOK$ or the schema $OrdinaryCarParkFull$. $OrdinaryEntry$ is an operation with no inputs. The only output is the report.

Whenever a real barrier-control system is constructed according to this specification, part of the system constructed must realize, or implement, the operation $OrdinaryEntry$. This is because $OrdinaryEntry$ is one of the operations mentioned in the informal requirements. In our specification $OrdinaryEntry$ is presented in terms of $OrdinaryEntryOK$ and $OrdinaryCarParkFull$. However, $OrdinaryEntryOK$ and $OrdinaryCarParkFull$ are not mentioned in the informal requirements and there is no similar requirement that these operations be implemented in any real system, such as with their own electronic circuits for example. $OrdinaryEntryOK$ and $OrdinaryCarParkFull$ were introduced simply for our convenience in presenting the specification.

The state invariant tell us that in every state in the state space the number of ordinary cars in the car park must be between zero and some maximum.

---

[6] Ξ is the 14th letter of the Greek alphabet, in upper case. $\Xi CarPark$ is pronounced 'xi car park'.

For every state, one of the two subcases of the operation *OrdinaryEntry* will apply. Thus, this operation is applicable to every state in the state space. When an operation satisfies this criterion we say it is *total*. This is a more precise counterpart to the argument we gave earlier that no special cases had been overlooked.

Let us examine more closely what has been established. When discussing the initial state we argued that such a state existed in the state space. The description of the operation given above describes after-states in terms of before-states. Having just argued that the description applies to every state in the state space, then it applies to the initial state, and defines a new state.

There is no requirement for operations in a formal specification to be total. An operation which is not total is *partial*. A partial operation is one for which the outcome in some states in the state space is not defined. In the case of the operation defining the admission of an ordinary customer, it is appropriate that the operation be total since we wish to say what happens under all circumstances. Whether the operations of a system need to be total, and whether they are in fact total, is an issue that needs consideration in every example. This issue is considered in greater depth in Chapter 6.

Ordinary customer departing

The first subcase of an ordinary customer leaving is one in which there is a change of state. The schema defining it is:

$$
\begin{array}{|l}
\hline
\_\,OrdinaryDepartureOK _____ \\
\Delta CarPark \\
r! : REPORT \\
\hline
ordinaryCars - ordinaryCars' = 1 \\
passesInUse' = passesInUse \\
r! = success \\
\hline
\end{array}
$$

Recall that this case applies when $ordinaryCars > 0$.

The second subcase is defined by the schema:

$$
\begin{array}{|l}
\hline
\_\,OrdinaryCarParkEmpty _____ \\
\Xi CarPark \\
r! : REPORT \\
\hline
ordinaryCars = 0 \\
r! = ordinaryCarParkEmpty \\
\hline
\end{array}
$$

The departure operation for ordinary customers comprises these two subcases:

$$OrdinaryDeparture \mathrel{\widehat{=}} OrdinaryDepartureOK \vee OrdinaryCarParkEmpty$$

OrdinaryDeparture is an operation with no input. The only output is the report.

Exercise 2.5 We argued above that the operation for the arrival of an ordinary customer was total. Give the corresponding argument for the operation for an ordinary customer leaving the car park.   □

Exercise 2.6 * Extend the specification we have presented so far to include an operation to enquire how many ordinary spaces remain.   □

Exercise 2.7 ** The car park model that we have identified keeps a count of the number of ordinary cars in the car park. Modify the model and partial specification we have presented so far so that, instead, it keeps track of the number of ordinary spaces that remain.   □

Pass holder arriving

The first subcase for the arrival of a pass holder involves a change of state:

$$
\begin{array}{l}
\_\,PassEntryOK\,\underline{\hspace{4cm}} \\
\Delta\,CarPark \\
arrivee? : PASS \\
r! : REPORT \\
\hline
arrivee? \notin passesInUse \\
passesInUse' = passesInUse \cup \{arrivee?\} \\
ordinaryCars' = ordinaryCars \\
r! = success
\end{array}
$$

This operation has an input, namely a pass, and this has been declared in the schema.

In the second subcase, there is no change of state:

$$
\begin{array}{l}
\_\,PassInUse\,\underline{\hspace{4cm}} \\
\Xi\,CarPark \\
arrivee? : PASS \\
r! : REPORT \\
\hline
arrivee? \in passesInUse \\
r! = passInUse
\end{array}
$$

The complete operation for the arrival of a pass holder is:

$$PassEntry \mathrel{\widehat{=}} PassEntryOK \lor PassInUse$$

PassEntry is an operation that takes a pass as input. The only output is the report.

Given a state of the car park, and the identity of a pass as input, either that pass is in the set of passes in use, or it is not. That is, for each state in the state space and each input one of the two subcases of the operation we have defined applies. In each case an after-state and a report are defined. Thus, the operation we have described is total.

Exercise 2.8 * Provide a Z specification of an operation to enquire whether a particular pass is in use. To do this you will require a type for the output. Recall how the type *REPORT* was defined. □

Exercise 2.9 * Provide a Z specification of an operation to output all of the passes currently in use. □

Pass holder departing

The first subcase for the departure of a pass holder defines a change of state.

```
┌─ PassDepartureOK ─────────────────────────────
│ ΔCarPark
│ departee? : PASS
│ r! : REPORT
├───────────────────────────────────────────────
│ departee? ∈ passesInUse
│ passesInUse' = passesInUse \ {departee?}
│ ordinaryCars' = ordinaryCars
│ r! = success
└───────────────────────────────────────────────
```

In the second subcase, there is no change of state.

```
┌─ PassNotInUse ────────────────────────────────
│ ΞCarPark
│ departee? : PASS
│ r! : REPORT
├───────────────────────────────────────────────
│ departee? ∉ passesInUse
│ r! = passNotInUse
└───────────────────────────────────────────────
```

The departure operation for pass holders is:

$$PassDeparture \mathrel{\widehat{=}} PassDepartureOK \lor PassNotInUse$$

PassDeparture is an operation that takes a pass as input. The only output is the report.

Exercise 2.10 Argue that the *PassDeparture* operation is total.   □

Exercise 2.11 ** Many car parks have an illuminated sign to indicate when there are spaces available. How would you extend the specification we have given to include this feature?   □

Exercise 2.12 ** Develop a specification of a bank account. You should include operations to make a deposit and to make a withdrawal. Any amount of money can be deposited but a withdrawal must not allow the account to go overdrawn.   □

2.4   Summary

In this chapter we have presented a small but complete specification in Z. We started by describing a simple mathematical model based on a number and a set and then expressed that model in the Z notation. We now turn our attention to studying the mathematics that underlies Z, logic, sets, relations, and so on. In covering these topics, we will use the Z notation presented so far and introduce additional notation as required.

Chapter 3

Logic

The central concern of logic is the description of situations by means of logical expressions, called predicates, and the determination of what other predicates must necessarily be true in the situation so described. The situation described may be the premises of an argument. In this case what follows, or what may be *deduced*, is a conclusion. In specification we shall be more concerned with situations that are models of systems, and in this case what follows is a property that the model must possess.

An important aspect of mathematical models is the description of relationships between values. For example, the state space is defined by a relationship between state observations, and operations are described in terms of relationships between two states. For example, the entry of an ordinary customer to the car park was described with the schema:

$$
\begin{array}{l}
\underline{\hspace{1em}OrdinaryEntryOK\hspace{8em}} \\
\Delta CarPark \\
r! : REPORT \\
\hline
ordinaryCars' - ordinaryCars = 1 \\
passesInUse' = passesInUse \\
r! = success
\end{array}
$$

If we list every predicate that is either explicit in this schema or implicit, because of the inclusion of $\Delta CarPark$ and reference to the global variable $carParkCapacity$, we find:

$$carParkCapacity \geq 0$$
$$ordinaryCars \leq carParkCapacity$$
$$ordinaryCars \geq 0$$
$$ordinaryCars' \leq carParkCapacity$$

$ordinaryCars' \geq 0$

$ordinaryCars' - ordinaryCars = 1$

$passesInUse' = passesInUse$

$r! = success$

Thus, the specification of a subcase of an operation is a description of a situation in terms of a set of predicates. Logic provides the vocabulary for constructing these predicates out of expressions. This vocabulary includes *relations*, such as $\leq$ and $=$. In addition, there are constructs not illustrated in this example, such as logical connectives and quantifiers.

As well as descriptions, logic is concerned with what predicates must follow on the basis of the description. This is one of the main advantages of express- ing the specification in mathematics. For example, we argued in Chapter 2 (page 34) that the subcase condition for the operation *OrdinaryEntryOK*:

$$ordinaryCars < carParkCapacity$$

followed from the description listed above. In this way we were able to confirm that the description had a property we required, and thus it was not necessary to express that property explicitly as part of the description.

In this chapter, we shall focus on the use of logic for building descriptions, and continue to rely on the informal style of justification used in the above example. In §3.4 we shall briefly consider the form that more rigorous justifi- cations may take.

3.1   Logic as a language for description

We shall explore the use of logic for describing situations by considering simple blocks scenes such as depicted in Figure 3.1. In a specification we will often be describing intangible things, such as numbers, but this is not significant. Our analysis of descriptions will work equally well for 'block b is on top of block a' and '3 is less than 4'.

In a blocks scene, blocks may be placed on top of each other to form towers of various heights, which stand on the floor. Giving a description of such a scene involves selecting an appropriate vocabulary. We shall consider individual blocks to be objects, that is, values. We shall refer to them by their names, a, b and so on. We shall not consider the floor to be an object, though it will feature in the description of the scene. As for properties and relationships, we shall allow ourselves to say that a block is 'on the floor', that a block is 'clear' (that is, it has nothing on top of it), that one block is (directly) 'on top of' another block, and that one block is 'above' another block. We may then describe the scene in Figure 3.1 by using these relationships in statements that are true of it. Part of the scene may be described by the following statements:

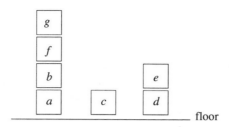

Figure 3.1: A simple blocks scene

block *d* is on the floor
block *e* is on top of block *d*
block *e* is above block *d*
block *e* is clear

Exercise 3.1 Complete the description of the blocks scene of Figure 3.1 in the style suggested above. □

There are general characteristics of the blocks scene that may be deduced from the description you gave in answer to Exercise 3.1. That is, they are true of the blocks scene but only implicit in its description. For example, 'anything that is above block *a* is not above block *c*'. This statement is true or false of the scene as a whole, rather than referring to particular blocks. This is because it refers to anything above block *a*. To represent this statement we must use a variable, *x* here, to stand for an arbitrary block:

if block *x* is above block *a*, then block *x* is not above block *c*

While this statement is true of the scene of Figure 3.1, it is not true of arbitrary blocks scenes. In contrast, the statements:

if block *x* is on top of block *y* then block *x* is above block *y*

if block *x* is above block *y* and block *y* is above block *z*
then block *x* is above block *z*

are true of any blocks scene. They express a relationship between 'on top of' and 'above' which holds for all blocks scenes. Stating this relationship explicitly for a scene will save giving a number of separate relationships about specific blocks.

Exercise 3.2 Amend your answer for Exercise 3.1 to take advantage of the general characteristic of blocks scenes given above. □

Exercise 3.2 shows that there may be alternative descriptions of the same blocks scene, even if they are based on the same vocabulary. If the same predicates may each be deduced from two descriptions then one description is redundant and can be discarded. Logic cannot tell us which description is superior, but we can apply factors external to logic, such as economy of expression, in order to decide between alternative descriptions.

There is further scope for variety of descriptions since we may select the vocabulary as well. Chapter 1 identified abstraction as important in modelling, and selecting the vocabulary for description is an important part of abstraction. For example, towers are not values in the descriptions of blocks scenes, nor is it possible to describe them explicitly.

The description of a situation must be accurate. That is, every statement in the description must be true. An accurate description of the blocks scene of Figure 3.1 could not include 'block *b* is clear', for example, since it is false. It is thus necessary for us to be able to judge the truth of statements. In this chapter we shall judge the truth of statements about blocks scenes informally by comparing them with the world they describe. In Chapter 4 (page 81) and Chapter 5 (page 114) we shall be able to give precise definitions of relations, and hence deal with the judgement of statements more rigorously.

There are further checks we can make on a description. For example, we can check that a predicate we would expect to follow from a description does in fact follow. If it does not, we might suspect the accuracy or completeness of our description. This kind of check plays an important role in formal specification. Similarly, we can check that a description is consistent (§ 1.4), that is, check that two contradictory predicates do not both follow from the description. If this is the case, the description is definitely inaccurate.

In simple cases such as blocks scenes it seems unlikely that we would make these kinds of mistake. In the description of complex systems, there is undoubtedly a much greater likelihood.

Exercise 3.3 * Draw a picture like that of Figure 3.1 for a blocks scene that involves blocks *a*, *b* and *c* and conforms to the following description:

> block *b* is on top of block *a*
>
> a block is on the floor unless it is on top of something
>
> a block is clear unless it has something on top of it

What can you say about block *b* that is not explicit in the description? How would you justify your answer simply on the basis of what you have been told about the scene? What can you say about block *c*?   □

3.2 The logical connectives

Consider the following argument or deduction:

Given   block b is clear or there is a block on top of it

                                 block b is not clear

it follows   there is a block on top of block b

It is clearly an example of good logical thinking, and we say the deduction is *valid*[1], but let us consider how we can be more precise about this observation. The first statement in the description has two constituents, separated by 'or'. Furthermore, the second statement asserts the opposite of one of these constituents. If we suppose that 'block b is clear' may be represented by the predicate P[2], and 'there is a block on top of b' may be represented by the predicate Q, then the deduction may be represented:

Given P or Q

                                not P

it follows Q

This reveals its underlying structure, and we see that the logical principles that justify it simply concern the roles of 'or' and 'not'. These are examples of *logical connectives*. The predicates P and Q may be true or false, and the validity of the deduction does not depend on what P and Q represent.

There are many possible logical connectives, although only five are required sufficiently often to merit inclusion in the basic Z language. The following table gives the symbols we shall use to denote the logical connectives, and a brief suggestion of the English words with which they are normally associated.

English	Symbol	Arity	Name
not, no	$\neg$	1	Negation
and, but	$\wedge$	2	Conjunction
or	$\vee$	2	Disjunction
implies, if ... then ...	$\Rightarrow$	2	Implication
implies and is implied by	$\Leftrightarrow$	2	Equivalence

The *arity* of a logical connective is the number of predicates it combines into a compound predicate. Negation is a *unary* connective; it has arity 1, and so creates the compound predicate $\neg\, P$ from the predicate P. A *binary* connective such as equivalence forms the compound predicate $P \Leftrightarrow Q$ from the predicates P and Q. Of these connectives, the one with which you may be least familiar is implication, and we shall consider it in more detail shortly.

Compound predicates may be nested arbitrarily. Example compound predicates are:

$$P \vee (\neg\, Q) \qquad (P \vee Q) \Leftrightarrow (R \Rightarrow (P \wedge Q))$$

---

[1] In Chapter 1 we talked of the validity of a model. The term we have just introduced has a different meaning. Both meanings of the term valid are in common use.

[2] We shall denote arbitrary predicates by single upper-case letters such as P, Q or R.

In the second example, two predicates, $P \vee Q$ and $R \Rightarrow (P \wedge Q)$ are combined with $\Leftrightarrow$. Similarly, $R \Rightarrow (P \wedge Q)$ is itself the result of combining R and $P \wedge Q$. To ensure that the structure of the overall predicate is clear, predicates are here enclosed in brackets each time they are used to make a larger predicate.

The components P and Q of the disjunction $P \vee Q$ are called *disjuncts*. The components P and Q of the conjunction $P \wedge Q$ are called *conjuncts*. Finally, in $P \Rightarrow Q$, P is the *antecedent* and Q is the *consequent*.

A predicate of any complexity will contain many brackets. For example:

$$(\neg (((\neg R) \wedge P) \vee Q)) \Rightarrow R$$

To improve readability, there are conventions that allow some brackets to be omitted. This is achieved by specifying the precedence, or binding power, of the logical connectives, and the associativity of the binary connectives.

Precedence	Connective	Associativity
Highest	$\neg$	
	$\wedge$	Left
	$\vee$	Left
	$\Rightarrow$	Right
Lowest	$\Leftrightarrow$	Left

Brackets that would be implied by the precedence rules may then be omitted. For example, just as $((-5) * 4) + 3$ may be written $-5 * 4 + 3$, $((\neg P) \wedge Q) \vee R$ may be written $\neg P \wedge Q \vee R$. In contrast, for example, $\neg (P \wedge Q)$ cannot be simplified: $\neg P \wedge Q$ is in fact $(\neg P) \wedge Q$ because $\neg$ has a higher precedence than $\wedge$.

Where a binary connective is repeated, the issue is settled by the associativity of the connective. For example, $P \Rightarrow (Q \Rightarrow R)$ may be written $P \Rightarrow Q \Rightarrow R$, since implication is right associative, but $(P \Rightarrow Q) \Rightarrow R$ may not be simplified. In contrast, since $\vee$ is left associative, $(P \vee Q) \vee R$ may be simplified according to these conventions, but $P \vee (Q \vee R)$ may not. We shall often include brackets in predicates where their omission, although sanctioned by these conventions, might nevertheless cause confusion.

Exercise 3.4 Simplify the following predicates by omitting as many brackets as possible.

   i. $(\neg (((\neg R) \wedge P) \vee Q)) \Rightarrow R$

  ii. $(\neg P) \Rightarrow (((P \Rightarrow Q) \Rightarrow R) \wedge S)$

$\square$

Exercise 3.5 Restore brackets to the following predicates.

   i. $P \Rightarrow Q \Leftrightarrow \neg Q \Rightarrow \neg P$

ii. $P \lor Q \land \neg R \lor Q \land P$

□

The meaning of the logical connectives

We mentioned in the introduction to this chapter that it should be possible to justify a deduction at increasing levels of detail. In the case of deductions that depend on the logical connectives it is possible to do this quite simply. This is achieved by giving truth values to the predicates involved, and defining the meaning of the logical connectives as functions over truth values.

Consider the conjunction 'block c is on the floor and block c is clear'. This would be accepted as true only when both the conjuncts 'block c is on the floor' and 'block c is clear' are true. If either of them is false, the conjunction would be false. We can summarize these properties of conjunction with the following *truth table*:

P	Q	$P \land Q$
T	T	T
T	F	F
F	T	F
F	F	F

in which the truth value 'true' is denoted T, the truth value 'false' is denoted F, and there is a row for each possible combination of truth values of P and Q.

This approach to the meaning of the connectives assumes that the truth value of a predicate such as $P \land Q$ depends only on the truth values of P and Q. We say logic is *truth functional*. In contrast, some uses of connectives in English are not truth functional. For example, suppose the conjunction 'John fell down and got up' is true. If this is the case, the conjuncts 'John fell down' and 'John got up' must both be true. In logic, the conjunction 'John got up' $\land$ 'John fell down' would then also be true. In practice, however, an English speaker would use the two statements 'John fell down and got up' and 'John got up and fell down' to mean quite different things. When we say the logical connectives are truth functional we are saying that such hidden dependence is not possible.

The truth tables for the remaining logical connectives are:

P	$\neg P$
T	F
F	T

P	Q	$P \lor Q$
T	T	T
T	F	T
F	T	T
F	F	F

P	Q	$P \Rightarrow Q$
T	T	T
T	F	F
F	T	T
F	F	T

P	Q	$P \Leftrightarrow Q$
T	T	T
T	F	F
F	T	F
F	F	T

The only truth table amongst these which warrants further consideration is that for implication. To justify this table, consider the statement 'if someone is in the police force then they are a state employee'. This statement is about people who are in the police force. It is not about people who are not in the police force. The statement should therefore be false only if one or more members of the police force are not state employees, that is, if the antecedent is true and the consequent is false. This justifies the single entry of F in the truth table for implication.

Logic also includes two predicates with constant truth values, denoted by *true* and *false*. Note that *true* and *false* are predicates and thus part of the language used to relate values in a model; they are not themselves values in the model. Only in very specialist applications in which the model being constructed is a model of a logic is it appropriate for *true* and *false* to denote values in the model. See also §6.1 for further discussion on this point. Of course, the constant *true* is always true, and the constant *false* is always false.

Given truth tables for the connectives, we may construct truth tables for predicates, as illustrated in the following example:

P	Q	R	$P \wedge Q$	$\neg (P \wedge Q)$	$R \Rightarrow P$	$\neg (P \wedge Q) \Rightarrow R \Rightarrow P$
T	T	T	T	F	T	T
T	T	F	T	F	T	T
T	F	T	F	T	T	T
T	F	F	F	T	T	T
F	T	T	F	T	F	F
F	T	F	F	T	T	T
F	F	T	F	T	F	F
F	F	F	F	T	T	T

Strictly speaking, the truth table for the predicate $\neg (P \wedge Q) \Rightarrow R \Rightarrow P$ would comprise the first three columns and the last column only. However, the above table has additional columns for the various predicates that comprise $\neg (P \wedge Q) \Rightarrow R \Rightarrow P$ to record how the final truth value of the predicate is determined in terms of the values of these constituents.

Exercise 3.6 * Construct the truth table for $(P \Rightarrow Q) \wedge (Q \Rightarrow P)$.   □

Since the requirements for a system may be expressed in English it is important to be able to translate English statements into logical predicates and to recognize which connectives are being used. In some cases explicit use of 'not', 'and', and 'or' are straightforward but some uses of connectives in English are not. Consider the statement:

The appliance will work unless there is a power cut.

We can identify the logical connective being used here if we identify the constituents of this statement and examine how the truth of the whole statement depends on the truth of these constituents. Let us denote the constituents 'the appliance will work' and 'there is a power cut' by AW and PC respectively, and for the sake of this example denote the whole statement as $AW?PC$. Let us consider each possible combination of truth values of AW and PC:

AW	PC	$AW?PC$
T	T	?
T	F	?
F	T	?
F	F	?

Consider a situation in which the appliance is working and there is a power cut, that is, when AW is true and PC is true. In this situation $AW?PC$ is false. If AW is true and PC is false then the statement $AW?PC$ is true. Continuing in this manner, we obtain:

AW	PC	$AW?PC$
T	T	F
T	F	T
F	T	T
F	F	F

This truth table does not correspond directly to any of the truth tables we gave earlier. It is, in fact, the negation of the equivalence truth table. Thus we should represent the statement as:

$\neg$ ('the appliance will work' $\Leftrightarrow$ 'there is a power cut')

Exercise 3.7 * What are the principle logical connectives in the following statements?

i. He is a millionaire, but never gives to charity.

ii. This car is available with a petrol or a diesel engine.

□

Tautologies and logical equivalences

A predicate that always takes the truth value true is called a *tautology*. For example, $(P \Rightarrow Q) \wedge (Q \Rightarrow R) \Rightarrow (P \Rightarrow R)$ is a tautology. This may be verified, of course, by constructing its truth table.

Exercise 3.8 * Show that $(P \vee Q) \wedge \neg P \Rightarrow Q$ is a tautology.   □

In §3.1 we discussed a number of desirable characteristics of descriptions. We may use the notion of tautology to clarify some of these characteristics.

Let us begin with the notion of deduction. Reconsider the deduction given on page 51 which we may now represent:

Given $P \vee Q$
          $\neg P$

it follows Q

This is valid if Q must be true whenever $P \vee Q$ and $\neg P$ are both true. That is, the deduction is valid if $(P \vee Q) \wedge \neg P \Rightarrow Q$ is a tautology. We saw in Exercise 3.8 that this is indeed the case.

More generally, if a description is given in terms of the predicates $P_1, \ldots, P_n$, then the predicate Q follows from the description if:

$P_1 \wedge \ldots \wedge P_n \Rightarrow Q$

is a tautology. If Q does follow from $P_1, \ldots, P_n$ then for the purposes of investigating what other predicates follow we may treat Q as if it was given in the original description. If we are viewing $P_1 \wedge \ldots \wedge P_n \Rightarrow Q$ as an argument, then we call $P_1, \ldots, P_n$ premises and Q the conclusion.

Some of the common justifications for deductions are embodied in the following tautologies:

$P \wedge Q \Rightarrow P$
$(P \vee Q) \wedge \neg P \Rightarrow Q$
$P \wedge (P \Rightarrow Q) \Rightarrow Q$
$(P \Rightarrow Q) \wedge (Q \Rightarrow R) \Rightarrow (P \Rightarrow R)$

Another characteristic of descriptions which the notion of tautology can clarify is the requirement that the description be consistent. A description is *consistent* if there is no predicate P such that both P and $\neg P$ follow from the description. A description that is not consistent is inconsistent. Since the following predicates are tautologies:

$P \wedge \neg P \Rightarrow false$
$false \Rightarrow Q$

we see that $P \wedge \neg P \Rightarrow Q$ for any predicate Q. That is, any predicate whatsoever follows from an inconsistent description. In terms of specification, if a specification is inconsistent we may deduce it has any property whatsoever. While this will include properties we want, it also includes properties we do not want. Such a description is useless as a specification.

Finally, the notion of a tautology is also useful for expressing the equivalence of logic predicates. Two predicates P and Q are *logically equivalent* if $P \Leftrightarrow Q$ is a tautology. That is, P and Q are logically equivalent if they have the same truth table. For example, $(\neg P \Rightarrow Q) \Leftrightarrow P \vee Q$ is a tautology so that $\neg P \Rightarrow Q$ and $P \vee Q$ are logically equivalent. Logical equivalences are useful for suggesting alternative ways in which a statement may be expressed, without changing its meaning. Reconsider the statement:

The appliance will work unless there is a power cut.

Since $\neg (P \Leftrightarrow Q) \Leftrightarrow (P \vee Q) \wedge \neg (P \wedge Q)$, this statement may be re-expressed:

The appliance will work or there is a power cut, but not both.

Re-expressing statements in this manner may help to clarify their truth-value properties.

Some laws about the logical connectives

The translation of predicates into equivalent predicates may always be justified by considering the relevant truth tables. Certain examples, however, arise so often that it is worth listing them. We do so in terms of logical equivalences, called *laws*. These laws are applicable where the truth value properties of the predicates depend only on the truth tables of the logical connectives.

The first laws state that disjunction and conjunction are commutative and associative:

$$P \vee Q \Leftrightarrow Q \vee P \qquad\qquad P \wedge Q \Leftrightarrow Q \wedge P$$
$$P \vee (Q \vee R) \Leftrightarrow (P \vee Q) \vee R \qquad\qquad P \wedge (Q \wedge R) \Leftrightarrow (P \wedge Q) \wedge R$$

The following laws show how negation interacts with disjunction and conjunction:

$$\neg (P \wedge Q) \Leftrightarrow \neg P \vee \neg Q \qquad\qquad \neg (P \vee Q) \Leftrightarrow \neg P \wedge \neg Q$$

Conjunction distributes over disjunction, and vice versa:

$P \wedge (Q \vee R) \Leftrightarrow P \wedge Q \vee P \wedge R$

$P \vee (Q \wedge R) \Leftrightarrow (P \vee Q) \wedge (P \vee R)$

The following laws show some of the ways in which various connectives may be defined in terms of each other:[3]

$P \Rightarrow Q \Leftrightarrow \neg Q \Rightarrow \neg P$

$P \Rightarrow Q \Leftrightarrow \neg P \vee Q$

$P \Leftrightarrow Q \Leftrightarrow (P \Rightarrow Q) \wedge (Q \Rightarrow P)$

$P \Leftrightarrow Q \Leftrightarrow (P \wedge Q) \vee (\neg P \wedge \neg Q)$

The following results are simplifications:

$P \vee P \Leftrightarrow P$	$P \wedge P \Leftrightarrow P$
$P \vee false \Leftrightarrow P$	$P \wedge true \Leftrightarrow P$
$P \vee true \Leftrightarrow true$	$P \wedge false \Leftrightarrow false$
$P \vee \neg P \Leftrightarrow true$	$P \wedge \neg P \Leftrightarrow false$
$\neg \neg P \Leftrightarrow P$	

Since two predicates which are logically equivalent have the same truth table, we may use logical equivalences to rewrite parts of predicates without changing their overall truth tables. For example, we may show that:[4]

$(P_1 \wedge Q_1 \Rightarrow R_1) \Leftrightarrow P_1 \Rightarrow (Q_1 \Rightarrow R_1)$

by gradually rewriting the left-hand side until we obtain the right-hand side. Using the law $P \Rightarrow Q \Leftrightarrow \neg P \vee Q$, with P as $P_1 \wedge Q_1$ and Q as R_1 we obtain:

$(P_1 \wedge Q_1 \Rightarrow R_1) \Leftrightarrow \neg (P_1 \wedge Q_1) \vee R_1$

Since $\neg (P \wedge Q) \Leftrightarrow \neg P \vee \neg Q$

$\neg (P_1 \wedge Q_1) \vee R_1 \Leftrightarrow (\neg P_1 \vee \neg Q_1) \vee R_1$

Using the law $P \vee (Q \vee R) \Leftrightarrow (P \vee Q) \vee R$

$(\neg P_1 \vee \neg Q_1) \vee R_1 \Leftrightarrow \neg P_1 \vee (\neg Q_1 \vee R_1)$

Since $P \Rightarrow Q \Leftrightarrow \neg P \vee Q$

$\neg P_1 \vee (\neg Q_1 \vee R_1) \Leftrightarrow \neg P_1 \vee (Q_1 \Rightarrow R_1)$

and finally by the same law

$\neg P_1 \vee (Q_1 \Rightarrow R_1) \Leftrightarrow P_1 \Rightarrow (Q_1 \Rightarrow R_1)$

---

[3] It can be shown that all connectives may be defined in terms of $\wedge$ and $\neg$ (or $\vee$ and $\neg$).

[4] The constituents in this predicate all have subscripts in order to distinguish them from the constituents of the laws.

Exercise 3.9 * Using the result just established, show that:

$$P \Rightarrow (Q \Rightarrow R) \Leftrightarrow Q \Rightarrow (P \Rightarrow R)$$

□

3.3 Relations and quantifiers

Not all valid deductions are amenable to analysis simply in terms of the logical connectives. Consider the deduction from the car park example of Chapter 2 which was discussed in the introduction to this chapter:

Given	$ordinaryCars' - ordinaryCars = 1$
	$ordinaryCars' \leq carParkCapacity$
it follows	$ordinaryCars < carParkCapacity$

There are no logical connectives involved in either premise or the conclusion of this argument; each predicate simply expresses a relationship between some values. Thus, if we were to attempt to analyse the validity of this argument in truth-table terms, each premise and the conclusion must be considered a distinct predicate and the argument would reduce to:

Given	P
	Q
it follows	R

Now $P \wedge Q \Rightarrow R$ is not a tautology. This means that although our argument is clearly valid, its validity cannot be established simply in terms of the logical connectives.

The situation is no different if the predicates involved in an argument do involve connectives. Consider the following deduction about a blocks scene:

Given	block b is on top of block a
	if a block is clear then there is no block on top of it
it follows	block a is not clear

in which the second premise includes $\Rightarrow$ and $\neg$, and the conclusion includes $\neg$. The first premise expresses a relationship between two particular blocks. The second premise does not refer explicitly to either of these blocks. Thus, if we were to consider the validity of this argument simply in terms of the connectives, the best we could do is consider the deduction to be:

Given P

              $Q \Rightarrow \neg\, R$

it follows $\neg\, S$

Once again, the validity of the deduction cannot be established in this manner. What we must note is that the validity of the deduction rests on the fact that the second premise expresses a property of any block which must hold for block a in particular. That is, the validity of the deduction depends not only on properties of the connective $\Rightarrow$, but also on interaction between the constituents of the implication and the other premise which cannot be captured in terms of connectives only. Thus, the representation we use must be capable of capturing that interaction.

Logic achieves this through the capability of denoting values by expressions, and expressing relationships between them. In this section we examine these in more detail. We also consider the quantifiers which are used to express general properties such as that illustrated in the above deduction.

The internal structure of predicates

Expressions

Perhaps the simplest means of denoting a value, at least in the case of integers, is to give the value explicitly. The type of the integers, $\mathbb{Z}$, is part of the Z library and so specifications may contain numbers such as 1, 99 and so forth. As we saw in Chapter 2 it is possible to introduce new types into a specification. For the blocks world, we shall need a type $BLOCK$ which is the set of all blocks of interest. The names a to g of the blocks are values of this type.

One of the most basic means of denoting a value in logic is with a *variable*. For example, in the specification of Chapter 2, the number of ordinary cars in the car park was denoted by the variable *ordinaryCars*.

As discussed in Chapter 2, a variable has a type, that is, a set of values which it might legally take, and it denotes a value of that type. The term 'variable' does not indicate that the value it denotes may be changed, but simply that its value may be any one of the values from the type. Variables are a very powerful tool in specifications, since they allow general statements to be made.

As well as denoting values with variables, we denoted values with expressions such as *ordinaryCars* $+ 1$. In this expression, $\_ + \_$ is a *function*.[5] Its use allows us to define an integer in terms of two other integers.

---

[5] The use of the underscore $\_$ is a convention in Z to show the arity of a function and to indicate where the arguments should be given. Thus $\_ + \_$ is a binary infix function. We shall drop the underscores if their position is clear from the context.

Example 3.1 The number of blocks above a block in a blocks scene may be given by a function *numberOfBlocksAbove* _. For example, in the blocks scene of Figure 3.1, *numberOfBlocksAbove b* = 2. □

The Z library provides a number of arithmetic functions which may be used in a specification, as summarized in the following table:

Symbol	Arity	Associativity	Meaning	Restriction
_ + _	2	Left	Addition	
_ − _	2	Left	Subtraction	
_ * _	2	Left	Multiplication	
_ div _	2	Left	Integer division	2nd argument ≠ 0
_ mod _	2	Left	Modulo	2nd argument ≠ 0
− _	1		Minus	

The functions + and − are of equal precedence. Likewise, *, div and mod are of equal precedence but higher than + or −.

It is possible to introduce further functions into a specification, indeed they will be an important modelling technique, but that is the topic of Chapter 7.

Relations

Properties of values and relationships between values are both described with *relations*. A relation has an arity, which is the number of expressions amongst that it expresses a relationship. There are also rules for each relation that state the type of the values to which it may be applied.

The most fundamental relation in specification in Z is equality, =, and this is part of the basic Z language. Two expressions of the same type are equal if they denote the same values. For example:

$2 * 3 = 55 \text{ div } 9$

$2 * ordinaryCars = ordinaryCars + ordinaryCars$

Two expressions of the same type are not equal if they denote different values. The equality of expressions of different types is not defined.

The Z library provides a number of binary arithmetic relations, $<$, $\leq$, $>$ and $\geq$, which express the obvious relationships:

$3 + 4 \geq 2 * 3 + 1$

$ordinaryCars < ordinaryCars + 1$

As with functions, it is possible to introduce relations into a specification. Relations, too, are an important modelling technique to which a separate chapter is devoted (Chapter 5). In this chapter we shall use relations, but we shall define them informally with logical equivalences only, or even rely on an English description. For example, we may define the property that a number is even as follows:

$$even \ x \Leftrightarrow x \bmod 2 = 0$$

Here, $even\_$ is a unary prefix relation. We may then construct the predicates:

$$even \ 143$$

$$even \ x \Rightarrow even \ y * x$$

Some of the predicates listed above are clearly true and some are false. For example, $2 * 3 = 55 \operatorname{div} 9$ is true, while $even \ 143$ is false. In contrast, the truth value of the predicate $3 = y \operatorname{div} 5$ cannot be determined yet. In order to give this predicate a truth value we must know a value for y. If $y = 49$, for example, it is false; if $y = 15$, it is true.

In §3.1 we chose some relations to be used to describe block scenes. We may now introduce names for these relations, and give their meaning:

Relation	Example	Intended meaning
$\_onTopOf\_$	$b \ onTopOf \ a$	b is directly on top of a
$\_above\_$	$f \ above \ a$	f is above a in a tower
$onFloor\_$	$onFloor \ c$	c is resting on the floor
$clear\_$	$clear \ c$	c has nothing on top of it

With these relations we can now represent simple statements about the blocks scene of Figure 3.1:

English

c is above e or on top of e

if x is on top of y then x is not on the floor

Logic

$c \ above \ e \lor c \ onTopOf \ e$

$x \ onTopOf \ y \Rightarrow \neg \ onFloor \ x$

Exercise 3.10 Represent the following statements in logic:

i. if b is on the floor then it is not on top of a

ii. a is on the floor, but b is not

$\square$

Consider the predicates:

$$x \le y \qquad x < y + 1 \qquad \neg (x > y)$$

These are each true for the same collections of values for x and y. Thus they are all interchangeable in the description of a situation. We say that these three predicates express the same *property*. Thus, with regard to constructing a model, the important thing about a predicate is the property it expresses, not the particular choice of relations involved in it. This is why when we consider operations we are interested in subcase properties rather than subcase predicates.

Quantifiers

Let us now consider how we might express general statements with terms and relations. For example, the statement 'every block on top of b is not on the floor' is a general statement about blocks on top of b, which is true in any blocks scene. A possible candidate is the predicate:

$$x \; onTopOf \; b \Rightarrow \neg \; onFloor \; x$$

but this does not have a single truth value. Only when we know values for x can we say if it is true or false. However, the statement we wish to represent is something that is true, irrespective of the value of x. Thus, this predicate does not properly represent the statement, and the logic must provide other constructs.

To represent 'every block on top of b is not on the floor' we must assert that $x \; onTopOf \; b \Rightarrow \neg \; onFloor \; x$ is true for all values of x. This is written:

$$\forall x : BLOCK \bullet x \; onTopOf \; b \Rightarrow \neg \; onFloor \; x$$

The symbol $\forall$ is the *universal quantifier*, and is pronounced 'for all'. Notice that we have included the type of the variable x, namely $BLOCK$, in the predicate. $\forall$ is called a quantifier because it is involved in specifying the extent to which a predicate holds for values of x. In the case of $\forall$ it must hold for all values.

More generally, supposing x is a variable and S is a set or type, then the universal quantification of P with respect to x is:

$$\forall x : S \bullet P$$

This predicate is true if P is true for all possible values of x in S, otherwise it is false. The variable x is said to be universally quantified. The predicate is pronounced 'for all values of x in S, P'.

Example 3.2 The statement 'any block on the floor is clear' would be represented as:

$$\forall x : BLOCK \bullet onFloor \; x \Rightarrow clear \; x$$

This predicate is false for the blocks scene of Figure 3.1 since, for example, a is on the floor but is not clear. It would be true in a blocks scene in which there were no towers.   □

The statement 'for any blocks x and y, if x is on top of y then y is not clear and x is not on the floor' may be represented by:

$$\forall \, x : BLOCK \bullet (\forall \, y : BLOCK \bullet$$
$$x \; onTopOf \; y \Rightarrow \neg \; clear \; y \wedge \neg \; onFloor \; x)$$

To make predicates more readable, repeated quantifiers over variables of the same type may be abbreviated:

$$\forall \, x, y : BLOCK \bullet x \; onTopOf \; y \Rightarrow \neg \; clear \; y \wedge \neg \; onFloor \; x$$

Where the adjacent quantifiers are over different types, the type information must be preserved. For example, the predicate:

$$\forall \, x : BLOCK \bullet \forall \, y : BLOCK \bullet \forall \, n : \mathbb{Z} \bullet P$$

becomes

$$\forall \, x, y : BLOCK; \; z : \mathbb{Z} \bullet P$$

in which a semicolon separates universally quantified variables of different types.

Exercise 3.11 Represent the statements:

> if block x is on top of block y then block x is above block y
>
> if block x is above block y and block y is above block z
> then block x is above block z

as predicates.   □

The statement 'there is a block on top of block a' is another kind of general statement. It says some block exists, without being specific about the identity of the block. This statement would be represented by the predicate:

$$\exists \, x : BLOCK \bullet x \; onTopOf \; a$$

The symbol $\exists$ is the *existential quantifier*, and is pronounced 'there exists'.

More generally, if x is a variable and S is a set or type, then existential quantification of a predicate P with respect to x is denoted:

$$\exists \, x : S \bullet P$$

This predicate is true if P is true for at least one value of x in S, otherwise it is false. The variable x is said to be existentially quantified. The predicate is pronounced 'there exists a value of x in S such that P'.

Example 3.3 The statement 'there is a block between a and f' could be represented by the predicate:

$$\exists \, x : BLOCK \bullet f \; onTopOf \; x \wedge x \; onTopOf \; a$$

                                                                                    □

Example 3.4 The predicate:

$$\exists\, x : \mathbb{Z} \bullet x > x + 1$$

asserts that there is an integer which is greater that itself plus 1. This is clearly false, although we must acknowledge that this judgement depends on consideration of all the integers. □

The statement of Example 3.3 is true of the blocks scene of Figure 3.1 and asserts that some block exists. We can, of course, see by inspection of Figure 3.1 that the block in question is block b. However, we will not always know which values, if any, make an existential quantification true.

For example, suppose S is a set of integers. The predicate:

$$\exists\, x : S \bullet 1 < x \wedge x < 5$$

asserts that there is a member of S strictly between 1 and 5. Without knowing more about S we cannot say if it is true or not. However, even if we are told it is true we do not know the value of x that makes it true. All we know of such a value of x is that it is a member of S and it has the properties expressed in the predicate $1 < x \wedge x < 5$. In general, an existential quantifier is used when you know the properties that a value must satisfy, but not the value itself. The use of the existential quantifier in a predicate in a schema to describe the properties of some value when its actual value cannot be known is one that causes novice Z users some difficulty.

Predicates involving adjacent existential quantifiers may be simplified in the same manner as predicates involving adjacent universal quantifiers.

An existentially quantified predicate $\exists\, x : T \bullet P$ is true if there is one or more values of x such that P is true. It does not mean that there is a unique (just one) such value. If we wish to assert that there is a unique value then we use the unique existential quantifier $\exists_1$ (or $\exists\,!$):

$$\exists_1 x : T \bullet P$$

This is pronounced 'there exists a unique x in T such that P'.

Example 3.5 We may assert that the equation $x^2 = 4$ has exactly one positive solution with either of the following predicates:

$$\exists_1 x : \mathbb{Z} \bullet x > 0 \wedge x * x = 4 \qquad\qquad \exists_1 x : \mathbb{N} \bullet x * x = 4$$

In the predicate on the right, $\mathbb{N}$ denotes the set of natural numbers, that is, $\mathbb{N} = \{0, 1, 2, \ldots\}$. $\mathbb{N}$ is included in the Z library. □

Exercise 3.12 Represent the statement 'every block is either clear or has a unique block on top of it'. □

In fact $\exists_1$ is just shorthand for a particular usage of the ordinary existential quantifier which we may illustrate by re-expressing $\exists_1 x : \mathbb{N} \bullet x * x = 4$ as:

$$\exists x : \mathbb{N} \bullet (x * x = 4 \wedge \forall y : \mathbb{N} \bullet y * y = 4 \Rightarrow y = x)$$

That is, there is a unique value with some property if there is a value x with that property, and all the values y with that property are in fact equal to x. This is a common approach to defining unique values; another example follows.

Example 3.6 Suppose $f\_$ is a prefix function from the integers to the integers. The property that $f\_$ has a maximum value is:

$$\exists \, max, x : \mathbb{Z} \bullet f \; x = max \wedge \forall y : \mathbb{Z} \bullet f \; y \le max$$

$\square$

Mixing quantifiers in a predicate

Universal and existential quantifiers may, of course, be mixed together in the same predicate, as we have already illustrated above.

Example 3.7 In the blocks scene the statement 'every block is on the floor or on top of another block' might be represented by:

$$\forall x : BLOCK \bullet (onFloor \; x \vee \exists y : BLOCK \bullet x \; onTopOf \; y)$$

$\square$

Notice that this predicate does not state that a block cannot be on top of itself, that is, it does not state that $x \neq y$. This is not necessarily a defect because the meaning of $x \; onTopOf \; y$ may be such that we can deduce $x \; onTopOf \; y \Rightarrow x \neq y$. For example, for the scene in Figure 3.1 we know that the following predicates are true:

$g \; onTopOf \; f$
$f \; onTopOf \; b$
$b \; onTopOf \; a$
$e \; onTopOf \; d$

and that they describe all the $onTopOf$ relationships in the scene. We can therefore deduce:

$$\forall x, y : BLOCK \bullet x \; onTopOf \; y \Rightarrow x \neq y$$

by case-by-case inspection for all possible values for x and y. If, however, we wish to state that for every scene no block can be on top of itself then we can include the predicate $x \neq y$.

Exercise 3.13 * Create a blocks scene in which the predicate:

$$\exists_1 \, y : BLOCK \bullet \forall \, x : BLOCK \bullet (\neg \ clear \ x \Rightarrow y \ onTopOf \ x)$$

is true. □

Special care must be taken when constructing a predicate involving both universal and existential quantifiers to ensure that they are used in the right order, since this can make quite a difference to the meaning of the predicate. Consider the ambiguous statement 'there is a block on top of every block that is not clear'. We will exploit this ambiguity as we consider how it might be represented in logic. One reading of the statement is 'there is some block on top of every block that is not clear', that is, it need not be the same block each time. This would be represented as:

$$\forall \, x : BLOCK \bullet \exists \, y : BLOCK \bullet (\neg \ clear \ x \Rightarrow y \ onTopOf \ x)$$

This predicate is true of any blocks world. We see this by noting that whatever the value of x, there will be a value of y such that y is on top of x if x is not clear.

The alternative reading is that 'there is some block which is on top of every block that is not clear' and it is the same block in each case. In logic this would be represented as:

$$\exists \, y : BLOCK \bullet \forall \, x : BLOCK \bullet (\neg \ clear \ x \Rightarrow y \ onTopOf \ x)$$

Notice that our use of $\exists$ rather than $\exists_1$ means that we are allowing the possibility that there is more than one block on top of another. This might be the case if some blocks are smaller than others. The predicate above is false regarding the blocks scene of Figure 3.1. We can see this by noting that there is no value of y such that, whatever the value of x, if x is not clear then y is on top of x. There are, however, possible blocks scenes for which it is true.

Free variables, bound variables, and scope

In the predicate:

$$\exists \, x : BLOCK \bullet x \ onTopOf \ y$$

the variable x occurs twice, once immediately following the $\exists$ and once in the predicate $x \ onTopOf \ y$. The occurrence in $x \ onTopOf \ y$ is said to be *bound*; it is subject to the existential quantifier. In contrast, the single occurrence of y is not subject to a quantifier.

More formally, in the predicate $\exists \, x : T \bullet P$ the predicate P is the *scope* of the variable x introduced by the $\exists$. That is, occurrences of x in this scope are the bound occurrences that are subject to the quantifier.[6] The x in $\exists\, x : T$ is called a *binding* occurrence. An occurrence of a variable in a predicate is *free* if it is not a binding occurrence or a bound occurrence.[7] Similar definitions apply to the universal quantifier.

The scope of a quantified variable begins at the • and extends as far right as possible. That is, you may think of a quantifier as a prefix operator with precedence lower than that of any of the logical connectives. We must include brackets if it is necessary to restrict the scope of a quantified variable.

The same variable name may have both free and bound occurrences in the same predicate. For example, in:

$$clear\ x \wedge \exists\, x : BLOCK\ \bullet\ x\ onTopOf\ y$$

x has a free occurrence in *clear x* and a bound occurrence in *x onTopOf y*. In this predicate the free occurrences of x correspond to a different variable than that of the bound occurrences of x.

Example 3.8 In the predicate:

$$(\forall\, x : \mathbb{Z}\ \bullet\ x < x + 1) \wedge (\forall\, x : \mathbb{Z}\ \bullet\ x < y)$$

the second, third and fifth occurrences of x are bound, and the first and fourth are binding occurrences. The fourth and fifth occurrences of x are instances of a different variable from the first, second and third.   □

Exercise 3.14 Identify the free, binding and bound occurrences of variables in the admittedly bizarre predicate:

$$\exists\, x : \mathbb{N}\ \bullet\ (x \geq y \wedge \forall\, x : \mathbb{N}\ \bullet\ (\exists\, y : \mathbb{N}\ \bullet\ x > y) \wedge x > y)$$

For the bound occurrences, say which quantifier binds them.   □

As we saw earlier, a predicate that contains free variables does not have a single fixed truth value. Rather, it has a truth value for each possible value of the free variables involved in it. For example, the predicate:

$$\exists\, x : BLOCK\ \bullet\ x\ onTopOf\ y$$

is true of the blocks scene illustrated in Figure 3.1 if $y = b$, but false if $y = e$. Thus, this predicate expresses the property 'block y has a block on top of it'. This property might also have been expressed by means of a unary relation. More generally, a predicate with n free variables expresses a property among n values just as an n-ary relation does.

---

[6]In the interests of simplicity, we ignore the possibility that some of the occurrences of x in P may be bound by a quantifier within P.

[7]It is possible in Z for a quantification to be over a set rather than a type. This raises the possibility of a predicate of the form $\exists\, x : y\ \bullet\ P$, where y is a set variable. In this predicate we shall say that the occurrence of y is a free occurrence.

Exercise 3.15 What property does the following predicate express?

$$\exists\, z : \mathbb{Z} \bullet z \geq 0 \land x = y + z$$

□

The property 'block y has a block on top of it' may also be expressed by the predicate:

$$\exists\, z : BLOCK \bullet z \; onTopOf \; y$$

Changing the name of the bound variable from x to z has had no impact on the property that the predicate expresses. Arbitrary changes to the name of a bound variable can have an impact, however, by changing structure. Consider the predicate:

$$\exists\, y : BLOCK \bullet y \; onTopOf \; y$$

Changing the name of the bound variable to y has resulted in what was originally a free variable being 'captured' by the quantifier. The result is a dramatic change in the property expressed by the predicate; it now expresses the same property as *false* since there is no block that is on top of itself.

Some laws about the quantifiers

As with the laws about the logical connectives, we expect in the simple examples in this book that you will be able to follow the manipulation of predicates that involve quantifiers from first principles, based on the informal meaning we have given for them. Once again, however, we list a range of laws that might be useful. Since the reasoning involved is now more sophisticated, we also justify a number of them.

The order of adjacent quantifiers of the same kind is not important:

$$(\forall\, x : X \bullet \forall\, y : Y \bullet P) \Leftrightarrow (\forall\, y : Y \bullet \forall\, x : X \bullet P)$$
$$(\exists\, x : X \bullet \exists\, y : Y \bullet P) \Leftrightarrow (\exists\, y : Y \bullet \exists\, x : X \bullet P)$$

as long as there is no variable capture. The danger of capture is illustrated in the predicates:

$$\exists\, x : \mathbb{P}\,\mathbb{Z} \bullet \exists\, y : x \bullet even \; y \qquad\qquad \exists\, y : x \bullet \exists\, x : \mathbb{P}\,\mathbb{Z} \bullet even \; y$$

The predicate on the left expresses the property 'there is some set of integers in which there is an even number'. Reversing the order of the quantifiers changes the role of x, and it is a free variable in the predicate on the right. Assuming x has the appropriate type, the predicate on the right expresses the property 'there is an even number'.

As we have seen, the order of mixed quantifiers is important. In general we may state only that:

$$(\exists\, y : Y \bullet \forall\, x : X \bullet P) \Rightarrow (\forall\, x : X \bullet \exists\, y : Y \bullet P)$$

provided that there is no variable capture as the result of the reordering.

The following results illustrate how negation interacts with the quantifiers:

$$\neg\,(\forall\, x : X \bullet P) \Leftrightarrow (\exists\, x : X \bullet \neg\, P)$$
$$\neg\,(\exists\, x : X \bullet P) \Leftrightarrow (\forall\, x : X \bullet \neg\, P)$$

The first of these says that if it is not the case that something is true for all x, then there must be values of x for which it is false.

Exercise 3.16 Is the following predicate true or false?

$$(\forall\, x : X \bullet P) \Rightarrow (\exists\, x : X \bullet P)$$

□

The remainder of the laws we present are motivated by the need to manipulate predicates when reasoning about specifications. This includes, in particular, the determination of the precondition of an operation, discussed in Chapter 6. The laws justify the consideration of a large predicate a fragment at a time, much as you might consider a large arithmetic calculation a fragment at a time. However, unlike an arithmetic calculation, care must be taken, when choosing fragments of a predicate, to ensure that they are not taken out of context. The general form of the kind of predicates we shall be considering is:

$$\exists\, x_1 : T_1; \ \ldots; \ x_n : T_n \bullet P_1 \wedge \ldots \wedge P_m$$

where $P_1, \ldots, P_m$ may contain free variables.

The first observation is that a quantifier affects only the parts of the predicate that involve free occurrences of the quantified variable. If P does not include free occurrences of x then:

$$(\exists\, x : T \bullet P \wedge Q) \Leftrightarrow P \wedge \exists\, x : T \bullet Q$$

Thus, when considering the validity of $\exists\, x : T \bullet P \wedge Q$ we could select out $\exists\, x : T \bullet Q$ for separate consideration. For example, given the predicate $\exists\, x : \mathbb{N} \bullet y > 0 \wedge x < y$ we may select out $\exists\, x : \mathbb{N} \bullet x < y$ for consideration separately from $y > 0$. The ability to do this helps to simplify the reasoning.

If the part of a predicate a quantifier affects involves several conjuncts they must all be considered together. This is because the existential quantifier does not distribute over conjunction. For example, of the following predicates:

$$\exists\, x : \mathbb{Z} \bullet (x > 0 \wedge x \leq 0) \qquad\qquad (\exists\, x : \mathbb{Z} \bullet x > 0) \wedge (\exists\, x : \mathbb{Z} \bullet x \leq 0)$$

the left is false, while the right is true. The existential quantifier does, however, distribute over disjunction. That is:

$$(\exists\, x : X \bullet P \vee Q) \Leftrightarrow (\exists\, x : X \bullet P) \vee (\exists\, x : X \bullet Q)$$

The universal quantifier distributes over conjunction, but not disjunction.

Exercise 3.17 * Give an example to show that the universal quantifier does not distribute over disjunction. □

The precondition of an operation, as described in Chapter 6, usually involves a number of equalities. A representative predicate might be:

$$\exists\, x', y' : \mathbb{Z} \bullet x < y \wedge y' = y \wedge x' = x + 1 \wedge x' < y'$$

Since the equality $x' = x + 1$ tells us the value of x', we may dispense with the quantifier for x' if we drop the equality and replace all bound instances of x' by $x + 1$. This yields:

$$\exists\, y' : \mathbb{Z} \bullet x < y \wedge y' = y \wedge x + 1 < y'$$

In a similar manner we may drop the quantification for y' to obtain:

$$x < y \wedge x + 1 < y$$

which is logically equivalent to $x + 1 < y$. In this way we have identified a simpler form of the property that underlies the original predicate.

3.4 The justification of deductions

Logic provides not only a language for writing predicates but also a means of reasoning with them. Let us look once again at the deduction from the car park example of Chapter 2 considered in the introduction to this chapter:

> Given $ordinaryCars' - ordinaryCars = 1$
> $ordinaryCars' \leq carParkCapacity$
> it follows $ordinaryCars < carParkCapacity$

It appealed to an intuitive understanding of $\leq$, $<$ and $+$. This is typical of the initial justification a mathematician would offer in favour of such a deduction. In deductions that rely on more complex interrelationships this kind of reasoning may be less persuasive. For example, is the following deduction valid?[8]

---

[8] See [9] for techniques that might help determine the validity of this deduction.

Given $u \leq 2 * v * v * v / (3 * v * v - 1)$

$y * y < (1 - x)(2 - 3)(3 - x) / x$

$u \geq v + x$

it follows $x > 0$

A concise justification that this deduction is sound, if such a thing is possible, must appeal to results that are not intuitive. In such circumstances we are likely to be sceptical, and would feel justified in asking for more detail. While this example is extreme, the same point is true of deductions made in the context of specification. In order to rule out the possibility of mistakes, we must be able to fall back onto increasingly more basic modes of reasoning. In the case of the justification for $ordinaryCars < carParkCapacity$ we might want to justify:

$$ordinaryCars + 1 \leq carParkCapacity$$
$$\Rightarrow ordinaryCars < carParkCapacity$$

whatever the values of $ordinaryCars$ and $carParkCapacity$. More abstractly, this is $\forall x, y : \mathbb{Z} \bullet x + 1 \leq y \Rightarrow x < y$.

Although the reader might feel that $\forall x, y : \mathbb{Z} \bullet x + 1 \leq y \Rightarrow x < y$ is obvious, how could one justify it? In the final assessment, the only possible approach is to say what $+$, $<$ and $\leq$ mean in such a way that the implication may be checked case by case. We can achieve this as follows. For the meaning of $+$ we give a set of triples:

$$\{\ldots, (-1, 0, -1), (0, 0, 0), (0, 1, 1), (1, 0, 1), (1, 1, 2), (2, 0, 2), \ldots\}$$

in which a triple (a, b, c) in this set means that $a + b = c$ is true. For $<$ we give a set of pairs:

$$\{\ldots, (0, 1), (0, 2), (0, 3) \ldots\}$$

in which a pair (a, b) means that $a < b$ is true. We give a similar set of pairs for $\leq$ and then we may state how the implication is to be checked: perform an exhaustive check of all the possible cases for the values of x and y. Of course, in practice we could not complete such a check, since there are an infinite number of possibilities.

We are forced to accept that the approach to justifying deductions with regard to meaning is fundamentally limited. It will, in general, leave us with cases which are far too numerous to check in practice. So logic considers another way of justifying deductions. This approach is based on using only laws of logic, and is reminiscent of the approach we used to show that $(P_1 \wedge Q_1 \Rightarrow R_1) \Leftrightarrow P_1 \Rightarrow (Q_1 \Rightarrow R_1)$ on page 58. The laws are used to rewrite predicates, in a purely syntactic manner, and no reference is made to truth tables. It is this approach to reasoning that is called *formal*. This topic is beyond the scope of this book, although we do make some further general comments in Chapter 12.

In this book, we are primarily concerned with logic as a language for description, and the informal style of justification that we have already illustrated will have to suffice. This acceptance of informality in the presentation of mathematics should not be misinterpreted, however. Informal reasoning is safe only in the hands of those who can, if necessary, pay greater attention to detail. The omission of material from this book should not be interpreted as a claim that it is not necessary; it is simply that this book is introductory.

Chapter 4

Sets

4.1 Informal example: car registration

The Metropolitan University of the Western World has a parking problem, and it is something that arouses strong feelings amongst the staff. As the Western World campus is fairly compact there are not enough parking spaces for the staff, never mind the students. To make matters worse, staff from the rival institution next door are in the habit of parking their cars on the Western World campus, since they are even more poorly provided for. A special committee was established to examine the issue. Amongst its recommendations was a proposal for a two-tier registration scheme, and Western World chose to implement this.

For a small annual fee, a Western World staff member can register his or her car and obtain a registration disc. This qualifies the staff member to park the registered vehicle on the campus if they can find a space. In future it will not be possible to park an unregistered vehicle on campus. The university hopes, of course, that being able to police more accurately which cars may park on the campus will bring about a general easing of the parking problem. For a more substantial annual fee[1], a Western World staff member can register his or her car and obtain a parking permit. This qualifies him or her to park in one of a number of specially designated car parks on the Western World campus. Those who have only a registration disc cannot park in these particular car parks. The total number of parking permits is, or course, limited so that permit holders will always be able to find a space.

Naturally, Western World needs to keep track of which cars are registered and which hold permits. We shall examine, at the end of this chapter, how to model a system suitable for this requirement. The core of the system will be a record of the registered cars, which can be modelled as a collection.

---

[1] But less than the price of a pint of beer a week.

4.2   Sets: the fundamentals

Specifications often involve collections. For example, the car park example of Chapter 2 involved the collection of season passes that had been issued. Sets are the mathematical objects used to model collections. A set is itself a collection of values or elements, each of which represents an element in the corresponding collection in the application. For example, consider the collection of George Eliot novels that I own. This may be modelled by a set of four elements which we list as follows:

$$\{adamBede, millOnTheFloss, middlemarch, romola\}$$

A set is an abstract, intangible mathematical object. It has no physical existence; you cannot, for example, see or feel a set. The set listed above is not a collection of books; it is a model of a collection of books. In fact, the printed symbols on this page are not the set either; they are merely a device we have used to communicate the members of the set to the reader.

Since a set is a mathematical object, it would be incorrect to speak of a set of George Eliot novels. Rather, we should use a term such as 'collection'. Nevertheless, this usage is common, and we may occasionally lapse into it ourselves, but it is not to be understood literally.

The power of sets as a modelling medium becomes apparent when we observe that real-world events as disparate as the acquisition of a new novel and the departure of a pass holder from a car park may be modelled by means of functions over sets.

Membership of a set

Suppose I wished to lend someone a particular George Eliot novel. This would be possible only if I owned a copy of it. In the model we have chosen, this condition is modelled using the *membership* relation, written $\in$ and pronounced 'is a member of'. For example:

$$middlemarch \in \{adamBede, millOnTheFloss, middlemarch, romola\}$$

is true if there is a copy of Middlemarch in my collection and we can see by inspection that it is indeed true. In contrast, *felixHolt* is not a member of this set.

This example illustrates how modelling a collection with a set allows us to model the individual identity of the elements in the collection. A simpler model of the collection, say the number of George Eliot novels I own, would not.

More generally, suppose S is a set and x is an element. The predicate $x \in S$, which is pronounced 'x is a member of S', is true if x is amongst the members of the set S. If S is presented by listing its members, we can judge $x \in S$ by looking down the list.

Example 4.1 The set of even integers strictly between 0 and 10 is $\{2, 4, 6, 8\}$ and we see that $6 \in \{2, 4, 6, 8\}$ is true, whereas $7 \in \{2, 4, 6, 8\}$ is false. □

Subset

Consider the sets $\{1, 3, 5\}$ and $\{1, 2, 3, 4, 5, 6\}$. Every value that is a member of the first set is also a member of the second set, and we say that $\{1, 3, 5\}$ is a *subset* of $\{1, 2, 3, 4, 5, 6\}$. This is written:

$$\{1, 3, 5\} \subseteq \{1, 2, 3, 4, 5, 6\}$$

Similarly

$$\{adamBede, romola\} \subseteq \{adamBede, middlemarch, romola\}$$

Specifying sets by enumeration

If, as we have done above, we define a set by listing its members, we are said to be defining the set by *enumeration*. In this section we investigate some of the implications of this approach.

The collection of Virginia Woolf novels I own may be modelled by the set:

$$\{orlando, the Waves\}$$

The outcome of inspecting this set to answer questions about membership would be the same if it was written:

$$\{the Waves, orlando\}$$

or even:

$$\{orlando, the Waves, orlando\}$$

The order in which the members of a set are listed is not significant: the members of the set are not ordered. It follows that it is not possible to talk of the first member of a set, for example. Furthermore, the number of times a member of a set is listed is not significant: it makes no sense to talk of an element being a member of a set more than once. It is conventional, however, to list the members of a set once. In summary, a set is determined entirely by the elements that are members of it.

Example 4.2 Sometimes it is not immediately apparent that a listing of the elements of a set does contain repetition. For example:

$$\{9, 3 * 3, 69 \text{ div } 7\}$$
$$\{f(1), f(2), f(3), f(4)\}$$

where $f(x) = 1$ for all x. □

While it is convenient to define a set initially by listing its members, if we want to refer to the set a number of times it will be helpful to be able to give the set a name. We can do this in Z by means of an *abbreviation definition*. We might, for example, want to define a set of numbers:

$$luckyNumbers == \{3, 7, 12, 15, 21, 28, 34, 41, 47, 55, 59, 64, 69, 72, 91\}$$

In the remainder of the specification we may now use the name of the set in place of the set itself. For example, we may write $n \in LuckyNumbers$ rather than $n \in \{3, 7, 12, 15, 21, 28, 34, 41, 47, 55, 59, 64, 69, 72, 91\}$. Something defined by abbreviation definition is a global constant in the specification.

There are two specific notations in Z for specifying sets by enumeration. The first notation we have met before and consists of a sequence of comma-separated expressions enclosed in $\{\}$. Note that a set description such as $\{10, 11, 12, \ldots\}$ is not defined in Z because it is not clear how to replace the ... and so must never appear in a specification. However, we will use it for explanatory purposes, and you should think of it as having the same status as English commentary.

The second notation is the *free type* definition. For example, the car park specification of Chapter 2 included:

$$
\begin{aligned}
REPORT ::= \ &success \\
| \ &ordinaryCarParkFull \\
| \ &ordinaryCarParkEmpty \\
| \ &passInUse \\
| \ &passNotInUse
\end{aligned}
$$

A definition by enumeration is also called *extensional*. An item is in the set because it is amongst the listed members of the set. The key property of an extensional definition of a set is that any question about the set, such as 'are all the members of the set $\{2, 4, 6\}$ even?', can be justified only by an examination of every member of the set.

Equality of sets

We saw above that two different representations may denote the same set. For example, $\{orlando, theWaves\}$ denotes the same set as $\{theWaves, orlando\}$. We express this explicitly in Z by means of the usual *equality* relation:

$$\{orlando, theWaves\} = \{theWaves, orlando\}$$

As you would expect, two sets are equal if and only if they have the same members. A complication arises if the sets are empty but we will deal with this when we consider the type of a set.

Small collections

Collections do not necessarily have many members, of course. For example, my collection of Winifred Holtby novels may be modelled by the set:

$\{southRiding\}$

A set such as this, with one member, is called a *singleton* set.

I do not own any novels by Barbara Cartland, so to model this collection we need a set with no members. We saw in the car park example of Chapter 2 that in the initial state the set of passes in use had no members, so it is necessary to model such collections. We call a set that has no members an *empty set*, and it is denoted:

$\varnothing$ or $\{\}$

In this book we shall always use $\varnothing$.

Example 4.3 The set of integers which are solutions of the equation $x * x = -1$ is empty. □

4.3 Sets and types

The underlying type of a set

In Z, all the elements of a set must be of the same type, and it is called the *underlying* type of the set. This type determines the possible values that may be members of the set. Whenever we represent a set it ought to be clear what its underlying type is. For example, in the set:

$\{orlando, theWaves\}$

we shall suppose that the members are all from some type $BOOK$, so that the underlying type of $\{orlando, theWaves\}$ is $BOOK$.

Example 4.4 The underlying type of the set $\{2, 4, 6, 8\}$ is the integers, $\mathbb{Z}$. □

Example 4.5 $\{1, southRiding, 2\}$ is not a set, because the 'members' of it are not all of the same type. □

The type of a set

The sets we have enumerated so far have been very simple: their members have been unstructured values. However, a set is itself a value and we may enumerate sets whose members are themselves sets. For example:

$\{\{orlando, theWaves\}, \{southRiding\}\}$

is a set in which the members are sets of elements from BOOK. This capability
would be useful for modelling collections of collections. What, however, is
the underlying type of this set? Equivalently, what is the type of the value
{ *southRiding* }? This value is a set with a member, so its type cannot be
BOOK, since values of *BOOK* are unstructured.

Each member of {{ *orlando, theWaves* }, { *southRiding* }} is a set of *BOOK*.
Furthermore, we could construct sets of this form taking any sets of *BOOK* as
members. Thus we need the type whose values are all possible sets of *BOOK*.
Thus, to provide a means of giving the underlying type of this set we must
introduce a way of building new types from existing types.

Given any type, the set of all possible sets of elements of that type forms
another type, called a *power set* type. The power set type of a type T is written
$\mathbb{P}\,T$. $\mathbb{P}$ is called a *type constructor*, for its role of making new types from existing
types. So, the underlying type of the set {{ *orlando, theWaves* }, { *southRiding* }},
which is the same as the type of the value { *southRiding* }, is $\mathbb{P}\,BOOK$, and
would normally be pronounced 'set of BOOK'.

Example 4.6

$$\mathbb{P}\{a, b, c\} = \{\varnothing, \{a\}, \{b\}, \{c\}, \{a, b\}, \{a, c\}, \{b, c\}, \{a, b, c\}\}$$

□

If the underlying type of {{ *orlando, theWaves* }, { *southRiding* }} is $\mathbb{P}\,BOOK$,
it follows that the type of the set {{ *orlando, theWaves* }, { *southRiding* }} is
$\mathbb{P}\,\mathbb{P}\,BOOK$.

Example 4.7 The underlying type of the set {{1}, {2, 3}, $\varnothing$} is $\mathbb{P}\,\mathbb{Z}$. The type
of the set {{1}, {2, 3}, $\varnothing$} is $\mathbb{P}\,\mathbb{P}\,\mathbb{Z}$.   □

Example 4.8 {2, {3}, 4} is not a set in Z, because the 'members' are not all
of the same type.   □

The type constructor $\mathbb{P}$ is an operator which may be applied to sets. It
follows that there must be type rules about its use. In particular, $\mathbb{P}\,S$ is meaningful only if S is a set.

Defining types in Z

Z provides a number of means of introducing types into a specification. As we
saw in Chapter 2, given sets are types. For example, the given set declaration:

[*PASS*]

introduced the type of passes. This kind of declaration introduces a type without specifying what any of its values are.

If we wish to specify the values of a type then we present an enumeration of the type by means of a *free type* definition. For example, the car park specification of Chapter 2 included the type:

$$REPORT ::= success$$
$$\mid\ ordinaryCarParkFull$$
$$\mid\ ordinaryCarParkEmpty$$
$$\mid\ passInUse$$
$$\mid\ passNotInUse$$

This style of definition is appropriate for the type *REPORT* since we actually want to state what the possible values are.

Revisiting equality and membership

Equality is used in Z for more than just equality of sets; it may be used between any two expressions of the same type. If E_1 and E_2 are expressions of the same type, $E_1 = E_2$ is true if and only if E_1 and E_2 have the same value. If E_1 and E_2 are not of the same type, then the equality $E_1 = E_2$ is meaningless. In particular, it is neither true nor false.

Given a variable x and a set S with underlying type T, the predicate $x \in S$ is well defined if x has type T. For example:

$$orlando \in \{orlando, theWaves\}$$

is well defined, and true, while:

$$middlemarch \in \{orlando, theWaves\}$$

is well defined, but false. In contrast, $4 \in \{orlando, theWaves\}$ is meaningless.

Defining unary relations

In Chapter 3, the meaning of relations was given informally. For example, we suggested that predicates about a blocks scene could be judged by inspection. Of course, this would not be acceptable with regard to a predicate in a specification. In the case of unary relations, the power set type may be used to give a precise definition. We shall be able to give precise definitions of other relations in Chapter 5 (page 114).

Let us consider the relation *clear_*, which is true of a block if it has no other block on top of it. By inspection of the blocks scene in Figure 3.1, we see that *clear x* is true if x is one of g, c or e. That is, *clear x* is true if $x \in \{g, c, e\}$. In order to use this as the basis of a definition, we must view *clear_* as a set of blocks, those for which it is true. The definition is:

$$clear\_ : \mathbb{P}\, BLOCK$$
$$\forall\, x : BLOCK \bullet$$
$$\quad clear\ x \Leftrightarrow x \in \{g, c, e\}$$

This defines the particular meaning of *clear* x with regard to Figure 3.1. In a different scene the relation may have a different meaning.

Exercise 4.1 Give a definition of the relation *onFloor_*.   □

4.4   Specifying sets by comprehension

The only means we have so far of specifying a set is by enumeration. An alternative approach is to specify the characteristics and properties that distinguish members of the set; for example, the description 'the even integers greater than 15'. This alternative approach to specifying a set is called an *intensional* definition.

A set is specified intensionally in Z by means of a *set comprehension*, and we shall approach the most general form of comprehension by way of several simpler cases. For the first case the description 'the even integers greater than 15' gives a good idea of what a simple set comprehension is like, particularly if we rephrase it as 'those integers that are both even and greater than 15'. Firstly the description mentions a set, in this case the integers, from which members of the set that is being specified are to be drawn. It then goes on to give properties that determine which of these potential members actually are members. In Z this would be written as:

$$\{y : \mathbb{Z} \mid even(y) \wedge y > 15\}$$

The general form of such a comprehension in Z is written:

$$\{x : S \mid P\}$$

This comprehension has two parts. The first part is the declaration $x : S$, where S is a type or set. The second part, P, is a predicate, and the set specified by this comprehension consists of all those values of x from S for which P is true. Since, in general, P selects some elements from S but not others, it is said to be a *filter*. The predicate P will normally include x as a free variable, though technically it need not.

Example 4.9 Suppose the unary relation *fiction_* is defined over the type *BOOK*, with the obvious meaning. If the set of books that John owns is *johnsBooks* then John's fiction books are:

$$johnsFiction = \{x : johnsBooks \mid fiction\ x\}$$

By these means we have defined a set without explicitly listing its members.
□

The *number range* is a Z library function. For example:

$$23 \mathbin{..} 27 = \{23, 24, 25, 26, 27\}$$

$23..27$ may be pronounced '23 up to 27'. More generally, if a and b are integers with $a \leq b$, the range $a \mathbin{..} b$ includes a, b and any integers in between.

Exercise 4.2 What set does the range $5 \mathbin{..} 5$ define? □

Exercise 4.3 What set does the range $5 \mathbin{..} 4$ define? Think about numbers greater than or equal to 5 and less than or equal to 4. □

Exercise 4.4 Give a set comprehension for each of the following sets:

i. the set of integers whose squares are in the range $1 \mathbin{..} 100$.

ii. the set of blocks that are not on the floor in a blocks scene such as considered in Chapter 3.

□

Exercise 4.5 * Describe the following set in English:

$$\{x : \mathbb{N} \mid \neg \, \exists \, y, z : \mathbb{N} \bullet y > 1 \wedge z > 1 \wedge x > 0 \wedge x = y * z\}$$

□

The description 'the squares of the integers' requires a slightly different formulation. In this description the elements of the set it describes are obtained from the integers by performing an operation on them, namely squaring. In Z this is written:

$$\{y : \mathbb{Z} \bullet y * y\}$$

and the set defined is $\{0, 1, 4, 9, 16, \ldots\}$. The general form of this kind of comprehension is:

$$\{x : S \bullet E\}$$

and again it has two parts, this time separated by $\bullet$[2]. As before, the declaration introduces a type or set S. The second part, this time, is an expression E. The set specified by this comprehension consists of the values of E for all $x \in S$. The expression E is called a *generator*, since it is a template that gives the form of the members of the comprehension. Once more we would normally expect the expression E to involve x as a free variable, though technically it need not.

---

[2] This is not the same use of $\bullet$ as in predicates with quantifiers.

Example 4.10 Suppose we have a unary function *author_* defined over BOOK, which defines the author of a book. The comprehension:

$$\{x : BOOK \bullet author\ x\} = \{georgeEliot, virginiaWoolf, \ldots\}$$

defines the set of authors of books. In this example the generator creates values of a type, say $PERSON$, which is different from the type of the variable x in the declaration. This is a powerful feature of comprehensions. $\square$

The most general form of a comprehension combines the two simpler forms we have already seen. For example, the description 'the squares of the even numbers greater than 15' may be formalized as:

$$\{x : \mathbb{Z} \mid even\ x \wedge x > 15 \bullet x * x\}$$

where *even_* is a unary relation. A set comprehension has the general form:

$$\{x : S \mid P \bullet E\}$$

The elements of the set specified in this manner are the values of E for all those values of x for which P is true.

Example 4.11 The authors of the fiction books are given by:

$$\{x : BOOK \mid fiction\ x \bullet author\ x\} = \{georgeEliot, \ldots\}$$

$\square$

Exercise 4.6 Give a set comprehension for the set of squares of the odd numbers in the set $1 \mathinner{.\,.} 100$. $\square$

So far the comprehensions we have presented have involved a single variable. It is possible in Z to have comprehensions involving more variables. In this section we illustrate these with a simple example. We return to this topic in Chapter 5 (page 128).

Example 4.12 The comprehension:

$$\{x, y : \mathbb{N} \mid x > 1 \wedge y > 1 \wedge x < y \bullet x * y\}$$

defines a set of natural numbers. Each element of this set is the product of two natural numbers greater than 1, one of which is less than the other. Some elements in the set defined by this comprehension are generated more than once. For example, $24 = 4 * 6 = 3 * 8$. This example illustrates that a description might quite naturally include repetition (recall related remarks on page 77). $\square$

Intensional definitions have several advantages over extensional definitions. Often in specifications we will know the properties of the elements that comprise a set, but not the individual identities. Since intensional definitions make the grounds for membership of a set explicit, reasoning about the set may be on the basis of the properties rather than the individual members. Intensional definitions of sets are of course particularly useful for infinite or very large sets, when an extensional definition is not possible or is too unwieldy.

Well-foundedness of set comprehensions in Z

In Z, a set comprehension defines a set in terms of some explicitly stated existing type or set. This is not an accidental feature of their definition which could be omitted.

Without the addition of a type for the members of a comprehension, some apparent comprehensions would be ambiguous. For example, it is not clear what $\{x \mid y \in x\}$ is supposed to be a set of.

More significantly, without this restriction it is possible to give what might appear to be set comprehensions but which in fact do not properly define a set at all. This discovery was made by Bertrand Russell in 1901, with an example called Russell's Paradox. By way of introduction to Russell's Paradox consider the following common analogy.

Large libraries hold many books that are catalogues of other books. For example, the Western World library holds a copy of *Catalogue of the Pepys Library at Magdalene College Cambridge*, R. McKitterick and R. Beadle (Eds), Cambridge (1992). Some of these catalogues, such as a catalogue of reference books and perhaps the Pepys Library Catalogue, will list themselves, while others will not. Suppose we decide to publish a catalogue of all catalogue books that do not list themselves. Should that catalogue list itself? If it does not then it satisfies the criterion for being listed in itself, so it ought to. So suppose it is listed in itself. It follows that it must be a catalogue that does not list itself. Clearly, while the description 'the catalogue of all catalogue books that do not list themselves' initially appears plausible, it is in fact an inconsistent description of a book.

If we draw the obvious analogy between a catalogue and a set, we see that the entries in the catalogue are analogous to members of the set. Thus the analogue of 'the catalogue of all catalogue books that do not list themselves' is 'the set of all sets that are not members of themselves': $\{X \mid X \notin X\}$. Following the argument about catalogues we see that this apparent comprehension cannot define a set.

The type rules for sets in Z rule out such problematical comprehensions. It is impossible to even approximate $\{X \mid X \notin X\}$ in Z since $X \notin X$ will always be ill-typed. A little more detail on this point is given by Woodcock and Loomes[22] (page 86).

4.5 Standard sets

Empty set: revisited

As we saw earlier, a set need not have any members and yet we stated that two sets are equal if they have the same members. It follows that there is just one empty set. This is not the case, however; in Z sets are typed and two sets are equal if they are of the same type and have the same members. This requires that there is an empty set of each underlying type.

Example 4.13 Suppose we have the declarations *johnsBooks* : $\mathbb{P}$ *BOOK* and *passesInUse* : $\mathbb{P}$ *PASS*. If we know that:

$$johnsBooks = \varnothing$$
$$passesInUse = \varnothing$$

we could not write down *johnsBooks = passesInUse* because this is not well defined.   □

Let S be a type or set. The empty set of type S is written $\varnothing[S]$. In this, S is an actual parameter. The definition of the empty set is given by means of a generic abbreviation definition:

$$\varnothing[T] == \{x : T \mid false\}$$

This is an abbreviation definition in which the left-hand side has *generic* parameters; in this case just one, T. This definition introduces a *generic constant*, which may be used anywhere in the remainder of the specification.

When using a global generic constant, the actual generic parameters may be supplied explicitly, or left implicit. It is usual in Z to omit the actual generic parameter, as we did earlier, if the reader of a predicate involving $\varnothing$ can determine the underlying type.

Power set: revisited

We saw earlier that the power set operator $\mathbb{P}$ is a necessary part of the type discipline in Z. $\mathbb{P}$ cannot be applied to something that is not a set; for example, we cannot write $\mathbb{P}\,4$.

Given a set S, the power set of S, denoted $\mathbb{P}\,S$, comprises all possible subsets of S. Thus, for example:

$$\mathbb{P}\{a, b, c\} = \{\varnothing, \{a\}, \{b\}, \{c\}, \{a, b\}, \{b, c\}, \{a, c\}, \{a, b, c\}\}$$

The defining property of the power set is characterized as:

$$S \in \mathbb{P}\,T \Leftrightarrow S \subseteq T$$

That is, something is a member of the power set of a set T if and only if it is a subset of T. From this we would be able to show that $T \in \mathbb{P}\,T$ and $\varnothing \in \mathbb{P}\,T$.

The notion of power set enables us to describe declarations properly. In a declaration of the form $x : X$, X must be a set of type $\mathbb{P}\,T$ for some type T, and x is introduced with type T.

Exercise 4.7 What are the power sets of the following sets?

  i. $\varnothing$

  ii. $\{\{a\}, \{a, b\}\}$

                                                                 □

Finite and infinite sets

Suppose we start to count the members of a set. If it is possible eventually to count all the members of the set, then we say the set is *finite*. What this means is that if a set is finite there is a member of the natural numbers, $\mathbb{N}$, that is the number of elements in the set. For example, $\{1, 2, 3, 4, 5, 6\}$ and $\{999, \ldots, 9999999\}$ are finite sets. If, on the other hand, it is not possible to complete the counting, because we would go on counting for ever, then we say the set is *infinite*. What this means is that if a set is infinite there is not a member of the natural numbers, $\mathbb{N}$, that is the number of elements in the set. For example, $\mathbb{Z}$ and $\mathbb{N}$ are infinite sets.

Particular care must be taken when infinite sets are concerned, since intuitions based on experience with finite sets do not always carry over. For example, if we add an element to a finite set we make the set bigger. However, adding an element into an infinite set does not make it bigger. For example, the set $\mathbb{N}_1 = \{1, 2, 3, \ldots\}$ is infinite. The set $\mathbb{N}$ may be obtained from $\mathbb{N}_1$ by adding one additional element, namely 0. But because we can pair off each element of $\mathbb{N}$ with an element of $\mathbb{N}_1$, for example (0,1), (1,2), ... it follows that $\mathbb{N}$ and $\mathbb{N}_1$ have the same number of elements, although this number is not finite.

If S has only a finite number of elements, deciding membership by inspection is possible. If a set has an infinite number of elements, such as $\{10, 11, 12, 13, \ldots\}$, this is not possible. If the element we are looking for is there, we would find it eventually and so we will be able to say it is a member. If the element in question is not there, we will never be able to conclude this on the basis of an element-by-element inspection. Such an inspection will never be complete. In practice, we can often decide such questions by exploiting some property that we can see the elements in the set possess. For example, 5 is not a member of $\{10, 11, 12, 13, \ldots\}$ since every element in this set is greater than 5.

The distinction between finite and infinite sets is important for modelling purposes. For example, consider the type *BOOK* introduced earlier, whose members are used to model books. As more books are published they will be modelled by further elements from the set *BOOK*. Suppose *BOOK* is a finite set. Since we may count its members, we will eventually use up all its elements in modelling books. However, what happens when a further book is published? The only conclusion we can reach is that *BOOK* must in fact be an infinite set, so that it is always possible to model a further book.

Now consider the collection of books an individual owns. It must be finite. Thus it should be modelled by a finite set. The type of such a set is $\mathbb{P}\,BOOK$. However, a set of type $\mathbb{P}\,BOOK$ is not necessarily finite, for example $BOOK \in \mathbb{P}\,BOOK$. The way around this is to be able to declare a variable as taking values which are any *finite subset* of some given set. In Z this is written:

$johnsBooks : \mathbb{F}\,BOOK$

Let U be a set. The set of all finite subsets of U is denoted $\mathbb{F}\,U$, and is pronounced 'the finite subsets of U'. However, $\mathbb{F}$ is not a type constructor. The declaration $x : \mathbb{F}\,U$ introduces x with the type $\mathbb{P}\,U$. The use of $\mathbb{F}$ in the declaration merely introduces the constraint that the set being declared is finite. A more formal definition of $\mathbb{F}$ is beyond the scope of this book, since it uses elements of Z that are not included in this book (see [20], page 111).

If a set S is finite, every possible subset of it is finite. That is, $\mathbb{P}\,S = \mathbb{F}\,S$. If S is infinite, then $\mathbb{P}\,S$ contains members that $\mathbb{F}\,S$ does not, and so they are not the same.

4.6   Relations over sets

We have already seen several relations over sets, namely set membership, $\in$, and set equality, $=$. In this section we consider three more relations which are useful in specifications.

In this section the definitions we present are to motivate and clarify the meaning of the relations. The definitions we present will be for specific types only. In Chapter 5 you will see how to give more general definitions.

Non-membership of a set

Recall that we assert that an element is a member of a set using the set membership relation $\in$. To assert that an element is not a member of a set we use the *non-membership* relation, which is written $\notin$. For example:

$3 \notin \{0, 2, 4, 6\}$

Example 4.14

$2117 \notin \{x : \mathbb{Z} \mid even(x) \wedge x > 15 \bullet x * x\}$

asserts that 2117 is not one of 'the squares of the even numbers greater than 15'.   □

Non-membership of a set is, of course, directly related to membership and $\notin$ may be defined in terms of $\in$:

$$x \notin S \Leftrightarrow \neg\,(x \in S)$$

where x must have some type T which is the underlying type of the set S. Thus, for example, $3 \notin \{\{4\}, \{5\}, \{6\}\}$ is ill-typed.

Inequality

Inequality, $\neq$, is a relation between expressions. If E_1 and E_2 are expressions of the same type, then $E_1 \neq E_2$ is true if the values of the two expressions are different. In particular, to say that two sets are not equal, we write:

$$\{1, 3, 5, 7, 9\} \neq \{2, 4, 6, 8\}$$

More formally, we may define inequality as follows:

$$E_1 \neq E_2 \Leftrightarrow \neg\,(E_1 = E_2)$$

This definition is specific to the type of the expressions E_1 and E_2. Two expressions of different types are neither equal nor not equal. Thus, in particular, two sets of different types are neither equal nor not equal.

Subset: revisited

Example 4.15 We saw earlier that the set of fiction books John owns is:

$$johnsFiction = \{b : johnsBooks \mid fiction\ b\} = \{adamBede, \ldots\}$$

Every fiction book John owns is, of course, a book John owns. It follows that $johnsFiction \subseteq johnsBooks$. □

More generally, suppose U and V are sets of the same type. U is a subset of V, written $U \subseteq V$, if every member of U is a member of V. This is illustrated in Figure 4.1. If U is a subset of V and U and V are not equal then U is said to be a *proper* subset of V, and this is written $U \subset V$. Thus, in Figure 4.1 $U \subset V$.

Example 4.16

$$\{2, 4, 6\} \subseteq \{2, 4, 6\}$$
$$\{256, 324, 1296, 2116\} \subset \{x : \mathbb{Z} \mid even(x) \wedge x > 15 \bullet x * x\}$$

□

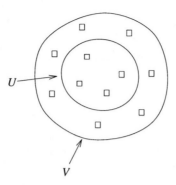

Figure 4.1: U is a subset of V

The modelling use of subset may be summarized as follows. Suppose we have two sets *these* and *those*. The predicate *these* $\subseteq$ *those* asserts that all *these* are *those*. Since in logic this would be represented by an implication, it should be no surprise that a more formal characterization of $\subseteq$ is as follows. Suppose $U, V : \mathbb{P}\, T$ then:

$$U \subseteq V \Leftrightarrow (\forall x : T \bullet x \in U \Rightarrow x \in V)$$

It follows that:

$$U \subset V \Leftrightarrow (U \subseteq V \wedge U \neq V)$$

If U and V are of different types then it does not make sense to consider whether one is a subset of the other.

Exercise 4.8 * Argue that for any set S, $\emptyset \subseteq S$.   □

4.7   Functions over sets

With the exception of the cardinality of a set, the functions described in this section are used in specifications to define new sets in terms of existing sets. The definitions of union, intersection and set difference we present are for specific types only. In Chapter 7 you will see how it is possible to give more general definitions.

Cardinality of a set

The number of elements in a finite set is called its *cardinality*. There is a Z library function, written #, that defines the cardinality of a finite set. For example:

$$\#\{15, 29, 146\} = 3$$

which may be pronounced 'the cardinality of the set $\{15, 29, 146\}$ is 3', or 'there are 3 elements in the set $\{15, 29, 146\}$'. The function $\#$ may be applied to a finite set of any type. The type of $\#S$ is $\mathbb{N}$. The function $\#$ is not defined for infinite sets such as $\mathbb{Z}$ since there is no member of $\mathbb{N}$ that would be appropriate, nor can $\#$ be applied to something that is not a set.

Example 4.17

$$\#\{15, 29, 146, 29\} = 3$$
$$\#\varnothing = 0$$
$$\#\{\varnothing, \{13, 42, 99\}\} = 2$$
$$\#\{2, 1 + 1, 4 - 2\} = 1$$

□

We shall omit the full definition of the function $\#$ since it makes use of a number of concepts we either have not yet covered or do not intend to cover in this book. You may find it in [20] (page 111).

Example 4.18 Suppose a mountaineering club has a membership limit of 30. If the set of members is *members*, this limit would be expressed by the predicate:

$$\#members \leq 30$$

□

Set union

Suppose U and V are sets of the same type. The set whose members are exactly those elements that are members of U or members of V (or both) is called the *union* of U and V, and it is written $U \cup V$. The union of the sets U and V is illustrated in Figure 4.2.

Example 4.19

$$\{1, 3\} \cup \{2, 4, 6\} = \{1, 2, 3, 4, 6\}$$
$$\{1, 3, 5\} \cup \{2, 3, 4\} = \{1, 2, 3, 4, 5\}$$

□

More formally, we have the following characterization of set union. Let $U, V : \mathbb{P}\, T$.

$$U \cup V = \{x : T \mid x \in U \vee x \in V\}$$

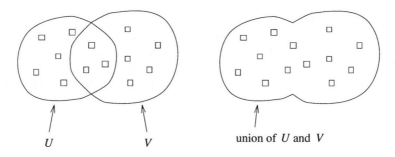

Figure 4.2: Set union

Thus, an element is a member of $U \cup V$ if and only if it is a member of U or it is a member of V. The type of the union of two sets is the same as the type of the two sets themselves.

Exercise 4.9 What are the values of the following expressions?

   i. $\{2, 4, 6, 8\} \cup \{4, 6, 7\}$

  ii. $\{2, 4, 6, 8\} \cup \varnothing$

                                                □

Exercise 4.10 * Is it always true that $\#(S \cup \{x\}) = \#S + 1$ where $S \cup \{x\}$ is well defined?   □

Set intersection

Suppose U and V are sets of the same type. The set whose members are exactly those elements that are members of both U and V is called the *intersection* of U and V, and is written $U \cap V$. The intersection of the sets U and V is illustrated in Figure 4.3.

Example 4.20

$$\{1, 3\} \cap \{2, 4, 6\} = \varnothing$$
$$\{1, 3, 5\} \cap \{2, 3, 4\} = \{3\}$$

                                                □

More formally, we have the following characterization of set intersection. Let $U, V : \mathbb{P}\, T$.

$$U \cap V = \{x : T \mid x \in U \land x \in V\}$$

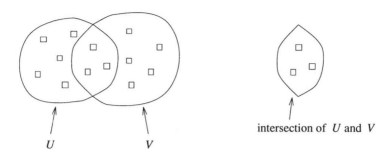

Figure 4.3: Set intersection

Thus, an element is a member of $U \cap V$ if and only if it is a member of U and it is a member of V. The type of the intersection of two sets is the same as the type of the two sets themselves.

Suppose U and V are sets of the same type. U and V are said to be *disjoint* if they do not have any members in common. That is, U and V are disjoint if $U \cap V = \varnothing$.

Example 4.21 The sets $\{2,4,6,8\}$ and $\{1,3,5,7,9\}$ are disjoint. □

Exercise 4.11 What are the values of the following expressions?

  i. $\{2,4,6,8\} \cap \{3,5,7\}$

 ii. $\{2,4,6,8\} \cap \{4,6,7\}$

iii. $\{2,4,6,8\} \cap \varnothing$

□

Set difference

Suppose U and V are sets of the same type. The set of elements that are members of U but not members of V is called the *difference* of U and V, and is written $U \setminus V$. The set difference of U and V is illustrated in Figure 4.4.

Example 4.22

$$\{1,3\} \setminus \{2,4,6\} = \{1,3\}$$
$$\{1,3,5\} \setminus \{2,3,4\} = \{1,5\}$$

□

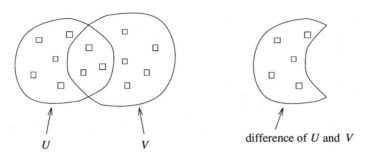

Figure 4.4: Set difference

More formally, we have the following characterization of set difference. Let $U, V : \mathbb{P}\, T$.

$$U \setminus V = \{x : T \mid x \in U \land x \notin V\}$$

Thus, an element is a member of $U \setminus V$ if and only if it is a member of U and it is not a member of V. The type of the difference of two sets is the same as the type of the two sets themselves.

Exercise 4.12 What are the values of the following expressions?

   i. $\{2, 4, 6, 8\} \setminus \{4, 6, 7\}$

  ii. $\{2, 4, 6, 8\} \setminus \varnothing$

 iii. $\{2, 4, 6, 8\} \setminus \{6\}$

  iv. $\varnothing \setminus \{5\}$

$\square$

Exercise 4.13 * Is it always true that $\#(S \setminus \{x\}) = \#S - 1$ where $S \setminus \{x\}$ is well defined? $\square$

Example 4.23 Suppose *hardback_* is a unary relation on books, with the obvious meaning. John's hardback books are given by:

$$johnsHardbacks = \{b : BOOK \mid hardback\ b\}$$

The collection of John's fiction or hardback books is then modelled by the set *johnsFiction* $\cup$ *johnsHardbacks*; John's hardback fiction is modelled by the set *johnsFiction* $\cap$ *johnsHardbacks*; and John's hardback non-fiction is modelled by the set *johnsHardbacks* $\setminus$ *johnsFiction*. $\square$

We may summarize the modelling purpose of the various functions over sets as follows. Suppose we have two sets *this* and *that* of the same type, such that the members of *this* have *this* property of interest, and the members of *that* have *that* property of interest. The elements that have the properties *this* and *that* are the members of *this* ∩ *that*; the elements that have the properties *this* or *that* are the members of *this* ∪ *that*; the elements that have the properties *this* but not *that* are the members of *this* \ *that*.

4.8   Defining recursive functions over sets

In each of the functions over sets we have so far defined, the definition has been given in terms of other constructs. For example, the definition of set union involved disjunction. For some functions, the most natural definition actually involves the function that is being defined. We explore such definitions in this section. The definitions covered in this section also illustrate how a value, namely a function, may be defined by the conjunction of several predicates.

Let us begin with a familiar function, exponentiation of integers, that is, x^n ($n \geq 1$). How should we define x^n, for any x and any n ($n \geq 1$)? We know it means form the product of n copies of x, but we cannot use that description in reasoning since it is informal. The key to the usual definition is to note that $x^1 = x$, $x^2 = x^1 * x$, $x^3 = x^2 * x$, and so on. More generally, $x^n = x^{n-1} * x$ ($n \geq 2$). Thus the usual definition is:

$$x^1 = x$$
$$x^n = x^{n-1} * x \quad (n \geq 2)$$

The key features of this definition are that there is a *base* case, where the value of the function is defined explicitly, and a *recursive* case where the value is given in terms of the function being defined applied to a simpler case, namely one less. Such a definition is said to be *recursive*.

In general, there may be several base cases in a recursive definition which apply under different criteria, and they may be more complex than the above example suggests. The key is that they do not involve the function being defined. There may also be several recursive cases, which may involve several applications of the function being defined. In order that such definitions are well founded, that is, they do define a value for the function for any argument, the recursive case must define the function in terms of simpler subcases, and as the recursive case is applied repeatedly progress is made towards one of the base cases. The power and elegance of this style of definition lies in the variety of ways in which simpler subcases may be identified.

Example 4.24 Recursive definitions are often elegant and economic ways of defining complex functions. Ackermann's function, $A(m, n)$, is defined as follows:

$$A(0, n) = n + 1 \qquad\qquad\qquad (n \geq 0)$$
$$A(m, 0) = A(m - 1, 1) \qquad\qquad (m > 0)$$
$$A(m, n) = A(m - 1, A(m, n - 1)) \qquad (m > 0, n > 0)$$

Verify that $A(1, 2) = 4$, and you will get an insight into the complexity of the computation defined by these three equations. If you require further confirmation, verify that $A(2, 3) = 9$. $\qquad\qquad\qquad\qquad\qquad\qquad\qquad$ □

Let us now turn to defining recursive functions over sets. The key to reducing a case to simpler subcases is to observe that any set may be expressed as the union of two other sets. For example:

$$\{1, 2, 3, 4\} = \{1, 3\} \cup \{2, 4\}$$

Suppose we wish to define a unary prefix function *sum_* which defines the sum of the members of any finite set of integers. For example:

$$sum\{1, 2, 3, 4\} = 10$$

Given the above decomposition of $\{1, 2, 3, 4\}$ into two sets we see that:

$$sum\{1, 2, 3, 4\} = sum(\{1, 3\} \cup \{2, 4\}) = sum\{1, 3\} + sum\{2, 4\}$$

This does not generalize, however, because:

$$\{1, 2, 3, 4\} = \{1, 2, 3\} \cup \{2, 3, 4\}$$

and now the simple mathematics illustrated above does not apply. The difficulty is that some members of $\{1, 2, 3, 4\}$ belong to both subsets, and so they get counted twice in $sum\{1, 2, 3\} + sum\{2, 3, 4\}$. Since we must count such elements once only, we must subtract one of the additional copies. That is:

$$sum\{1, 2, 3, 4\}$$
$$= sum(\{1, 2, 3\} \cup \{2, 3, 4\})$$
$$= sum\{1, 2, 3\} + sum\{2, 3, 4\} - sum(\{1, 2, 3\} \cap \{2, 3, 4\})$$

This is now an instance of a general rule:

$$sum(X \cup Y) = sumX + sumY - sum(X \cap Y)$$

which holds for all finite sets X and Y. This rule relates the definition of a function for a given set to the function applied to other sets. We suggested above that in a recursive definition the function should be applied to simpler cases. The decomposition of a set into the union of two other sets does not guarantee that the two subsets are simpler, since $Z = Z \cup \varnothing$ for example. However, the above equality holds for any X and Y, and so this includes all the possible cases where the decomposition is into simpler cases.

In order to complete the definition of *sum_* we must give the base case or cases. These are cases where the sum of the elements involved may be defined explicitly, without attempting to define it in terms of simpler cases. These are:

$$sum \varnothing = 0$$
$$sum\{x\} = x$$

In neither of these cases would it be possible to give a definition of the sum in which the sets in question were broken down into simpler sets. Thus the complete definition of the sum of the elements of a finite set of integers is:

$$sum \varnothing = 0$$
$$sum\{x\} = x$$
$$sum(X \cup Y) = sumX + sumY - sum(X \cap Y)$$

Exercise 4.14 * Modify the definition of *sum_* to obtain an appropriate definition of a function *count_* which determines the cardinality of a finite set. For example, $count\{1, 2, 3, 4\} = 4$. The cardinality function # given in the Z library is not defined in this manner. □

The function *sum_* is not defined for infinite sets. This is because the value of the function on a set is to be a member of $\mathbb{Z}$, and in general we can guarantee there is a suitable member of $\mathbb{Z}$ only if the set in question is finite. This restriction to finite sets is not obvious in the defining equations for *sum_*, so you should take care when attempting to define values in this manner. More generally, you should be warned that recursive definitions involving infinite sets are not necessarily well defined (see [20], page 84).

4.9 Some laws about sets

In this chapter we have presented a range of functions over sets, and shown how they may be used to express certain relationships between sets. Often, a particular set or a relationship between sets may be specified in a range of ways that are equivalent. For example:

$$A \setminus (B \cup C) = (A \setminus B) \setminus C$$

It is important for anyone reading or writing a specification to be aware of such laws and we list a few in the remainder of this section.

It is beyond the scope of this book to present a comprehensive list of such laws or to justify them individually but many of the laws we have chosen to list are plausible. Where the law is an equality, it may be used to rewrite arbitrary parts of predicates.

Set union and intersection are *commutative*. That is, the order in that two sets are listed in a union or intersection is not significant:

$$A \cup B = B \cup A$$
$$A \cap B = B \cap A$$

Set union and intersection are *associative*. That is, the bracketing used when three or more sets are combined with union or intersection is not significant:

$$A \cup (B \cup C) = (A \cup B) \cup C$$
$$A \cap (B \cap C) = (A \cap B) \cap C$$

We may thus write $A \cup B \cup C$, for example, without ambiguity.

Set union and intersection are *idempotent*. That is, the union or intersection of a set with itself leaves it unchanged:

$$A \cup A = A$$
$$A \cap A = A$$

In contrast to union and intersection, set difference is not commutative, not associative and not idempotent. The following examples illustrate this:

$$\{a, b\} \setminus \{a\} = \{b\}$$
$$\{a\} \setminus \{a, b\} = \varnothing$$
$$\{a, b\} \setminus (\{a, b\} \setminus \{a\}) = \{a\}$$
$$(\{a, b\} \setminus \{a, b\}) \setminus \{a\} = \varnothing$$
$$A \setminus A = \varnothing$$

Set union and intersection each distributes over the other. For example:

$$A \cup (B \cap C) = (A \cup B) \cap (A \cup C)$$
$$A \cap (B \cup C) = (A \cap B) \cup (A \cap C)$$

Properties of the empty set include:

$$A \cup \varnothing = A$$
$$A \cap \varnothing = \varnothing$$
$$A \setminus \varnothing = A$$

Some properties of the subset relation are:

$$\varnothing \subseteq A$$
$$A \subseteq A$$
$$A \subseteq B \wedge B \subseteq C \Rightarrow A \subseteq C$$
$$A \subseteq B \wedge B \subseteq A \Rightarrow A = B$$

4.10   Sets in logic

Since predicates in a specification may now include constructs like $x \in \{a, b, c\}$ it might appear as if set notation is a proper extension of the logic of Chapter 3. In fact, the only really new ingredient is the relation $\in$. Formulae that involve sets specified by enumeration or comprehension may be replaced by an equivalent predicate of logic that does not include set-like constructs apart from $\in$. Further details of this are given in [22], for example.

4.11   Car registration: revisited

Returning to the Western World car park example, we shall construct a specification to maintain records of which cars are registered and which hold parking permits. The system we specify will be able to record the registration of a vehicle, the issue of a parking permit and the cancellation of registration and of a parking permit, and will be able to answer a query about the status of any vehicle. We shall begin by identifying an appropriate state space.

In this system every vehicle must be considered a distinct entity, so that the modelling technique we select must distinguish identity. Since the order in which cars are registered is of no concern, it is sufficient to maintain a set of registered cars. Parking permits may have been issued for some of the cars that are registered and we shall require a second set to record these. Thus we make two observations of the state of the registration system:

- a set of cars registered, and

- a set of cars for which parking permits have been issued.

Since every car that holds a parking permit must also be registered, the state space is defined by the invariant

- The set of cars with parking permits is a subset of the set of registered cars.

On the basis of this state space, the operations we shall specify are summarized in Table 4.1. The operations to register, deregister, add a permit and delete a permit naturally have cases to do with whether a car is already registered or already holds a parking permit. The description of each operation will include a report that defines the outcome of the operation.

Since a permit can be held for a car only if it is first registered, there is some dependence between the various subcase properties for the operations of the proposed system. This dependence also means that we need to consider what happens if there is an attempt to deregister a car for which a permit is

Operation	Input	Subcase property	State change	Output	Report
Register car	Car	Not registered	Add to set of registered cars	*None*	Success
		Registered	*None*	*None*	Already registered
Deregister car	Car	Registered; no permit	Remove from registered cars	*None*	Success
		Registered; permit holder	Remove from registered cars and permits	*None*	Permit cancelled also
		Not registered	*None*	*None*	Not registered
Record permit	Car	Registered; no permit; permits left	Add to set of permits	*None*	Success
		Not registered	*None*	*None*	Not registered
		Registered; no permit; no permits left	*None*	*None*	No permits left
		Registered; permit holder	*None*	*None*	Permit already
Cancel permit	Car	Registered; permit holder	Remove from set of permits	*None*	Success
		Registered; not permit holder	*None*	*None*	Not permit holder
		Not registered	*None*	*None*	Not registered
Enquire	Car	Not registered	*None*	Not registered	Success
		Registered; no permit	*None*	Registered only	Success
		Registered; permit	*None*	Permit holder	Success

Table 4.1: The operations required for the car registration system

already held. We have chosen to cancel the permit as well. However, cancelling a permit will not entail cancelling the registration as well.

The *enquire* operation must output the status of a car. This could be achieved through the report for the operation, but we have chosen not to do that. The report is used solely to define the outcome of the operation, and the outcome of a query about the status of a car will always be 'success'. The status of the car will be given as a separate output.

The specification

Basics

Since we shall be recording only whether a car is registered, any values may be used to model cars. We thus assume a given set of cars:

$[CAR]$

We shall assume that this set contains a member for all possible cars that are of interest to the system.

There is a limit on the number of parking permits that may be on issue at any one time, although the requirements do not say what its value is. This limit will thus be a parameter of the specification. This will be achieved by means of an axiomatic definition of a global variable:

$$\mid permitLimit : \mathbb{N}$$

The constraint on the value of *permitLimit* that it be non-negative is specified by using the set $\mathbb{N}$ in the declaration, rather than $\mathbb{Z}$. There is no other constraint on the value of *permitLimit* so the axiomatic definition has a simpler form; the predicate part is omitted.

Exercise 4.15 Give the axiomatic definition of *permitLimit* in which its declaration involves the type $\mathbb{Z}$. □

Responding to the enquire operation requires that the system can output names for the specific categories. So we have the type:

$STATUS ::= noRegistration \mid registeredCar \mid permitHolder$

Finally, we need to specify the range of responses we can get in an operation and so we have the type:

$$
\begin{aligned}
REPORT ::=\ & success \\
\mid\ & alreadyRegistered \\
\mid\ & permitCancelledAlso \\
\mid\ & notRegistered \\
\mid\ & noPermitsLeft \\
\mid\ & permitAlready \\
\mid\ & notPermitHolder
\end{aligned}
$$

Note that the data types *STATUS* and *REPORT* must be disjoint, since they are distinct types.

State of the system

The state of the car registration system is a set of registered cars, some of which have permits. The limit on the number of permits held is *permitLimit*. The state is thus:

```
┌─ RegistrationDB ────────────────────────────────────
│ registered, permits : F CAR
├──────────────────────────────────────────────────────
│ permits ⊆ registered
│ #permits ≤ permitLimit
└──────────────────────────────────────────────────────
```

Observe that *registered* and *permits* are finite subsets of the type *CAR*. This is realistic for the system being specified, and also necessary in the case of *permits* since the state invariant involves the cardinality function applied to *permits*.

Initial state

Cars can be registered so it is simplest, as well as adequate, to begin with no cars registered:

$$registered' = \varnothing$$

The state invariant tells us:

$$permits' \subseteq registered'$$

and $permits' = \varnothing$ is a logical consequence of these two predicates. Thus we need not explicitly state a value for *permits'*.

```
┌─ InitRegistrationDB ────────────────────────────────
│ RegistrationDB'
├──────────────────────────────────────────────────────
│ registered' = ∅
└──────────────────────────────────────────────────────
```

It is clear that a state exists satisfying this schema.

Registering a car

Registering a car requires the input of an identifier for the car. We begin with a successful transaction:

```
┌─ RegisterOK ─────────────────────────────────────
│ ΔRegistrationDB
│ c? : CAR
├──────────────────────────────────────────────────
│ c? ∉ registered
│ registered' = registered ∪ {c?}
│ permits' = permits
└──────────────────────────────────────────────────
```

The predicate part of the schema records the subcase property that the new car must not already be registered. The set of cars registered after this operation is all those registered before with the addition of the new car. The set of permit holders after the operations is the same as it was before.

Exercise 4.16 Would it be sufficient if the predicate part of *RegisterOK* took the following form?

$c? \notin registered$

$c? \in registered'$

□

The operation is successful in this subcase, although we have not defined a report in the above schema. Instead we take this opportunity to illustrate how the definition of a subcase may be given in several parts which are subsequently combined. The required report is defined in a schema:

```
┌─ Success ────────────────────────────────────────
│ r! : REPORT
├──────────────────────────────────────────────────
│ r! = success
└──────────────────────────────────────────────────
```

The complete definition of this subcase of the operation is then:

$RegisterOK \land Success$

In this, ∧ is *schema conjunction*, and the effect is that *RegisterOK* ∧ *Success* defines a subcase of the operation satisfying both *RegisterOK* and *Success*. An advantage of this approach is that the schema *Success* may be reused in the remainder of the specification.

The following schema specifies what happens when there is an attempt to register a car that is already registered.

```
┌─ AlreadyRegistered ──────────────────────────────
│ ΞRegistrationDB
│ c? : CAR
│ r! : REPORT
├──────────────────────────────────────────────────
│ c? ∈ registered
│ r! = alreadyRegistered
└──────────────────────────────────────────────────
```

The full registration operation, *Register*, is then:

$$Register \mathrel{\widehat{=}} RegisterOK \wedge Success \vee AlreadyRegistered$$

The operation has a single input and produces a single output. For each state in the state space and for each input $c?$, either $c? \notin registered$ or $c? \in registered$. In each case a suitable after-state and report is defined. Thus this operation is total.

Deregistering a car

It is possible to cancel the registration of a registered car only. We have to be careful of the possibility that a permit may be held as well. In the first case, no permit is held (a property captured with set difference).

```
┌─ DeregisterOK ─────────────────────────────
│ Δ RegistrationDB
│ c? : CAR
├────────────────────────────────────────────
│ c? ∈ registered \ permits
│ registered' = registered \ { c? }
│ permits' = permits
└────────────────────────────────────────────
```

The predicate $c? \in registered \setminus permits$ is true only if $c?$ is registered, but not a permit holder.

In the event that a car holds a permit as well, we cancel that at the same time. We alert the operator that this has taken place.

```
┌─ DeregisterPlusPermit ─────────────────────
│ Δ RegistrationDB
│ c? : CAR
│ r! : REPORT
├────────────────────────────────────────────
│ c? ∈ permits
│ registered' = registered \ { c? }
│ permits' = permits \ { c? }
│ r! = permitCancelledAlso
└────────────────────────────────────────────
```

Given the state invariant $permits \subseteq registered$, $c? \in registered$ follows from $c? \in permits$ and so this part of the subcase property need not be expressed explicitly.

Exercise 4.17 * On the basis of $registered' = registered \setminus \{c?\}$, we have that $c? \notin registered'$. Given that $permits' \subseteq registered'$, we can conclude that $c? \notin permits'$. So, if this is the case, would it be possible to omit the predicate $permits' = permits \setminus \{c?\}$ from the schema *DeregisterPlusPermit*?   □

We cannot cancel the registration of a car that is not registered.

```
┌─ NotRegistered ─────────────────────────────────
│ ΞRegistrationDB
│ c? : CAR
│ r! : REPORT
├─────────────────────────────────
│ c? ∉ registered
│ r! = notRegistered
└─────────────────────────────────
```

The full operation for cancelling a car registration is:

$$Deregister \mathrel{\widehat{=}} DeregisterOK \wedge Success$$
$$\vee\ DeregisterPlusPermit$$
$$\vee\ NotRegistered$$

This operation has a single input and a single output.

Exercise 4.18 Investigate the totality of this operation. □

Exercise 4.19 Amend the operation for deregistering a car, so that a car can be deregistered only if there is no valid permit held. □

Record a permit being issued

To issue a permit the car has to be registered and must not yet hold a permit. This is formalized as:

$$c? \in registered \setminus permits$$

If $c? \in permits$ then $c? \notin registered \setminus permits$, so it follows that $c? \notin permits$. Recording the issue of the additional permit to the car $c?$ is defined as:

$$permits' = permits \cup \{c?\}$$

and, because $c? \notin permits$, it follows that:

$$\#permits' = \#(permits \cup \{c?\}) = \#permits + 1$$

By the state invariant,

$$\#permits' \leq permitLimit$$

and it follows that $\#permits + 1 \leq permitLimit$, that is, $\#permits < permitLimit$. Thus, we cannot make the state transition in which a new permit is issued unless there is one available to issue and so this part of the subcase property need not be stated explicitly.

```
┌─ PermitOK ─────────────────────────────────────────
│ ΔRegistrationDB
│ c? : CAR
├────────────────────────────────────────────────────
│ c? ∈ registered \ permits
│ registered' = registered
│ permits' = permits ∪ {c?}
└────────────────────────────────────────────────────
```

If a car is not already registered, then a permit cannot be issued. Such states have been dealt with before when considering deregistering a car, so we shall reuse the schema introduced there.

If a car already has a permit then we do not record it again.

```
┌─ PermitAlready ────────────────────────────────────
│ ΞRegistrationDB
│ c? : CAR
│ r! : REPORT
├────────────────────────────────────────────────────
│ c? ∈ permits
│ r! = permitAlready
└────────────────────────────────────────────────────
```

If there are no permits left, then we cannot record another one.

```
┌─ NoPermitsLeft ────────────────────────────────────
│ ΞRegistrationDB
│ c? : CAR
│ r! : REPORT
├────────────────────────────────────────────────────
│ c? ∈ registered \ permits
│ #permits = permitLimit
│ r! = noPermitsLeft
└────────────────────────────────────────────────────
```

The full operation for recording a permit is:

$$Permit \mathrel{\widehat{=}} PermitOK \land Success$$
$$\lor NotRegistered$$
$$\lor PermitAlready$$
$$\lor NoPermitsLeft$$

This operation has an input and an output.

Exercise 4.20 Investigate the totality of this operation.   □

Exercise 4.21 * Add an operation to the system to enquire how many permits remain.   □

Cancelling a permit

In the first case, a permit can be cancelled if one is held. Registration does not change.

```
┌─ CancelPermitOK ────────────────────────────────
│ ΔRegistrationDB
│ c? : CAR
├──────────────────────────────────────────────────
│ c? ∈ permits
│ registered' = registered
│ permits' = permits \ {c?}
└──────────────────────────────────────────────────
```

If a permit is not held, it cannot be cancelled.

```
┌─ NotPermitHolder ───────────────────────────────
│ ΞRegistrationDB
│ c? : CAR
│ r! : REPORT
├──────────────────────────────────────────────────
│ c? ∈ registered \ permits
│ r! = notPermitHolder
└──────────────────────────────────────────────────
```

The other case is where the car is not registered, which we have seen before.

The full operation for cancelling a permit is:

$$CancelPermit \mathrel{\widehat{=}} CancelPermitOK \land Success$$
$$\lor\ NotPermitHolder$$
$$\lor\ NotRegistered$$

This is an operation with a single input and a single output. There are three cases in the predicate part.

Exercise 4.22 Investigate the totality of this operation. □

Enquiring about the status of a car

There are three possible cases: an unregistered car; a registered car; a car for which a permit is held. These cases are treated separately.

```
┌─ RegisteredOnly ────────────────────────────────
│ ΞRegistrationDB
│ c? : CAR
│ s! : STATUS
├──────────────────────────────────────────────────
│ c? ∈ registered \ permits
│ s! = registeredCar
└──────────────────────────────────────────────────
```

Exercise 4.23 Specify the remaining two subcases of this operation and hence define *Enquire*.   □

Exercise 4.24 ** Fees must be paid for a registration disc and a parking permit, and there are no refunds when registration or a permit is cancelled. Modify the specification to keep a record of the total amount of fees paid for registration discs and parking permits, and add an operation to enquire what the current total is.   □

Exercise 4.25 ** A second-hand book shops buys and sells books. Model the collection of books in the shop at any one time, and use this as the basis of a specification. There should be an operation to buy a collection of books, and an operation to sell an individual book.   □

Chapter 5

Relations

In Chapter 3, relationships between values were described with relations. Relations are important modelling techniques and in this chapter we shall explore them in greater detail. We begin with an example.

In line with many other universities, the Metropolitan University of the Western World plans to move to modular degree schemes and to teach in two 15-week semesters rather than three 10-week terms. The Western World has about 8000 students and offers about 200 degree courses, involving perhaps 2500 modules. With this volume and variety, it is believed that a successful modularization scheme will require increased central administrative support.

In this chapter we shall consider a very small part of the problem. To register for a module, students must satisfy any stated prerequisites. These prerequisites will be expressed in terms of modules for which credits must be held. The system component we consider in this chapter is concerned with maintaining records of module prerequisites and querying the recorded information.

5.1 Ordered pairs

The Western World Informatics Department teaches a variety of programming languages. Let us suppose, for the sake of discussion, that the type of programming languages is:

$$LANGUAGE ::= prolog \mid pascal \mid modula2 \mid occam \mid haskell \mid smalltalk80$$

and that the teaching staff may be modelled by the type:

$$STAFF ::= rabhi \mid rayner \mid jones \mid bottaci \mid grubb \mid brookes \mid phillips$$

Suppose we wish to model which members of staff teach which programming languages. Let us begin by considering how we might represent the fact that Dr Grubb teaches Modula-2. We cannot achieve this with a set, for several reasons. Firstly, $\{grubb, modula2\}$ is not a set in Z, because $grubb$ and $modula2$ are not values of the same type. Secondly, since the members of a set are not ordered, even if $\{grubb, modula2\}$ was a set we would not be able to distinguish the language from the lecturer.

We need a construct in which it is possible to consistently ascribe a role to the components, possibly of different types. One of the possible ways of achieving this exploits position, and the construct in Z that satisfies our requirements is the *ordered pair*. We may thus represent the fact that Dr Grubb teaches Modula-2 by the ordered pair:

$$(grubb, modula2) \qquad \text{or} \qquad grubb \mapsto modula2$$

The first notation is the standard notation for an ordered pair in Z. The second, *maplet*, notation is often preferred. The above pair may be pronounced 'grubb maps to modula2', or, since we know what we intend the pair to model, 'grubb teaches modula2'.

The complete information about the teaching of programming at Western World would comprise a number of ordered pairs. Since there is no additional relationship between pairs that must be modelled, we use a set of pairs:

$$teachesProgramming = \{jones \mapsto prolog, bottaci \mapsto prolog,$$
$$bottaci \mapsto smalltalk80, grubb \mapsto modula2,$$
$$rabhi \mapsto occam\}$$

A set of pairs such as this is called a *binary relation*, or simply a relation. Since the first element of each pair is of type $STAFF$ and the second element is of type $LANGUAGE$ we talk of the relation being *from STAFF to LANGUAGE*.

Exercise 5.1 Model the information on the teaching of programming as a relation from $LANGUAGE$ to $STAFF$.   □

The *teachesProgramming* relation is illustrated in Figure 5.1. An arrow between two items indicates that the corresponding pair is in the relation. Observe that some elements in the set on the left have several arrows emanating from them, and some elements in the set on the right have several arrows terminating at them. A relation in which there is this kind of multiplicity is said to be *many to many*. Also observe that some elements on the left and right do not take part in pairs in the relation. For example, no one teaches *pascal*, and Professor Phillips does not teach programming.

The model *teachesProgramming* may be used in a variety of ways. Since a relation is a set we may use some of the techniques discussed in Chapter 4. For example, the set of programming languages that Dr Bottaci teaches is:

$$\{l : LANGUAGE \mid bottaci \mapsto l \in teachesProgramming\}$$

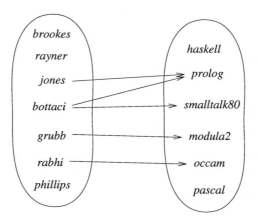

Figure 5.1: The *teachesProgramming* relation

and we see by inspection that this is {*prolog, smalltalk*80}. To assert that no one teaches Pascal we would write:

$$\neg\ \exists\, s : STAFF \bullet s \mapsto pascal \in teachesProgramming$$

Example 5.1 Laboratory practical sessions are associated with each module that covers programming. The relationship between a language and the number of laboratory sessions is represented by the following relation from *LANGUAGE* to ℕ:

> *hoursPractical*
> $$= \{prolog \mapsto 10, modula2 \mapsto 40, occam \mapsto 10, smalltalk80 \mapsto 10\}$$

This relation is *many to one*, since a given language can have only one total of practical sessions, although several languages may be supported by the same number of practical sessions. □

Example 5.2 A three-year degree comprises six semesters. Let us suppose the type of semesters is:

> $$SEMESTER ::= sem1 \mid sem2 \mid sem3 \mid sem4 \mid sem5 \mid sem6$$

We can represent the semesters in which the various programming languages are taught by a relation from *LANGUAGE* to *SEMESTER*:

> $$programmingSemesters = \{modula2 \mapsto sem1, modula2 \mapsto sem2,$$
> $$prolog \mapsto sem3, occam \mapsto sem4,$$
> $$smalltalk80 \mapsto sem5\}$$

A relation such as this is said to be *one to many* since some languages are taught in several semesters, but there is only one language taught in any given semester.   □

Exercise 5.2 Give a picture of the *programmingSemesters* relation in the style of Figure 5.1.   □

The definition of a binary relation does not require that the two types involved are different. Indeed, there are many interesting relations where they are the same. If this is the case, we talk of a relation *on* a set or type.

Example 5.3 Teaching staff in the Western World Informatics Department are lucky enough to have individual offices. We may model which staff have adjacent offices as a relation on *STAFF*:

$$neighbours = \{rayner \mapsto jones, jones \mapsto rayner, jones \mapsto bottaci,$$
$$bottaci \mapsto jones, grubb \mapsto rabhi, rabhi \mapsto grubb\}$$

The pair *rayner* $\mapsto$ *jones* models the fact that Dr Rayner has an office next to Dr Jones. It follows, of course, that Dr Jones has an office next to Dr Rayner, and so the relation also contains the pair *jones* $\mapsto$ *rayner*. This regularity in structure is a property of what is being modelled. This relation is many to many.   □

The relations we have considered so far have been defined extensionally. We may define relations intensionally if we make the generator of a comprehension a maplet.

Example 5.4 Let T be a type. The relation from $\mathbb{F}\, T$ to $\mathbb{N}$ in which a finite set is mapped to its cardinality is:

$$\{x : \mathbb{F}\, T \bullet x \mapsto \#x\}$$

                                                                                    □

Exercise 5.3 Why was the type involved in Example 5.4 $\mathbb{F}\, T$ rather than $\mathbb{P}\, T$?   □

Example 5.5 The relation on the integers that maps an integer to its square is:

$$square = \{x : \mathbb{Z} \bullet x \mapsto x * x\}$$

For example, $3 \mapsto 9 \in square$. Since $-3 \mapsto 9 \in square$, this relation is many to one.   □

Exercise 5.4 Suppose A is a set. A relation on $\mathbb{F}\ A$ may be defined as follows: two elements of $\mathbb{F}\ A$ are related if the first has strictly fewer members than the second. Express this relation intensionally by means of a set comprehension. Is this relation many to many, one to many or many to one? □

In order to give an intensional definition of a relation from X to Y the declaration part of a comprehension may need to involve two variables. This is possible in Z, and a typical comprehension for a relation has the form:

$$\{x : X;\ y : Y \mid P \bullet x \mapsto y\}$$

for some predicate P, which we would normally expect to involve x and y. We consider comprehensions involving a number of variables in more detail on page 128.

5.2 Type of a relation

A relation is a set of pairs. We know from Chapter 4 that the type of a set is $\mathbb{P}\ T$ for some T. However, what is T in this case? That is, what is the type of an ordered pair?

Reconsider the relation *teachesProgramming*:

$$
\begin{aligned}
teachesProgramming = \{ &jones \mapsto prolog, bottaci \mapsto prolog, \\
&bottaci \mapsto smalltalk80, grubb \mapsto modula2, \\
&rabhi \mapsto occam \}
\end{aligned}
$$

The type of the first element of a pair is $STAFF$, and the type of the second element is $LANGUAGE$. The actual value we have illustrated for this relation is coincidental; it may have included pairs with any value of type $STAFF$ in the first place, and any value of type $LANGUAGE$ in the second place. Thus the underlying type of this relation is the set whose members are any value of type $STAFF$ paired with any value of type $LANGUAGE$. This is a type we have not met before. To define the type we must introduce a new type constructor, written $\times$, called the *Cartesian product*. The type of the pair *jones $\mapsto$ prolog* is then:

$$STAFF \times LANGUAGE$$

This type is pronounced '$STAFF$ cross $LANGUAGE$'. The values of this type are all the ordered pairs that can be made from the two component types.

Example 5.6

$$
\begin{aligned}
\{a, b\} \times \{one, two, three\} = \{ &a \mapsto one, a \mapsto two, a \mapsto three, \\
&b \mapsto one, b \mapsto two, b \mapsto three \}
\end{aligned}
$$

□

Two ordered pairs of the same type are equal if they have the same first element and the same second element. Thus for example:

$$jones \mapsto prolog = jones \mapsto prolog$$
$$jones \mapsto prolog \neq bottaci \mapsto prolog$$

Two pairs of different types are neither equal nor not equal.

The relation *teachesProgramming* is a set of ordered pairs of type $STAFF \times LANGUAGE$, and so it has the type $\mathbb{P}(STAFF \times LANGUAGE)$. Relations are used sufficiently often in specifications to warrant a standard abbreviation for their type:

$$A \leftrightarrow B == \mathbb{P}(A \times B)$$

Thus, the type of *teachesProgramming* may be written $STAFF \leftrightarrow LANGUAGE$, which may be pronounced 'relation from $STAFF$ to $LANGUAGE$'. It is as if $\leftrightarrow$ is another type constructor, although as we have seen it is actually defined in terms of the existing type constructors $\times$ and $\mathbb{P}$.

Exercise 5.5 What is the type of a relation on a set A?   □

Example 5.7 For some relations it is convenient to write them in infix form. This is particularly true, of course, for the common arithmetic relations such as $<$ and $\leq$. In order to do this the definition of the relation must be given in a particular form, which we shall illustrate with the relation *square* of Example 5.5. In the following axiomatic definition:

$$\begin{array}{|l}
\_\, square\, \_ : \mathbb{Z} \leftrightarrow \mathbb{Z} \\
\hline
\forall\, x, y : \mathbb{Z} \bullet \\
\quad x\; square\; y \Leftrightarrow y = x * x
\end{array}$$

the name of the relation is given in the form $\_\, square\, \_$. The underscores, $\_$, indicate where the arguments should appear. In this case the relation is defined as infix, although it is possible to define prefix or postfix unary relations. With this definition, we may write $3\; square\; 9$ instead of $3 \mapsto 9 \in square$.   □

We may now give precise definitions of the binary relations used in Chapter 3 to describe blocks scenes, namely $\_onTopOf\_$ and $\_above\_$. Recalling how unary relations were defined in Chapter 4 (page 81), we view $\_onTopOf\_$ as a set of pairs, those for which it is true. This is of course consistent with the definition of a relation in this chapter. The appropriate definition of $\_onTopOf\_$ with regard to the blocks scene of Figure 3.1 is:

$$\begin{array}{|l}
\_onTopOf\_ : BLOCK \leftrightarrow BLOCK \\
\hline
\forall\, x, y : BLOCK \bullet \\
\quad x\; onTopOf\; y \Leftrightarrow x \mapsto y \in \{b \mapsto a, f \mapsto b, g \mapsto f, e \mapsto d\}
\end{array}$$

Exercise 5.6 Define the relation $\_above\_$?   □

5.3 Standard relations

Subset relation: generic definition

In Chapter 4 (page 89) we described the subset relation, $\subseteq$. Now that we have the relation type, we may present a formal definition of $\subseteq$. The formal definition of $\subseteq$ involves a further aspect of Z, in that the form of definition used allows a single definition to introduce a relation for any type. The definition is:

$$
\begin{array}{|l}
\hline = [T] =\!=\!=\!=\!=\!=\!=\!=\!=\!=\!= \\
\hline \quad \_ \subseteq \_ : \mathbb{P}\, T \leftrightarrow \mathbb{P}\, T \\
\hline \quad \forall\, U, V : \mathbb{P}\, T \bullet \\
\qquad U \subseteq V \Leftrightarrow \forall\, x : T \bullet x \in U \Rightarrow x \in V \\
\hline
\end{array}
$$

The form of the declaration $\_ \subseteq \_ : \mathbb{P}\, T \leftrightarrow \mathbb{P}\, T$ tells us that the symbol $\subseteq$ will be written infix. The fact that this definition introduces a relation for any type is indicated by the appearance of a type parameter in the top line of the definition. Such a definition is called a *generic definition* or *generic constant* . The declaration part of the definition gives the type of the relation, in terms of the formal parameter T, and the predicate part restricts the value to the required relation. Compare the predicate part of this generic schema with the description of subset given in Chapter 4.

The generic definition introduces a whole family of global constants, one for each possible value of T. Formally, if we want to indicate a specific constant we have to supply the appropriate type parameter. For example, the subset relation over the type $STAFF$ would, formally, be denoted $\subseteq [STAFF]$, and we might pedantically write:

$$\{jones, bottaci\} \subseteq [STAFF]\{jones, bottaci, brookes, phillips\}$$

However, as we have been doing already, it is common practice to omit the explicit type parameters where they can be deduced from the types of the expressions involved.

Exercise 5.7 Give a generic definition of the proper subset relation $\subset$. □

Non-membership and inequality: revisited

Complete definitions of these relations introduced in Chapter 4 may be given by means of generic definitions. The definition of non-membership is:

$$
\begin{array}{|l}
\hline = [T] =\!=\!=\!=\!=\!=\!=\!=\!=\!=\!= \\
\hline \quad \_ \notin \_ : T \leftrightarrow \mathbb{P}\, T \\
\hline \quad \forall\, x : T;\ S : \mathbb{P}\, T \bullet x \notin S \Leftrightarrow \neg\, (x \in S) \\
\hline
\end{array}
$$

For a given type T this definition gives $\notin$ a unique value, as required.

Exercise 5.8 Give a generic definition of $\neq$.   □

Identity relation

Given a set X, the relation that relates every element of X just to itself is called the *identity relation* on X. It may be defined with the following abbreviation definition

$$\mathrm{id}\, X == \{x : X \mid x \mapsto x\}$$

On the left-hand side of the definition, X appears as a formal parameter and the definition applies for any type or set X.

Example 5.8 $\mathrm{id}\{1, 2, 3\} = \{1 \mapsto 1, 2 \mapsto 2, 3 \mapsto 3\}$ □

The identity relation is unlikely to be of great interest in itself for modelling purposes, because of its very simple and regular structure. Its role is more important when expressing properties of various operations applied to relations. In this sense its role is somewhat like that of 1 with regard to multiplication.

Empty relation

The *empty relation* from A to B is the empty set of type $A \leftrightarrow B$. This relation is useful in specifying initial states of systems that involve an observation that is a relation.

5.4   Functions over relations

Some of the functions discussed in this section may be defined in Z using the techniques of Chapter 7.

Standard set functions

A relation is a set of pairs, so that we can define new relations in terms of existing relations using set functions such as union and intersection.

For example, we can define a new relation which includes all the pairs from *teachesProgramming* and the additional pair *rabhi* $\mapsto$ *haskell* by:

$$teachesProgramming \cup \{rabhi \mapsto haskell\}$$

We may define a relation which is the same as *teachesProgramming* except that Professor Phillips teaches *occam* rather than Dr Rabhi as follows:

$$(teachesProgramming \setminus \{rabhi \mapsto occam\}) \cup \{phillips \mapsto occam\}$$

First and second

The Z library provides two functions for accessing the two components of a pair, called *first* and *second*. Thus:

$$first(x, y) = x$$
$$second(x, y) = y$$

Clearly, the type of $first(x, y)$ is the type of x.

The need for two functions *first* and *second* is in contrast with the membership predicate for sets, and this difference emphasizes the significance of order in pairs. For example, consider the predicates:

$$1 \in \{1, 2\}$$
$$2 \in \{1, 2\}$$

Each of these is true. Now consider the predicates:

$$1 = first(1, 2)$$
$$2 = first(1, 2)$$

Only the first of these is true; the second is false.

In specifications in which pairs are presented explicitly there is no need for *first* and *second*. They are useful, though, when the elements of a pair are not explicit.

Example 5.9 Given the relation *teachesProgramming*, the property that a given programming language p is taught is:

$$\exists t : STAFF \times LANGUAGE \bullet t \in teachesProgramming \land second\ t = p$$

□

Source, target, domain and range

Given that the relation *teachesProgramming* is of type $STAFF \leftrightarrow LANGUAGE$, $STAFF$ is called the *source* of the relation and $LANGUAGE$ is called the *target*.

More often than not a relation does not include every possible ordered pair. Under these circumstances it can be convenient to be able to refer to those elements of the source that are related to an element in the target, and vice versa. Two prefix functions are provided in the Z library for this purpose. If $R : A \leftrightarrow B$ is a relation:

$$\text{dom}\,R = \{x : A;\ y : B \mid x \mapsto y \in R \bullet x\}$$
$$\text{ran}\,R = \{x : A;\ y : B \mid x \mapsto y \in R \bullet y\}$$

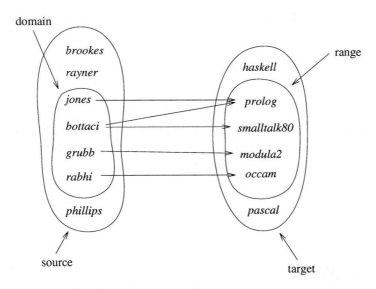

Figure 5.2: Source, target, domain and range of *teachesProgramming*

dom R is called the *domain* of R, and consists of all those elements of the source that are first elements of a pair in R. ran R is called the *range* of R, and consists of all those elements of the target that are second elements of a pair in R. These sets are illustrated in Figure 5.2.

Exercise 5.9 Let $A = \{1, 2, 3, 4, 5, 6\}$, $B = \{two, three, four, five, six, seven\}$, and $R : A \leftrightarrow B$ be:

$$R = \{1 \mapsto two, 2 \mapsto three, 4 \mapsto five, 5 \mapsto five\}$$

What are dom R and ran R?   □

We can express the restriction that the value of a variable s of type $STAFF$ is a person who teaches programming as follows:

$$s \in \text{dom } teachesProgramming$$

Exercise 5.10 Suppose $p1$ and $p2$ are of type $LANGUAGE$. How would we express the restriction that the value of $p1$ is a programming language that is taught? What if you want to make sure that the value of $p2$ is a language that is not taught?   □

Exercise 5.11 If $R : A \leftrightarrow B$, what is the type of dom R? What is the type of ran R? When is dom $R \cup$ ran R well defined?   □

Relational composition

The relation *teachesProgramming* is from *STAFF* to *LANGUAGE*, while the relation *programmingSemesters* is from *LANGUAGE* to *SEMESTER*. Thus the target of *teachesProgramming* and the source of *programmingSemesters* are the same set. For this reason it is possible to illustrate these two relations in one diagram in Figure 5.3.

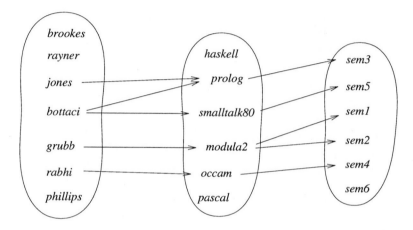

Figure 5.3: *teachesProgramming* and *programmingSemesters*

The diagram combining the two relations suggests how we might define a new relation, from *STAFF* to *SEMESTER*. A pair $x \mapsto y$ is in the new relation if x is a member of staff, y is a semester and it is possible to traverse arrows from x to y in Figure 5.3. The relation defined in this way models the information about the semesters in which members of staff teach programming. For example, Dr Bottaci teaches programming in semester 3 and semester 5. The complete relation arising out of *teachesProgramming* and *programmingSemesters* is:

$$\{grubb \mapsto sem1, grubb \mapsto sem2, jones \mapsto sem3,$$
$$bottaci \mapsto sem3, bottaci \mapsto sem4, rabhi \mapsto sem4\}$$

This relation is the *relational composition* of the relations *teachesProgramming* and *programmingSemesters*, and it is denoted:

$$teachesProgramming \; \S \; programmingSemesters$$

More formally, suppose $R : X \leftrightarrow Y$ and $S : Y \leftrightarrow Z$. The relational composition of R and S, denoted $R \, \S \, S$ and pronounced 'R composed with S', is defined as follows:

$$R \, \mathring{,} \, S = \{x : X; \; y : Y; \; z : Z \mid x \mapsto y \in R \land y \mapsto z \in S \bullet x \mapsto z\}$$

$R \, \mathring{,} \, S$ is of type $X \leftrightarrow Z$.

Example 5.10 Let $A = \{a, b, c\}$, $B = \{1, 2\}$ and $C = \{one, two, three, four\}$. Supposing $R = \{a \mapsto 1, b \mapsto 2, c \mapsto 2\}$ and $S = \{1 \mapsto two, 2 \mapsto three\}$, then:

$$R \, \mathring{,} \, S = \{a \mapsto two, b \mapsto three, c \mapsto three\}$$

The resulting relation in this case is illustrated in Figure 5.4. Note that in this example, $S \, \mathring{,} \, R$ is not well defined.   □

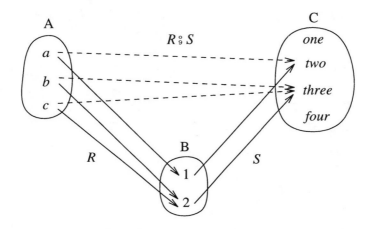

Figure 5.4: The composition of R and S

Exercise 5.12 * Suppose we have the following relation defined over the integers, $\mathbb{Z}$:

$$plus5 = \{x : \mathbb{Z} \bullet x \mapsto x + 5\}$$

We can compose this with the relation *square* either way round. What are *square* $\mathring{,}$ *plus5* and *plus5* $\mathring{,}$ *square*? Try to give your answers in the form of comprehensions.   □

Relational composition is an infix function over relations. It has the same precedence as intersection (see [20], page 46). Relational composition is associative. That is, for any relations R, S and T which are type-compatible:

$$(R \, \mathring{,} \, S) \, \mathring{,} \, T = R \, \mathring{,} \, (S \, \mathring{,} \, T)$$

We may thus write $R \, \mathring{,} \, S \, \mathring{,} \, T$, if we wish, without ambiguity. Exercise 5.12 shows that relational composition is not commutative.

Relational image of a set

The set of programming languages that Drs Jones, Bottaci and Rayner teach is $\{prolog, smalltalk80\}$. It is given by the comprehension:

$$\{l : LANGUAGE \mid jones \mapsto l \in teachesProgramming$$
$$\vee bottaci \mapsto l \in teachesProgramming$$
$$\vee rayner \mapsto l \in teachesProgramming\}$$

The set $\{prolog, smalltalk80\}$ is the *relational image of* $\{jones, bottaci, rayner\}$ *through teachesProgramming*. This is illustrated in Figure 5.5. Observe that since *rayner* is not in the domain of *teachesProgramming* the relational image of $\{jones, bottaci, rayner\}$ is the same as the relational image of $\{jones, bottaci\}$.

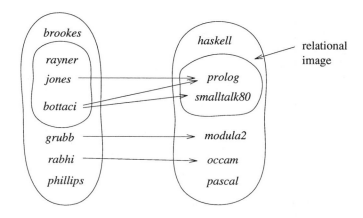

Figure 5.5: Relational image of $\{jones, bottaci, rayner\}$ through *teachesProgramming*

More formally, given a relation $R : X \leftrightarrow Y$ and a set $U \subseteq X$, the relational image of U through R, denoted $R(\!|U|\!)$, is the set of elements of Y that are related by R to some element of U. That is:

$$R(\!|U|\!) = \{x : X; \; y : Y \mid x \in U \wedge x \mapsto y \in R \bullet y\}$$

This description is particular to the relation R and the set U.

Example 5.11 Consider the relation *propertiesOfNumbers* from $A = \{3, 6, 37\}$ to $B = \{small, large, odd, even, prime\}$ given by:

$$propertiesOfNumbers = \{3 \mapsto small, 3 \mapsto odd, 3 \mapsto prime, 6 \mapsto small,$$
$$6 \mapsto even, 37 \mapsto large, 37 \mapsto prime\}$$

Then:

$$propertiesOfNumbers(\!|\{3,6\}|\!) = \{small, odd, even, prime\}$$

□

Exercise 5.13 What is $propertiesOfNumbers(\!|\{3,37\}|\!)$?   □

Inverse of a relation

Given the relation *teachesProgramming* and a subset of *STAFF* we may use the relational image operator to find the set of languages taught by those staff. What if, instead, we wish to know which staff teach a given set of languages? We could not immediately use the relational image to answer this question, since we would be trying to apply it in the opposite direction. To overcome this problem we could define a relational pre-image, but instead we will define the more general notion of inverting a relation. This will then allow us to exploit the relational image.

The *inverse* of *teachesProgramming* is the relation *teachesProgramming*~ from *LANGUAGE* to *STAFF* obtained from *teachesProgramming* by reversing all the maplets. That is:

$$teachesProgramming^{\sim} = \{prolog \mapsto jones, prolog \mapsto bottaci,$$
$$modula2 \mapsto grubb, occam \mapsto rabhi,$$
$$smalltalk80 \mapsto bottaci\}$$

Given this relation, the set of staff who teach Prolog or Modula-2 is:

$$teachesProgramming^{\sim}(\!|\{prolog, modula2\}|\!) = \{jones, bottaci, grubb\}$$

More formally, for $R : A \leftrightarrow B$ the inverse of R, written $R^{\sim}$, is defined by:

$$R^{\sim} = \{x : A; \ y : B \mid x \mapsto y \in R \bullet y \mapsto x\}$$

This definition is particular to the relation R. A more general definition will be given in Chapter 7 on functions.

Example 5.12 The set of staff teaching programming in the second semester is:

$$(teachesProgramming \,\fatsemi\, programmingSemesters)^{\sim}(\!|\{sem2\}|\!)$$

□

Example 5.13 The inverse of $square = \{x : \mathbb{Z} \bullet x \mapsto x * x\}$ is:

$$square^{\sim} = \{x : \mathbb{Z} \bullet x * x \mapsto x\}$$

The only change is to reverse the order of the components in the generator part of the comprehension. This is appropriate because the underlying correspondence between two elements is to be the same; only the order is different. □

Example 5.14 We may compose any relation with its own inverse. For example, the relation *teachesProgramming* ⨾ *teachesProgramming*$^{\sim}$ is:

$$\{jones \mapsto jones, jones \mapsto bottaci, bottaci \mapsto bottaci,$$
$$bottaci \mapsto jones, grubb \mapsto grubb, rabhi \mapsto rabhi\}$$

First note that this relation is not the identity relation on *STAFF*, nor even the identity relation on dom *teachesProgramming*. This relation relates members of staff to staff who teach the same programming language. Through the means by which this relation was defined this includes relating individuals to themselves. More interestingly it shows that Drs Bottaci and Jones share the teaching of one or more languages. Inspection of *teachesProgramming* shows that it is Prolog. □

Exercise 5.14 The relation *propertiesOfNumbers* was defined in Example 5.11. What are:

 i. *propertiesOfNumbers*$^{\sim}$(|{*small, prime*}|)
 ii. *propertiesOfNumbers* ⨾ *propertiesOfNumbers*$^{\sim}$

  □

Transitive closure of a relation

The Western World Informatics Department offers a range of degrees, and some individual modules are present in several degrees. Under the examination regime that existed prior to modularization, an examination paper examined several modules. This inevitably led to situations where the same module had to be examined in different examination papers for different degrees[1]. It was clearly cost-effective as far as the staff were concerned if the examination papers that examined the same module were taken at the same time, so that only one set of examination questions needed to be written. If the type of an examination paper is *EXAM* then the information about which papers share questions can be modelled using a relation on *EXAM*:

$$shareQues = \{paper1 \mapsto paper2, paper2 \mapsto paper1,$$
$$paper2 \mapsto paper3, paper3 \mapsto paper2,$$
$$paper4 \mapsto paper5, paper5 \mapsto paper4\}$$

---

[1]Semesterization of the degrees and the adoption of a full module system will do away with this problem, since in the future each module will be examined separately.

The intended meaning of $x \mapsto y \in shareQues$ is that the papers x and y share examination questions.

Let us say that examination papers that must be taken at the same time are concurrent. Since $paper1$ and $paper2$ share questions they are concurrent. We also see that $paper2$ and $paper3$ are concurrent. It follows that $paper1$ and $paper3$ must be concurrent even though there is no question shared by these two papers (observe that $paper1 \mapsto paper3 \notin shareQues$). Thus concurrent examination papers are not simply those that share examination questions.

Figure 5.6 illustrates the various relationships between $paper1$, $paper2$ and $paper3$. The dotted lines between $paper1$ and $paper3$ are the additional concurrency information. The pairs $paper1 \mapsto paper3$ and $paper3 \mapsto paper1$ would arise from the composition of $shareQues$ with itself.

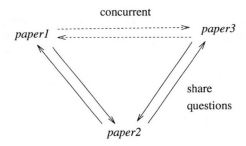

Figure 5.6: Various relationships between $paper1$, $paper2$ and $paper3$

If we compose $shareQues$ with itself, we obtain the relation:

$shareQues \, \fatsemi \, shareQues$
$$= \{paper1 \mapsto paper1, paper2 \mapsto paper2, paper3 \mapsto paper3,$$
$$paper4 \mapsto paper4, paper5 \mapsto paper5, paper1 \mapsto paper3,$$
$$paper3 \mapsto paper1\}$$

This is illustrated in Figure 5.7. Pairs in the composition may be read off from Figure 5.7 by following two arrows from left to right. This composition will identify all implicit concurrencies in $shareQues$ through pairs of the form $x \mapsto y$ and $y \mapsto z$. Observe that $shareQues \nsubseteq shareQues \, \fatsemi \, shareQues$.

The complete information we have so far on concurrency of examinations is given by:

$$shareQues \cup (shareQues \, \fatsemi \, shareQues)$$

In this particular example, this set comprises all the necessary concurrencies. In more complex examples it may be necessary to consider also:

$$shareQues \, \fatsemi \, shareQues \, \fatsemi \, shareQues$$

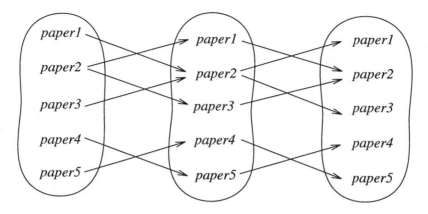

Figure 5.7: The relation *shareQues* composed with itself

or:

$$shareQues \,\S\, shareQues \,\S\, shareQues \,\S\, shareQues$$

and so on.

Exercise 5.15 Extend *shareQues* so that the derivation of all necessary concurrencies requires $shareQues \,\S\, shareQues \,\S\, shareQues$. □

For a given relation we cannot tell in advance how many times we will have to compose it in order to extract all the information of interest. To overcome this problem, the Z library provides an operator that repeatedly composes a relation until no new information may be obtained by further composition. This operator forms the *transitive closure* of a relation. Given the relation *shareQues* the transitive closure is written $shareQues^+$. In this example $shareQues^+ = shareQues \cup (shareQues \,\S\, shareQues)$ although, as we have already observed, this is not a general result.

Given a relation R on a set A, R^+ is also a relation on A. Informally it is given by:

$$R^+ = R \cup (R \,\S\, R) \cup (R \,\S\, R \,\S\, R) \cup (R \,\S\, R \,\S\, R \,\S\, R) \cup \ldots$$

We may define the concurrent examination papers simply as:

$$concurrencies = shareQues^+$$

This definition is appropriate whatever the structure of *shareQues*.

Exercise 5.16 Recall the relation *square* on $\mathbb{Z}$ from Example 5.5. What is $square \,\S\, square$? □

Example 5.15 Let $R = \{1 \mapsto 1, 2 \mapsto 2, 3 \mapsto 3\}$. Then $R = R^+$.   □

A relation R which is equal to its transitive closure is said to be *transitive*. Such a relation has the property that whenever $x \mapsto y \in R$ and $y \mapsto z \in R$ it must be the case that $x \mapsto z \in R$.

We can extend the idea of transitive closure to that of a set being closed under an operation. For example, the integers are closed under addition. This means that the result of the function $+$ applied to two arbitrary members of $\mathbb{Z}$ is itself a member of $\mathbb{Z}$. Obviously not all sets are closed under all operations. For example, $\mathbb{N}$ is not closed under subtraction, and $\mathbb{Z}$ is not closed under division. In the context of transitive closure we are talking of the closure of a set with respect to a property. A set is closed under a property if, given elements in the set, any other element that is required to ensure that the given property holds is also in the set. In forming the closure of a relation under a property, we are effectively saying 'add whatever maplets are necessary for the relation to have the specified property'.

Thus transitive closure is an operation that takes a relation and makes it transitive. It does so in a minimal way; that is, by adding as few new pairs as are required. It is, of course, a feature of the particular example chosen that transitive closure results in a relation that has such an immediate and intuitive interpretation. Transitive closure can be applied to arbitrary relations, but there is no guarantee that the resulting relations are particularly useful in the application.

There are other properties of relations, besides transitivity, that are of interest, and a rich theory about relations that satisfy various combinations of these properties. The value of such theory is that if we know that the relations we are using in a specification satisfy the required properties we can immediately exploit the theoretical results to tell us further properties. Unfortunately, this material is beyond the scope of this book. The interested reader may consult a book on discrete mathematics, such as [10], for more detail.

5.5   Some laws about relations

As relations are sets, they satisfy the laws about sets given in Chapter 4. In this section we list some further laws which relate specifically to relations. As in previous chapters, the laws we list are relatively intuitive, and we shall not justify them. Suppose $R, R_1, R_2 : A \leftrightarrow B$.

$$\mathrm{dom}\,\varnothing = \varnothing$$
$$\mathrm{ran}\,\varnothing = \varnothing$$

$$\mathrm{dom}\,R \subseteq A$$

$\operatorname{ran} R \subseteq B$

$\operatorname{dom} R = \varnothing \Rightarrow R = \varnothing$

$\operatorname{ran} R = \varnothing \Rightarrow R = \varnothing$

$\operatorname{dom}(R_1 \cup R_2) = (\operatorname{dom} R_1) \cup (\operatorname{dom} R_2)$

$\operatorname{ran}(R_1 \cup R_2) = (\operatorname{ran} R_1) \cup (\operatorname{ran} R_2)$

$\operatorname{dom}(R_1 \cap R_2) \subseteq (\operatorname{dom} R_1) \cap (\operatorname{dom} R_2)$

$\operatorname{ran}(R_1 \cap R_2) \subseteq (\operatorname{ran} R_1) \cap (\operatorname{ran} R_2)$

Example 5.16 Let $R_1, R_2 : \{a\} \leftrightarrow \{1, 2\}$ be such that $R_1 = \{a \mapsto 1\}$ and $R_2 = \{a \mapsto 2\}$. $R_1 \cap R_2 = \varnothing$, so that $\operatorname{dom}(R_1 \cap R_2) = \varnothing$. However, $\operatorname{dom} R_1 = \{a\}$ and $\operatorname{dom} R_2 = \{a\}$, so that $(\operatorname{dom} R_1) \cap (\operatorname{dom} R_2) = \{a\}$. This shows that $(\operatorname{dom} R_1) \cap (\operatorname{dom} R_2) \subseteq \operatorname{dom}(R_1 \cap R_2)$ is not generally true. □

Exercise 5.17 Construct an example to demonstrate that:

$$(\operatorname{ran} R_1) \cap (\operatorname{ran} R_2) \subseteq \operatorname{ran}(R_1 \cap R_2)$$

is not generally true. □

Relational composition is associative. That is, for any relations R, S and T which are type-compatible:

$$(R \mathbin{\substack{\circ\\\circ}} S) \mathbin{\substack{\circ\\\circ}} T = R \mathbin{\substack{\circ\\\circ}} (S \mathbin{\substack{\circ\\\circ}} T)$$

$$(R^\sim)^\sim = R$$

$$(R \mathbin{\substack{\circ\\\circ}} S)^\sim = S^\sim \mathbin{\substack{\circ\\\circ}} R^\sim$$

$$\operatorname{dom}(R^\sim) = \operatorname{ran} R$$

$$\operatorname{ran}(R^\sim) = \operatorname{dom} R$$

$$R(\!|\varnothing|\!) = \varnothing$$

$$R(\!|S \cup T|\!) = R(\!|S|\!) \cup (\!|T|\!)$$

$$R(\!|S \cap T|\!) \subseteq R(\!|S|\!) \cap R(\!|T|\!)$$

$$R(\!|\operatorname{dom} R|\!) = \operatorname{ran} R$$

Exercise 5.18 Construct an example which demonstrates that:

$$R(\!|S|\!) \cap R(\!|T|\!) \subseteq R(\!|S \cap T|\!)$$

is not generally true. □

5.6   Tuples

Ordered pairs are, in fact, simply a special case of *ordered n-tuples* (or simply tuples). An ordered *n*-tuple comprising the elements a_1, a_2, ..., a_n ($n \geq 2$) is written:

$$(a_1, a_2, \ldots, a_n)$$

If a_i has the type A_i ($i = 1, \ldots, n$) then the *n*-tuple $(a_1, \ldots, a_n)$ has the type $A_1 \times A_2 \ldots \times A_n$. The values of this type are all the possible *n*-tuples that may be constructed by taking an element of A_i as the *i*th element of the tuple ($i = 1, \ldots, n$). The sets A_1, ..., A_n need not all be different. For $A_1 \times A_2 \ldots \times A_n$ to be well typed, A_1, ..., A_n must be types (or sets).

Example 5.17

$$
\begin{aligned}
\{a, b\} \times \{1, 2, 3\} \times \{one, two\} = \{ & (a, 1, one), (a, 1, two), (a, 2, one), \\
& (a, 2, two), (a, 3, one), (a, 3, two), \\
& (b, 1, one), (b, 1, two), (b, 2, one), \\
& (b, 2, two), (b, 3, one), (b, 3, two)\}
\end{aligned}
$$

□

Two *n*-tuples of the same type are equal if the corresponding pairs of elements are equal:

$$(x_1, \ldots, x_n) = (y_1, \ldots, y_n) \Leftrightarrow x_1 = y_1 \wedge \ldots \wedge x_n = y_n$$

Recall that $x \neq y \Leftrightarrow \neg (x = y)$ and so:

$$(x_1, \ldots, x_n) \neq (y_1, \ldots, y_n) \Leftrightarrow \neg (x_1 = y_1 \wedge \ldots \wedge x_n = y_n)$$

That is:

$$(x_1, \ldots, x_n) \neq (y_1, \ldots, y_n) \Leftrightarrow x_1 \neq y_1 \vee \ldots \vee x_n \neq y_n$$

Thus, two tuples of the same type are not equal if one or more corresponding pairs of elements are not equal. Two *n*-tuples in which a pair of corresponding components have different types are not of the same type, and so are neither equal nor not equal. Two tuples with different numbers of elements are not of the same type.

The notion of tuple allows us to consider comprehensions in which there are more than two variables. If the comprehension includes *n* variables then it specifies a set of *n*-tuples.

Example 5.18 The comprehension:

$$\{x, y, z : \mathbb{Z} \mid x < y \wedge y < z \bullet (x, y, z)\}$$

defines a set of ordered triples in which the three components of each triple are in strict numerical order.   □

5.7   Relations over non-basic types

Applicants to study Informatics at the Western World are invited to visit the university on an open afternoon. While they are there they are taken on tours of the university and department, and are interviewed. In order to allow as many applicants as possible to see as much as possible there is a fairly elaborate schedule for an open afternoon. For the sake of simplicity let us suppose that the schedule is given by the following table:

	Slot 1	Slot 2
Group A	Tour	Interview
Group B	Interview	Tour

Thus, applicants are divided into two groups, there are two time slots and there are two activities. The kind of structure in this problem is typical of a range of situations in which multiple groups of people are undertaking multiple activities which need time-tabling; for example, teaching in schools and universities, or schedules for conferences and workshops.

Suppose we have the types:

$GROUP ::= groupA \mid groupB$

$ACTIVITY ::= tour \mid interview$

$SLOT ::= slot1 \mid slot2$

It would be possible to represent this information with triples such as:

$(groupA, slot1, interview)$

However, we shall instead represent it as a pair, one of whose components is a pair:

$(groupA, slot1) \mapsto interview$

We have employed a mixture of the two possible notations for a pair, to emphasize the structure involved. The type of $(groupA, slot1) \mapsto tour$ is $(GROUP \times SLOT) \times ACTIVITY$. This is a different type from that of the triple $(groupA, slot1, interview)$, which is $GROUP \times SLOT \times ACTIVITY$.

The complete information for the open afternoon is then:

$$schedule = \{(groupA, slot1) \mapsto tour, (groupA, slot2) \mapsto interview,$$
$$(groupB, slot1) \mapsto interview, (groupB, slot2) \mapsto tour\}$$

The type of *schedule* is $(GROUP \times SLOT) \leftrightarrow ACTIVITY$.

The schedule for *groupA* for the afternoon is:

$$\{s : SLOT;\ a : ACTIVITY \mid (groupA, s) \mapsto a \in schedule \bullet s \mapsto a\}$$
$$= \{slot1 \mapsto tour, slot2 \mapsto interview\}$$

The schedule for tours is:

$$\{x : GROUP \times SLOT \mid x \mapsto tour \in schedule\}$$

Exercise 5.19 Give a comprehension that identifies which activities are scheduled for which groups in slot 2. $\square$

There are some natural restrictions on the table given above. For example, no group may be scheduled for different activities during the same session.

$$\forall x : GROUP \times SLOT \bullet \exists_1 y : ACTIVITY \bullet x \mapsto y \in schedule$$

Exercise 5.20 Express the restriction that every group does every activity. $\square$

More generally, suppose A, B and C are types. We may form three distinct types $A \times B \times C$, $A \times (B \times C)$ and $(A \times B) \times C$. Values of the type $A \times B \times C$ are triples, while values of the other two types are pairs. For example, if $a \in A$, $b \in B$ and $c \in C$ then:

$$(a, b, c) \in A \times B \times C$$
$$(a, (b, c)) \in A \times (B \times C)$$
$$((a, b), c) \in (A \times B) \times C$$

We may, of course, define more complex product types such as $(A \times B) \times (C \times D)$ if we wish.

Exercise 5.21 Given $A = \{1, 2\}$, $B = \{a, b, c\}$ and $C = \{four\}$, determine $A \times (B \times C)$, $(A \times B) \times C$, and $A \times B \times C$. $\square$

Exercise 5.22 If $a \in A$, $b \in B$ and $c \in C$, what can you say about $(a, (b, c)) \in (A \times B) \times C$? $\square$

Exercise 5.23 The information modelled by *teachesProgramming* may also be represented by:

$$\{prolog \mapsto \{jones, bottaci\}, modula2 \mapsto \{grubb\},$$
$$smalltalk80 \mapsto \{bottaci\}, occam \mapsto \{rabhi\}\}$$

What is the type of this relation? $\square$

5.8   Module prerequisites: revisited

We shall be specifying a system to maintain prerequisite information about modules. Clearly we must be able to modify the information recorded as well as use it, so the operations we might expect are:

Add: add information to the database

Delete: remove information from the database

Query: select information from the database

Let us consider adding information to the database. Suppose that Western World modules are identified by codes such as *CS*113 and *CS*205. Figure 5.8 illustrates a part of the information that needs to be recorded. In this figure an arrow from one module to another indicates that the former module is a prerequisite for the latter. Thus, for example, *CS*113 is a prerequisite for *CS*203.

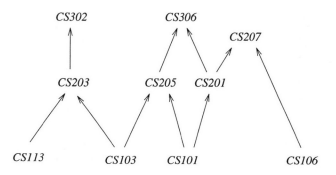

Figure 5.8: Prerequisite information for a selection of informatics modules

Let us consider what happens when we add further arcs to Figure 5.8. Suppose, for the sake of example, that we decide that *CS*205 should be a prerequisite for *CS*302. The extra arc can simply be added into Figure 5.8 to record this. Now suppose that we add arcs from *CS*201 to *CS*101 and from *CS*302 to *CS*103. In Figure 5.9 we illustrate part of the prerequisite information which results from these additions. Let us explore this briefly.

If *CS*101 is a prerequisite for *CS*201, it means that a student who wishes to take *CS*201 must already have achieved the credits for *CS*101. Yet *CS*201 is also a prerequisite for *CS*101, in which case the student must have the credits for *CS*201 before taking *CS*101. Clearly this is an impossible situation; in order to take *CS*201 a student must already hold the credits for *CS*201. A similar analysis applies to the addition of the arc from *CS*302 to *CS*103; in order to take *CS*302 a student must already hold the credits for *CS*302. Clearly it must not be possible to record such information in the prerequisites database. Let us say that information that includes such possibilities is inconsistent. It is clear that the prerequisites database must always be consistent.

To motivate the query operations, let us consider the information that may usefully be extracted from the prerequisites information. Figure 5.8 emphasizes

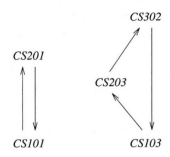

Figure 5.9: Examples of inconsistent information

dependencies between modules which are not explicit in the notion of prerequisite. For example: a student who does not have the credits for $CS113$ will be unable to take $CS203$ and hence $CS302$; a student who wishes to take $CS207$ must gain the credits for $CS106$ and $CS201$, and hence for $CS101$.

We shall include enquiry operations to determine all of these hidden dependencies, and a little terminology to distinguish between the various possibilities will be helpful. The modules that quote a given module as prerequisite will be called its *offspring*. For a given module, its offspring and offspring of its offspring and so on will be called its *descendants*. If one module is a descendant of another, then the latter module will be called an *ancestor* of the former module. For example, in Figure 5.8 the offspring of $CS101$ are $CS205$ and $CS201$, while the descendants of $CS101$ are $CS205$, $CS201$, $CS207$ and $CS306$. The ancestors of $CS306$ are $CS205$, $CS201$, $CS103$ and $CS101$.

It is now appropriate to consider how the information will be recorded. The only observation we need to make concerns the prerequisite information, and it seems clear that it is a relation between modules. So, we shall need a type $MODULE$. With this choice, we might expect the add operation to be specified with set union, and the delete operation with set difference. We might hope to specify the query operation with functions over relations, such as relational image.

Let us consider how the consistency of the information may be characterized. In the example inconsistency examined above, a student who wishes to take $CS201$ must already have the credits for $CS201$. A similar argument would lead to the conclusion that a student who wishes to take $CS101$ must already have the credits for $CS101$. Obviously, the identity of the particular module is not crucial here; what is important is that the inconsistency arises when a student must hold the credits for a given module in order to take that module. This should not be possible in a consistent database. The examples above show that it is not as simple as saying that there must be no module that is a prerequisite for itself. The same problem can arise through following chains of arcs. This suggests that composition of the relation with itself may be appropriate. Since we cannot know how many arcs we shall need to follow, we should in fact consider the closure of the prerequisites database. So, a consistent database is one in which:

- no module is mapped to itself in the closure of the prerequisite database.

This is the state invariant.

Inconsistency can be created only though the addition of information. When a new pair is added, the combination of the database and the new pair may be consistent, and so the add operation will have two subcases. This issue does not arise in the delete operation, and we can make do with one subcase. The operations of the system are summarized in Table 5.1.

Operation	Input	Subcase property	State change	Output	Report
Add prerequisite	Two modules	Database with new pair consistent	Add in	*None*	Success
		Database with new pair inconsistent	*None*	*None*	Inconsistent
Delete prerequisite	Two modules	*None*	Remove pair	*None*	*None*
Prerequisites	Module	*None*	*None*	Set of modules	*None*
Ancestors	Module	*None*	*None*	Set of modules	*None*
Offspring	Module	*None*	*None*	Set of modules	*None*
Descendants	Module	*None*	*None*	Set of modules	*None*

Table 5.1: The operations of the prerequisites database

Basics

The fundamental entities in the system are modules. The specification of the system need say nothing about how they are represented. So, we simply have a type:

$[MODULE]$

We shall assume that this type has values for every module that is required.

The type for reports has two values:

$REPORT ::= success \mid inconsistent$

The state of the system

The state will comprise a relation $prerequisites : MODULE \leftrightarrow MODULE$, in which a pair $m_1 \mapsto m_2$ means that m_1 is a prerequisite of m_2. The state invariant is that no module is mapped to itself in the closure of the prerequisite database. Given these ingredients, the state schema is:

$$
\begin{array}{l}
\rule{4cm}{0.4pt}\; PrerequisitesDB \rule{4cm}{0.4pt} \\
prerequisites : MODULE \leftrightarrow MODULE \\
\rule{6cm}{0.4pt} \\
\neg\; \exists\, m : MODULE \bullet m \mapsto m \in prerequisites^+
\end{array}
$$

Initial state

For the initial state, since we shall be able to add prerequisite information it is adequate to begin with an empty prerequisites relation.

$$
\begin{array}{l}
\rule{3cm}{0.4pt}\; InitPrerequisitesDB \rule{3cm}{0.4pt} \\
PrerequisitesDB' \\
\rule{5cm}{0.4pt} \\
prerequisites' = \varnothing
\end{array}
$$

It is clear that a state exists satisfying this specification.

Creating the database

Add a prerequisite

Suppose the two modules input are m_1 and m_2. To add this new pair into the prerequisites database we use set union:

$$prerequisites' = prerequisites \cup \{m_1? \mapsto m_2?\}$$

If the pair is already present then this definition does not define a state change. The after-state invariant tells us that $prerequisites'$ is consistent, so that this case applies only when $prerequisites \cup \{m_1? \mapsto m_2?\}$ is consistent. There is thus no need to include explicitly the subcase property that $prerequisites \cup \{m_1? \mapsto m_2?\}$ is consistent.

```
┌─ AddPairOK ─────────────────────────────────────────────
│ Δ PrerequisitesDB
│ m₁?, m₂? : MODULE
│ r! : REPORT
├─────────────────────────────────────────────────────────
│ prerequisites' = prerequisites ∪ {m₁? ↦ m₂?}
│ r! = success
└─────────────────────────────────────────────────────────
```

The other possibility is that the addition of the input pair would make the prerequisites database inconsistent, that is, $prerequisites \cup \{m_1? \mapsto m_2?\}$ would be inconsistent. $prerequisites \cup \{m_1? \mapsto m_2?\}$ is inconsistent if its closure includes a module mapped to itself.

```
┌─ InconsistentPair ──────────────────────────────────────
│ Ξ PrerequisitesDB
│ m₁?, m₂? : MODULE
│ r! : REPORT
├─────────────────────────────────────────────────────────
│ ∃ m : MODULE • m ↦ m ∈ (prerequisites ∪ {m₁? ↦ m₂?})⁺
│ r! = inconsistent
└─────────────────────────────────────────────────────────
```

The operation for adding a prerequisite record is:

$$AddPair \mathrel{\hat=} AddPairOK \lor InconsistentPair$$

Consider an arbitrary state in the state space and two input modules m_1 and m_2. Either the state of the database with the addition of the pair $m_1 \mapsto m_2$ is consistent or it is not. In each case there is a schema that defines a suitable after-state and report, and so this operation is total.

Delete a prerequisite

The input to this operation is again a pair of modules, m_1 and m_2. We may remove this pair from the database as follows:

$$prerequisites' = prerequisites \setminus \{m_1? \mapsto m_2?\}$$

Irrespective of whether $m_1? \mapsto m_2? \in prerequisites$, this predicate defines the correct value for $prerequisites'$. The operation is thus:

```
┌─ DeletePair ────────────────────────────────────────────
│ Δ PrerequisitesDB
│ m₁?, m₂? : MODULE
├─────────────────────────────────────────────────────────
│ prerequisites' = prerequisites \ {m₁? ↦ m₂?}
└─────────────────────────────────────────────────────────
```

This operation clearly applies in every state in the state space and defines a suitable after-state and report; hence the operation is total.

Query the database

Enquiring about prerequisites

This operation requires an input module $m?$. The output will be a set of modules which are recorded as prerequisites of the specified module, that is, all those modules which are first elements of a pair for a given second element. We can specify this using the relational image as $prerequisites^{\sim}(\!|\{m?\}|\!)$.

The complete operation is then:

$$
\begin{array}{|l}
\hline
\;Prerequisites \underline{\hspace{6cm}} \\
\;\Xi PrerequisitesDB \\
\;m? : MODULE \\
\;ms! : \mathbb{P}\, MODULE \\
\;\rule{10cm}{0.4pt} \\
\;ms! = prerequisites^{\sim}(\!|\{m?\}|\!) \\
\hline
\end{array}
$$

Recall that the query operations do not include reports. You should consider the totality of this operation.

Exercise 5.24 Specify an operation for enquiring about the prerequisites of a set of modules.   □

Enquiring about ancestors

This is similar to enquiring about prerequisites, except that it is necessary to follow chains of prerequisites. We achieve this by forming the transitive closure of *prerequisites*. None of the cases of this operation change the state of the system.

$$
\begin{array}{|l}
\hline
\;Ancestors \underline{\hspace{6cm}} \\
\;\Xi PrerequisitesDB \\
\;m? : MODULE \\
\;ms! : \mathbb{P}\, MODULE \\
\;\rule{10cm}{0.4pt} \\
\;ms! = (prerequisites^{+})^{\sim}(\!|\{m?\}|\!) \\
\hline
\end{array}
$$

You should consider the totality of this operation.

Enquiring about offspring

Exercise 5.25 Specify the operation for enquiring about offspring of a given module.   □

Enquiring about descendants

Exercise 5.26 Specify the operation for enquiring about descendants of a given module.   □

Exercise 5.27 ** In systems such as the prerequisites database it can be helpful to build in checks on the information that is input. For example, if it was known which modules were actually on offer at Western World then the operations of the system could ensure that no reference was made to a module that was not being offered. Modify the specification of the prerequisites database to include these checks.   □

Chapter 6

A Closer Look at Z

In our first example of the use of Z, the car park example from Chapter 2, we gave an overview of the Z notation by presenting a small specification. In this chapter we present the Z notation, starting from the basic elements and leading towards the more complex constructions. We do not expect the reader to fully appreciate the significance of all the material in this chapter on a first reading, but to return to this chapter from time to time as necessary.

6.1 Types

The majority of readers will have a reasonably good intuitive understanding of the concept of a type, an understanding that we have so far exploited in order to get across an impression of Z without the distraction of the details required for rigour. Students, however, are often confused, for example, by the fact that whereas $\mathbb{Z}$ is a type, $\mathbb{N}$ is not. In addition, students may not be fully aware of why types are useful. In this section we will consider types in some detail and provide answers to these questions.

Intuitively we think of a type as a set. Although strictly speaking this is incorrect, for most purposes, including those of this book, there is no harm in thinking of a type as a set.

In Z every value must belong to exactly one type. Consider, for example, the integer value 3. This value belongs to many sets, including $\{1, 2, 3, 4\}$, $\mathbb{N}$ and $\mathbb{Z}$, but only one of these can be the type of 3. This means that although a type is a set, not every set is a type. One can think of the type of a value as the largest set to which it belongs.

The Z library contains the type $\mathbb{Z}$ (the integers) and Z allows the user to introduce other types as necessary. The Z library does not include the type *Boolean* which is common in programming languages. The reason for this is that it is unnecessary. If we want to specify, for example, that x is greater than zero we simply state the predicate:

$x > 0$

rather than attempt the predicate:

$(x > 0) = boolTrue$

where *boolTrue* is a Boolean value rather than the predicate *true*. In fact $x > 0$ is not a value at all; it is a predicate and so it cannot take part in an equality relationship with a value.

Types fall into one of two categories, basic types or composite types.

Basic types

$\mathbb{Z}$ is a basic type. This is because each element of the type is atomic, which is to say, indivisible, and thus has no internal structure. Another way of saying the same thing is to say that there is no information inside an atomic object. Another example of a basic type is the given set *PASS*, which was used in the car park example in Chapter 2 to model car park passes. A given set is a basic type introduced by the user. It is always possible to test any two values belonging to the same basic type for equality. This does not provide us with very much scope for manipulating elements of basic types but often it is all that is needed. By convention, the names of given sets are written in upper case.

Given that every value belongs to exactly one type, it follows that all types are disjoint or non-intersecting sets. This means that declaring new basic types does not 'interfere' with any existing types and is the reason why users can introduce basic types as necessary.

Free types

Z provides a notation for introducing a basic type consisting of a few specified values. We met an example of such a type in the car park example of Chapter 2:

$REPORT ::= success$
$\qquad\quad | \quad ordinaryCarParkFull$
$\qquad\quad | \quad ordinaryCarParkEmpty$
$\qquad\quad | \quad passInUse$
$\qquad\quad | \quad passNotInUse$

Recall that a declaration such as that of *REPORT* is called a *free type* definition.[1]

---

[1] The free type definition facility is actually more powerful than the above example illustrates but a full discussion would be beyond the scope of this book; see [20].

Readers familiar with the concept of an enumerated type in a programming language will notice a similarity between a free type and an enumerated type. In many programming languages, however, the values of an enumerated type are ordered; this is not so for a free type.

Composite types

Composite types, in contrast to basic types, are types that are constructed from other types. For example, a common way of forming a composite type is to use the Cartesian product type constructor. Given the type $\mathbb{Z}$, the Cartesian product type constructor can be used to construct the type:

$$\mathbb{Z} \times \mathbb{Z}$$

and given this constructed type it can be used again to construct the type:

$$\mathbb{Z} \times (\mathbb{Z} \times \mathbb{Z})$$

and so on. The power set type constructor is another means of constructing types. This constructor allows us to construct the type:

$$\mathbb{P}\,\mathbb{Z}$$

and, in conjunction with the Cartesian product type constructor, the two distinct types:

$$\mathbb{P}(\mathbb{Z} \times \mathbb{Z}) \qquad (\mathbb{P}\,\mathbb{Z}) \times \mathbb{Z}$$

and so on. The Z type constructors can be applied repeatedly to obtain more and more complex types and the elements of these types will have more and more complex internal structure. Z has just three type constructors. In addition to the constructors for Cartesian products and power sets, there is the schema type constructor.

Utility of types

Types are essentially a means of organizing values by grouping them into sets. Recall that every value belongs to exactly one type. Values are organized in this way in order to help us check that specifications are meaningful. For example, the following expression:

$$2 + \varnothing$$

is meaningless because there is no value that can be represented as $2 + \varnothing$. If we think about how we can determine that $2 + \varnothing$ is meaningless we realize that it is to do with the fact that the operation $+$ is defined exclusively on the type

$\mathbb{Z}$. In other words, the reason that $2 + \varnothing$ is not well defined is that it is not well typed. The following are more examples of expressions that are not well typed.

$\{1, 2, 3\} \cup 4$

$3 + \{2\}$

$\{5\} \in \{1, 2, 3, 4, 5\}$

The fact that the third expression above is regarded as ill-typed rather than simply false is interesting because it illustrates the difference between the meaning of the $\in$ relation in set theory and the everyday notion of an object belonging to a set. Consider an analogous example: if we were to ask ourselves the question:

Is this book a member of the United Nations?

we would almost certainly say 'no' first and then perhaps point out that the question is a little bizarre. We might thus be tempted to take the value of $\{5\} \in \{1, 2, 3, 4, 5\}$ to be false whereas in fact it does not have a value.

By separating values into disjoint sets, we can specify precisely the values to which a function or predicate can or cannot be applied. We can thus analyse any expression and determine whether it is well typed. If we find that the expression is not well typed then we know that it does not represent a value.

The practical benefit of using types is substantial because it is possible to test any expression systematically and determine whether is well typed. This checking is done by a computer program known as a *type checker*.

The crucial feature that makes a type checker so useful is that it can be guaranteed to detect all ill-typed expressions. In technical terms, the question of whether or not an expression is well typed is said to be *decidable*. In general, if a question is decidable then it simply means that there is some procedure or algorithm that can provide the answer to the question in a finite number of simple well-defined steps. For example, the question of whether every number in the set $\{2, 4, 6, 8, 9, 10\}$ is even, or equivalently, the truth of the predicate:

$\forall x : \mathbb{Z} \bullet x \in \{2, 4, 6, 8, 9, 10\} \Rightarrow x \bmod 2 = 0$

is decidable because we can test each of the numbers in the set $\{2, 4, 6, 8, 9, 10\}$ one by one and complete this testing in a finite number of steps.

One might be forgiven for thinking that since mathematics is concerned fundamentally with well-defined, unambiguous, statements, all mathematical questions are decidable. Interestingly, this is not the case. Many quite basic mathematical questions are not decidable, and of particular relevance to us is the fact that the question of whether an expression in Z has a particular value is, in general, undecidable. For example, the question of whether two predicates express the same property, that is, the truth of:

$$\{x : \mathbb{Z} \mid P(x)\} = \{x : \mathbb{Z} \mid Q(x)\}$$

is not decidable for all predicates P and Q. The undecidability is due to the fact that the equality statement concerns every member of the infinite set $\mathbb{Z}$. This means that if we are particularly devious we can choose P and Q in such a way that we would be forced to examine every member of $\mathbb{Z}$ before being able to answer the question. This would violate the condition that a decidable question must be answered in a finite number of steps.

The implication of this undecidability is that we cannot rely on evaluation (working out the value of an expression) as a means of establishing whether expressions are well defined. The type system of Z, however, is specifically designed so that the determination of the type of any expression is decidable.

You should not think that a type checker can spot all kinds of meaningless values; it cannot. We know that if an expression is ill-typed then it does not represent a value but the converse is not true. In other words, it is not true that if an expression is meaningless then it must be ill-typed. There are many expressions that are meaningless but are perfectly well typed. For example:

$$57689782 \operatorname{div} (6786 - 6786)$$

is a meaningless expression because it requires division by zero. It is, however, well typed because the arithmetic operations involved in the expression are defined on the type $\mathbb{Z}$, which includes the integer zero.

The reader might be tempted to argue that this example simply shows that we have not defined the division operation correctly. We perhaps ought to define a special type consisting of the elements:

$$\mathbb{Z} \setminus \{0\}$$

and use this type in the definition of the division operation. Unfortunately, this approach will not work and it shows that we cannot choose whatever sets we like as types if we want to retain the benefits of type checking. To see why this is so, consider how we might go about checking that the expression:

$$57689782 \operatorname{div} (6786 - 6786)$$

is ill-typed according to our new type which excludes zero. We would need to establish that the expression $6786 - 6786$ is not a member of our new type, but we can do this only by establishing that it is zero, that is, by evaluating the expression. Now we know that the evaluation of expressions in Z is not in general decidable and so type checking with our new type would not be decidable.[2] The result is that our type checker would no longer be guaranteed to find every type error.

---

[2] The reader who thinks that checking for zero might be decidable if we employ rules such as $x - x = 0$ should consider the value of $\#\{x : \mathbb{Z} \mid P(x)\}$ for some arbitrary P.

We can now see that only certain kinds of set can qualify as a type. If we try to choose our types in such a way as to make too fine distinctions between values then we find that these types are of little use for checking for meaningless expressions.

6.2   Use of names in Z

Names are always used to denote some value. A name is usually used because it is more convenient than giving a representation of the value itself. Names and the values they denote are completely interchangeable in the sense that the meaning of the specification is not altered. In practice, names that are used as variables cannot usually be replaced by a value because we do not know the value denoted by the name. For example, in the car park example in Chapter 2 we used the name *carParkCapacity* to denote an unspecified number and so we could not replace this name. In fact the car park specification is more generally applicable because we have not specified the value of *carParkCapacity*.

If the type checker is to do its job then it must know the type of every name used in a Z specification. This means that every name used in a Z specification must be declared at the point at which the name is first introduced. Usually, a name is declared by listing the name and associating it with a type. The value denoted by the name must of course belong to this type. For example, the declaration:

$$x : \mathbb{Z}$$

introduces the name x and gives its type as $\mathbb{Z}$, which means that x will denote an integer.

The scope of a name is the region of the specification in which that name can be used to denote some object. The issue of scope was first introduced in §3.3 in the logic chapter. The scope of a name can be essentially determined from the position within the specification of the declaration of that name. For example, certain names in a Z specification are declared outside a schema. Examples of such names from the car park example in Chapter 2 include:

carParkCapacity	a variable, the capacity of the car park
PASS	a given set
REPORT	a free type definition
CarPark	the name of the schema describing the state
PassDeparture	the name of a schema describing an operation
$\mathbb{Z}$	a basic type
$<$	a relation

The scope of such names, excluding $\mathbb{Z}$ and $<$ which are declared in the Z library, begins at the point in the specification where they are declared and continues up to the end of the specification. In particular, (apart from a qualification that we will give below) the scope includes the declarative and predicate parts of any schema following the declaration. Any name declared outside a schema is known as a global name because of the 'global' extent of its scope. In contrast to global names, a name declared inside a schema has a scope that does not extend outside the schema.

Constants and variables

All names fall into one of two categories, variables or constants. If the value of a name is not known precisely, that is, it is some value in a set of values, then we say the name is a variable. If the value denoted by a name is known precisely, we say the name is a constant.

Note that Z variables have little in common with programming language variables. It is not possible to change the value of a Z variable. If we write:

$$x = 4$$
$$x = 5$$

then we have two inconsistent predicates.

Exercise 6.1 Identify the constants in the previously given list of names taken from the car park example. □

Global names

Z provides specific means for declaring global constants and global variables.

Axiomatic description

A variable is a name used to denote a value that we do not know precisely. For example:

$$luckyNumber : \mathbb{Z}$$
$$luckyNumber \in \{3, 7, 12, 15, 21, 28, 34, 41, 47, 55, 59, 64, 69, 72, 91\}$$

This definition states that the value denoted by *luckyNumber* is one of the numbers in the set $\{3, 7, 12, 15, 21, 28, 34, 41, 47, 55, 59, 64, 69, 72, 91\}$. We cannot give the precise value denoted by *luckyNumber* but we can state predicates such as:

$$luckyNumber \leq 100$$

In the car park example from Chapter 2 the maximum number of cars without passes allowed into the car park is the value of *carParkCapacity*, introduced using an axiomatic description.

$$
\begin{array}{|l}
carParkCapacity : \mathbb{Z} \\
\hline
carParkCapacity \geq 0
\end{array}
$$

In this example we did not give the value of *carParkCapacity* because we wanted to specify a car park system that would be applicable for a large number of possible car parks of different capacities.

Abbreviation definition

The use of names to denote precisely known values is essentially one of convenience. If the name was not used we would need to give a possibly lengthy expression to denote the value in question. For example, the following abbreviation definition declares a name for a specific set of numbers:

$$luckyNumbers == \{3, 7, 12, 15, 21, 28, 34, 41, 47, 55, 59, 64, 69, 72, 91\}$$

The abbreviation definition (symbol '==') is used to declare a name to denote the value of a given expression.

The above declaration is equivalent to the declaration:

$$luckyNumbers : \mathbb{P}\,\mathbb{Z}$$

and the predicate:

$$luckyNumbers = \{3, 7, 12, 15, 21, 28, 34, 41, 47, 55, 59, 64, 69, 72, 91\}$$

This suggests that instead of an abbreviation definition we could have used an axiomatic description:

$$
\begin{array}{|l}
luckyNumbers : \mathbb{P}\,\mathbb{Z} \\
\hline
luckyNumbers = \{3, 7, 12, 15, 21, 28, 34, 41, 47, 55, 59, 64, 69, 72, 91\}
\end{array}
$$

However, in a situation where we can define precisely the value we wish to name, an abbreviation definition is more appropriate because it can be used only when the value we wish to name is known exactly.

Other examples of names that denote precisely known values are: the name $\mathbb{N}$ which denotes the natural numbers, the name $+$ which denotes the addition function, and the relation $<$; there are many others. These names are all examples of constants. Abbreviation definitions are in fact special cases of generic constants.

Generic constants

A special group of constants are the generic constants. Generic constants may appear to be variables but they are in fact constants. For example, the empty set is a generic constant. Each use of the $\varnothing$ name denotes a known empty set. For example, in the two following expressions:

$$3 \notin \varnothing$$
$$(2 \mapsto 4) \setminus (2 \mapsto 4) = \varnothing$$

the first occurrence of $\varnothing$ denotes the empty set of integers and the second occurrence the empty set of integer pairs.

We can often determine which empty set we mean by referring to the types of the other part of the expression in which the $\varnothing$ symbol occurs. If this is not possible then we must explicitly give the type as in:

$$A \setminus B = \varnothing[\mathbb{Z} \times \mathbb{Z}]$$

Z provides a notation for creating generic constants, which is illustrated in the following example definition of the $\varnothing$ generic constant:

$$
\begin{array}{|l}
\hline\!\!\!\![X]\!=\!\!=\!\!=\!\!=\!\!=\!\!=\!\!=\!\!=\!\!=\!\!=\!\!=\!\!=\!\!= \\
\;\; \varnothing : \mathbb{P}\, X \\
\hline
\;\; \varnothing = \{x : X \mid x \neq x\} \\
\hline
\end{array}
$$

The parameters of the generic definition are enclosed in [ ] in the double lines at the top of the schema box; otherwise the definition is like a schema definition. Another example of a generic constant is the subset relation introduced in §5.3:

$$
\begin{array}{|l}
\hline\!\!\!\![X]\!=\!\!=\!\!=\!\!=\!\!=\!\!=\!\!=\!\!=\!\!=\!\!=\!\!=\!\!=\!\!= \\
\;\; \_\subseteq\_ : \mathbb{P}\, X \leftrightarrow \mathbb{P}\, X \\
\hline
\;\; \forall\, U, V : \mathbb{P}\, X \bullet \\
\;\;\;\;\;\;\;\; U \subseteq V \Leftrightarrow \forall\, x : X \bullet x \in U \Rightarrow x \in V \\
\hline
\end{array}
$$

Again, the appearance of a type parameter in the double lines of the definition indicates that this definition introduces a relation for many types. In both of these examples there is just one type parameter, X, although there may be more than one in general. It is also possible to give a set rather than a type as the actual parameter.

The definition of a generic constant must be such that for each substitution of the formal parameters, the value of the definition must be precisely determined. It is for this reason that generic definitions are known as generic constants. The following is an example of an unsound definition:

$$
\begin{array}{|l}
\underline{[X]} \\
\hline
pickAny : \mathbb{P}\,X \nrightarrow X \\
\hline
\forall s : \mathbb{P}\,X \bullet s \neq \varnothing \Rightarrow pickAny(s) \in s \\
\hline
\end{array}
$$

The function *pickAny* maps a set to some member but, for a given type, the definition does not specify which member. This means that we cannot determine whether:

$$pickAny\ \{1,2,3\} = pickAny\ \{1,2,3\}$$

To ensure that the equality relation retains it's usual properties, such generic definitions are not allowed.[3]

The abbreviation definitions that we have seen so far can be thought of as generic constants with no parameters. In fact, parameters can be included in an abbreviation definition, for example:

$$\varnothing[X] == \{x : X \mid x \neq x\}$$

Which form is used is simply a matter of presentation.

6.3   Schemas

We first encountered a schema in the specification of the car park system in Chapter 2. One of those schemas is reproduced here.

$$
\begin{array}{|l}
\underline{CarPark} \\
ordinaryCars : \mathbb{Z} \\
passesInUse : \mathbb{P}\,PASS \\
\hline
ordinaryCars \geq 0 \\
ordinaryCars \leq carParkCapacity \\
\hline
\end{array}
$$

This schema was used to specify the state observations of the barrier-controlled car park system. The variable *ordinaryCars* represents a number of cars in the car park and thus must be a value between zero and the car park capacity. Schemas have also been used for a quite different purpose, namely the description of operations, and in fact schemas can be used for a variety of purposes. To be able to use schemas effectively and with confidence, however, we must understand the meaning of a schema within the Z notation.

Within Z, the schema is used to write structured mathematical theories. Strictly speaking, such a theory describes a collection of mathematical values and nothing more, but in practice we will be looking to use the values to build

---

[3]See [19] for more information on this.

a model. Let us ignore for the moment the fact that we wish to describe a state space or an operation and consider the schema:

$$
\begin{array}{|l}
\hline
S \\\hline
s : \mathbb{P}\,\mathbb{Z} \\
x : \mathbb{N} \\\hline
x \in s \\\hline
\end{array}
$$

Now we ask the question 'what does this schema mean?' We do not want to answer this question by pointing out what x and s stand for in some model; after all, we can understand an expression such as $x + 3 = 7$ without knowing that x represents the number of cars in a car park, say. We would like to understand a schema such as S in terms of the Z notation alone. When we have succeeded in doing this we will be able to give two descriptions of a schema. Firstly, we will be able to describe the schema as a means of defining an aspect of a state-based model, for example the state space, and secondly, we will be able to describe the same schema from the point of view of the Z notation.

Schema definition

Within Z, a schema is a fragment of mathematical text in which some variables are declared and some additional predicates may be provided to restrict the possible values of those variables. The general form for a schema is given below.

$$
\begin{array}{|l}
\hline
SchemaName \\\hline
declaration\ part \\\hline
predicate\ part \\\hline
\end{array}
$$

Let us consider the various parts of this general schema form.

1. The name of the schema, *SchemaName*, is embedded in the upper line of the open box. The name is used to denote the schema throughout the specification and cannot be used to denote any other element. By convention, the names of schemas begin with a capital letter.

2. One or more variables are declared in the declaration part. Each variable is declared to be of a particular type. This does not necessarily mean that each variable must be declared to be of some explicitly given type. A variable can be declared using any set expression; for example, the declaration:

   $s : \mathbb{P}(\mathbb{N} \times \mathbb{N})$

   is equivalent to the declaration:

   $s : \mathbb{P}(\mathbb{Z} \times \mathbb{Z})$

and the predicate:

$$\forall\, x, y : \mathbb{Z} \bullet (x, y) \in s \Rightarrow (x \geq 0 \wedge y \geq 0)$$

Not every variable declared in the declaration part need be explicitly listed; see the topic of schema inclusion on page 156.

The variables declared in the declaration part are known as the components of the schema. There is no significance to the order in which the components of a schema are declared. The scope of variables declared in the declaration part is local to the schema, which means that they are usable within the predicate part only. See §6.2 and §6.7 for a complete discussion of this topic. The declarations introduced in the declarative part of a schema constitute the *signature* for the schema. A signature is simply a collection of variables and their types.

3. The predicate part is written using zero or more lines. On each line, a predicate appears. Predicates written on separate lines are assumed to be conjoined with each other as if there was a logical conjunction inserted between each of the lines. If a single predicate extends over several lines then subsequent lines should be indented and these lines are not assumed to be conjoined. The predicate can involve variables other than those declared in the declaration part provided these variables have been declared and introduced in a way that is compatible with the scope rules (§6.2). For example, in the *CarPark* schema the global variable *carParkCapacity* is involved in the predicate part.

The predicates stated in the predicate part of a schema, together with any introduced as a constraint in a declaration, are used to express a property which has the effect of restricting the possible values of the variables that are the components of the schema. The components of a schema may take only those values for which the property of the schema is true. A useful way of understanding this is to think of a schema as a description of a set of bindings. A binding is a one-to-one correspondence between a collection of variables and associated values. The variables in question are those in the signature or the components of the schema. Let us reconsider the schema S:

```
┌─ S ──────────────────────────────────────
│ s : ℙ ℤ
│ x : ℕ
├───────────────────────────────────────────
│ x ∈ s
└───────────────────────────────────────────
```

The binding in which s denotes $\{1, 2, 3\}$ and x denotes 2 is consistent with the constraints imposed by the property of S. In contrast, the binding in which s denotes $\{1, 2, 3\}$ and x denotes 0 is not, that is, the property of the schema is false for this binding.

It is possible to have a schema that does not restrict the values of the components, that is, a schema with a property equivalent to the predicate true. Such a schema might be written without a predicate part, that is:

```
 ___ SchemaName _____
|  declaration part
|
|_____
```

We should remember, however, that a schema without a predicate part may nonetheless have a property that restricts the values of the components. This results from constraints introduced in the declaration part.

Schema normalization

Clearly, it is important to be able to identify the property of a schema. In some cases, the property of a schema is the property expressed by the conjunction of the predicates appearing in the predicate part of the schema. In other cases, the property of a schema includes predicates which are not present in the predicate part but have been introduced by a declaration given in the declaration part of a schema. This situation is illustrated in the schema below.

```
 ___ S _____
|  s : \mathbb{P}\,\mathbb{Z}
|  x : \mathbb{N}
|_____
|  x \in s
|_____
```

The predicate part contains the single predicate $x \in s$ but this is not the only restriction on the value of x. In the declarative part, x is declared as $x : \mathbb{N}$ which constrains x to be greater than or equal to zero. Implicit predicates introduced by declarations given in the declarative part, known as *constraints*, can be made explicit by adding them to the predicate part. The schema T given below is equivalent to S above, but the predicates included in the predicate part express the property of the schema.

```
 ___ T _____
|  s : \mathbb{P}\,\mathbb{Z}
|  x : \mathbb{Z}
|_____
|  x \geq 0
|  x \in s
|_____
```

The rewriting of a schema in order to make explicit all the predicates of the property is known as *schema normalization*.

6.4   The use of schemas to represent sets of states

In the previous section we said that from the Z notation view, the meaning of a schema definition is the set of bindings for which the property of the schema is true. If we now wish to consider how schemas can be used to build specifications of state-based models, we must relate the Z notation view to the state-based model view. In this section we consider how schemas can be used to describe the set of states that can be occupied by a state-based model, that is, the state space.

In the car park example from Chapter 2, the state consisted of two observations: the number of ordinary cars in the car park and the set of passes in use. Each observation is modelled as a component of the state space schema.

$$
\begin{array}{|l}
\underline{\ CarPark\ } \\
ordinaryCars : \mathbb{Z} \\
passesInUse : \mathbb{P}\ PASS \\
\hline
ordinaryCars \geq 0 \\
ordinaryCars \leq carParkCapacity \\
\end{array}
$$

The predicates in the predicate part ensure that the values of the components are appropriate for the observations they represent.

If, in terms of the Z notation, we say that a binding satisfies the property of a state space schema then from the point of view of the state-based model, we can say that there is a state in the state space. Moreover, the values of the components of the binding are the values of the observations of the state. If the property of the state space schema is false for all bindings then the state space is empty. If the property of the state space schema is true for all bindings then the state space consists of all possible values for each observation.

6.5   Use of schemas for defining operations

We have used schemas to define the state space but we know that the state space is an entirely different concept to that of an operation. The former is a description of the range of states that a state-based model can occupy and the latter is a description of a small part of the behaviour or function of a state-based model. An operation, in its most general form, has a number of inputs, produces a number of outputs and is associated with a change of state. Operations that do not involve a change of state include the condition that the before-state is equal to the after-state.

Before considering how schemas can be used to define operations let us explore the meaning of an operation in terms of the state-based model. In

§1.5 we described the bank cash dispensing machine as a suitable subject for a state-based model. The cash machine can be in a number of states but at any one time it is in a specific state, the current state. Intuitively, we think of an operation as something that is performed in the current state in order to advance the cash machine to a new current state. This way of thinking is sensible in terms of the state-based model and is certainly how state-based systems function in practice. We can easily envisage a process in which a system moves from state to state as a consequence of performing various operations.

Within the Z notation, however, there is nothing that corresponds to the current state or to a process in which a model moves from state to state. The Z notation, and the logic and mathematics upon which it is built, is not a language that contains any intrinsic facility for modelling change. In the English language, for example, we can say that someone is running, that someone ran and that someone will run. There is a rich vocabulary and grammar that allows us to describe activities with reference to time. There are no ready-made facilities for constructing such descriptions in Z. Z, and certainly the underlying logic and set theory on which Z is based, is a very simple language; it is essentially a language for describing properties of objects and the relationships between objects, and nothing more. These objects exist, if that is the right word, in some abstract timeless world.

The simplicity of Z brings some crucial advantages which we do not want to lose. This simplicity ultimately means, for example, that we can construct specifications with a precision that is impossible to achieve in a natural language. Fortunately, we can describe change in a very simple way without extending the Z language; we do this by exploiting the notion of state.

Use of schemas for state change descriptions

In a state-based model, behaviour is modelled as changes of state. Each change is described using two states, the before-state and the after-state. Let us now consider the details of how this kind of state change description is specified in Z. We have seen how a schema can be used to model the range of possible states by interpreting each binding that satisfies a schema as a collection of observations and corresponding values of a particular state. There is no reason why we cannot use a schema to model two collections of states, the before-states and after-states that are required to define an operation.

Let us consider an example state with two observations, one a set of integers, the other an integer. The schema below describes the state space.

$$
\begin{array}{|l}
\hline
\_SetAndNumber _____ \\
\; s : \mathbb{P}\,\mathbb{Z} \\
\; i : \mathbb{N} \\
\hline
\; i = \#s \\
\hline
\end{array}
$$

Notice that the value of the integer is constrained to be a natural number and further restricted to be equal to the number of elements in the set. A change of state is illustrated in Figure 6.1.

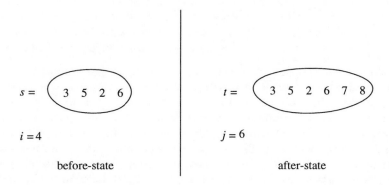

before-state   after-state

Figure 6.1: A change of state is represented in terms of the state before the change and the state after the change

We could describe this change of state by giving two state descriptions, using a schema to describe each state. The before-state would be described by the schema:

$$\begin{array}{|l}
\hline
\;\textit{SetAndNumberState1} \underline{\hspace{6cm}} \\
\; s : \mathbb{P}\,\mathbb{Z} \\
\; i : \mathbb{N} \\
\hline
\; s = \{3, 5, 2, 6\} \\
\; i = 4 \\
\hline
\end{array}$$

and the after-state would be described by the schema:

$$\begin{array}{|l}
\hline
\;\textit{SetAndNumberState2} \underline{\hspace{6cm}} \\
\; t : \mathbb{P}\,\mathbb{Z} \\
\; j : \mathbb{N} \\
\hline
\; t = \{3, 5, 2, 6, 7, 8\} \\
\; j = 6 \\
\hline
\end{array}$$

There are a number of important points to notice about this state change description. There are two observations in the state but four components (two in each schema) are used to describe the state change. The identical state change is specified irrespective of the variables used to name the components. It is the value of the set, the members it contains, that is important, not what we call it. The variable names s, i, t and j are of course local to their respective schemas and cannot be used outside these schemas. Even though we know that for any state the integer observation should always be equal to the size of the set observation, no predicate in either of the two schemas specifies this general fact.

One of the problems with using a separate schema for the before-state and the after-state is that it is necessary to specify in some way that one schema is to be interpreted as the before-state and the other as the after-state. Given that a schema is simply a way of grouping a collection of variables and restrictions on the values of those variables, one way to overcome this problem is to place the four variables into a single schema:

$$
\begin{array}{l}
\underline{\quad SetAndNumberState1andState2 \underline{}} \\
\quad s, t : \mathbb{P}\,\mathbb{Z} \\
\quad i, j : \mathbb{N} \\
\rule{6cm}{0.4pt} \\
\quad s = \{3, 5, 2, 6\} \\
\quad i = 4 \\
\quad t = \{3, 5, 2, 6, 7, 8\} \\
\quad j = 6 \\
\end{array}
$$

and provide an indication of which components describe the before-state and which describe the after-state. This brings us to the topic of variable decoration.

Variable decoration

By convention in Z, if a variable, say s, is used to denote the value of a state observation before a state change, then the variable s' (an entirely different variable to s) is used to denote the value of the same observation after the state change. If we adhere to this convention then the schema we require is:

$$
\begin{array}{l}
\underline{\quad SetAndNumberState1andState2 \underline{}} \\
\quad s, s' : \mathbb{P}\,\mathbb{Z} \\
\quad i, i' : \mathbb{N} \\
\rule{6cm}{0.4pt} \\
\quad s = \{3, 5, 2, 6\} \\
\quad i = 4 \\
\quad s' = \{3, 5, 2, 6, 7, 8\} \\
\quad i' = 6 \\
\end{array}
$$

The convention is designed to provide a convenient means of writing schemas that describe state changes. It is important to remember that in terms of the Z notation, this schema describes a set of bindings with each binding containing four variables. The four variables all have the same status; they are simply components of a schema. The concept of a before-state with two observations and an after-state with two observations is not present within the Z notation. It is simply a matter of convention that the s and i components are interpreted as before-state observations and the s' and i' components as after-state observations.

Creating variable names by adding characters to the end of an existing name is a general notational device in Z. The Z notation allows a name to be followed by the characters '?', '!' and '′' (the prime character). When such a character is added to a name we say the name is *decorated*.

There is no formal relationship between a name and the same name with a decoration. They are two distinct names and the value denoted by one name is independent of the value denoted by the other. Decoration is simply a device to tell the reader what sort of thing the names should stand for in the subject or application that is being modelled. In addition to the use of '′' for after-state variables, variables decorated with a '?' represent inputs and variables decorated with an '!' represent outputs.

Exercise 6.2 Is x''' a legal name in Z?   □

Schema inclusion

A schema provides a way of naming a collection of variables so that the collection can be treated as a single entity, and as such it is a structuring facility. To make full use of this structuring facility, we would expect to be able to denote schemas by their names. To appreciate the advantages of doing this, let us suppose that we need to describe a large number of state changes. In this situation, we would need to declare the four variables, s, s', i and i', in a large number of schemas. There are a number of practical problems with doing this. Firstly, we might make a mistake in the one of the schemas, for example declaring:

$$s, s' : \mathbb{P}\,\mathbb{Z}$$
$$i, i' : \mathbb{Z}$$

Secondly, anyone reading the schemas and wishing to check that the variables were declared equivalently in each schema would have to laboriously check all the schemas that declared these variables. Thirdly, if we wanted to change the declaration of these variables we would need to change the declarations in a large number of schemas.

The solution adopted in Z is to declare the variables in a single schema and then include that schema in any other schema in which the variables are required. A schema can be included in another by placing its name in the declaration part of this other schema. The effect is to introduce the declarations and predicates into the including schema. So for example, given that s and i are declared in the *SetAndNumber* schema:

$$\begin{array}{l} \underline{\quad SetAndNumber \quad\quad\quad\quad\quad\quad\quad\quad\quad\quad\quad\quad} \\ s : \mathbb{P}\,\mathbb{Z} \\ i : \mathbb{N} \\ \underline{\quad\quad\quad\quad\quad} \\ i = \#s \end{array}$$

we can implicitly declare s and i in our earlier state change by writing:

$$\begin{array}{l} \underline{\quad SetAndNumberState1andState2 \quad\quad\quad\quad\quad\quad\quad} \\ SetAndNumber \\ s' : \mathbb{P}\,\mathbb{Z} \\ i' : \mathbb{N} \\ \underline{\quad\quad\quad\quad\quad} \\ s = \{3, 5, 2, 6\} \\ i = 4 \\ s' = \{3, 5, 2, 6, 7, 8\} \\ i' = 6 \end{array}$$

Schema inclusion is a form of declaration and thus such we must take care that the declaration made is meaningful. For example, given:

$$\begin{array}{l} \underline{\quad S \quad\quad\quad\quad\quad\quad\quad\quad\quad\quad\quad\quad\quad\quad\quad} \\ x : \mathbb{N} \end{array}$$

and:

$$\begin{array}{l} \underline{\quad T \quad\quad\quad\quad\quad\quad\quad\quad\quad\quad\quad\quad\quad\quad\quad} \\ x : \mathbb{P}\,\mathbb{Z} \end{array}$$

we cannot write:

$$\begin{array}{l} \underline{\quad SinT \quad\quad\quad\quad\quad\quad\quad\quad\quad\quad\quad\quad\quad\quad} \\ S \\ x : \mathbb{P}\,\mathbb{Z} \end{array}$$

because x is declared twice, each declaration being of a different type.

Schema decoration

The inclusion of the *SetAndNumber* schema solves the problem of declaring s and i but we have a similar problem with s' and i'. Moreover, in a state change specification, there should be a one-to-one correspondence between the decorated variables and the undecorated variables. The Z notation provides a simple means of declaring these decorated variables and ensuring the one-to-one correspondence.

If the name of a schema is decorated with a symbol (say $''$) then this is the name of another schema which is obtained by taking the variables and predicates of the original and decorating all the variables declared in the declaration part with the same symbol. All occurrences in both the declaration part and the predicate part are decorated. For example, if S is the schema:

$$
\begin{array}{|l}
\hline
\textit{S} \\\hline
s : \mathbb{P}\,\mathbb{Z} \\
i : \mathbb{N} \\\hline
i = \#s \\
\exists\, i : \mathbb{Z} \bullet i \in s \\\hline
\end{array}
$$

then S' is the schema:

$$
\begin{array}{|l}
\hline
\textit{S'} \\\hline
s' : \mathbb{P}\,\mathbb{Z} \\
i' : \mathbb{N} \\\hline
i' = \#s' \\
\exists\, i : \mathbb{Z} \bullet i \in s' \\\hline
\end{array}
$$

Notice that the bound occurrences of i in the predicate part are not occurrences of the component i and so are not decorated (see §3.3).

By making use of schema decoration and schema inclusion, we can now specify our state change as the schema:

$$
\begin{array}{|l}
\hline
\textit{SetAndNumberState1andState2} \\\hline
\textit{SetAndNumber} \\
\textit{SetAndNumber'} \\\hline
s = \{3, 5, 2, 6\} \\
i = 4 \\
s' = \{3, 5, 2, 6, 7, 8\} \\
i' = 6 \\\hline
\end{array}
$$

Since this pattern of schema inclusion, a schema and its decorated counterpart, is so common in the specification of state changes, there is a convention within Z that for any schema *SchemaName*, Δ*SchemaName* is defined[4] as follows:

$$
\begin{array}{|l}
\hline
\Delta\textit{SchemaName} \\\hline
\textit{SchemaName} \\
\textit{SchemaName'} \\\hline
\end{array}
$$

---

[4] Since this is a convention, it is possible to redefine the schema Δ*SchemaName*.

The use of Δ, the capital δ, is a mnemonic for change. Finally, we can give the conventional schema description of the state change as:

$$
\begin{array}{|l}
\underline{\;SetAndNumberState1\,andState2\;}\underline{}\\
\Delta SetAndNumber\\
\hline
s = \{3, 5, 2, 6\}\\
i = 4\\
s' = \{3, 5, 2, 6, 7, 8\}\\
i' = 6\\
\end{array}
$$

The above example of a state change operation is very specific. It relates one specific state to one other specific state. In practice, state change specifications tend to be more general in that they are applicable to many states. The following schema is an example of such a specification; it specifies an operation to include elements in a set.

$$
\begin{array}{|l}
\underline{\;SetAndNumberStateChange\;}\underline{}\\
\Delta SetAndNumber\\
s? : \mathbb{P}\,\mathbb{Z}\\
\hline
s' = s \cup s?\\
\end{array}
$$

Let us summarize our understanding of the above schema. Within Z we think of a schema as a set of bindings. In order to identify these bindings more easily we make explicit the components and property of the schema by normalising it to obtain:

$$
\begin{array}{|l}
\underline{\;SetAndNumberStateChange\;}\underline{}\\
s, s', s? : \mathbb{P}\,\mathbb{Z}\\
i, i' : \mathbb{Z}\\
\hline
i \geq 0\\
i' \geq 0\\
i = \#s\\
i' = \#s'\\
s' = s \cup s?\\
\end{array}
$$

It is now straightforward to determine, for example, that for the above schema the binding:

Variable	Value
i	2
i'	5

s	$\{7,8\}$
s'	$\{4,5,6,7,8\}$
$s?$	$\{4,5,6\}$

satisfies the property, but that the binding:

Variable	Value
i	2
i'	5
s	$\{7,8\}$
s'	$\{4,5,6,7,8\}$
$s?$	$\{1,2,3\}$

does not satisfy the property because of the false predicate:

$$s' = s \cup s?$$

Each binding that satisfies the property of this schema can be interpreted as a possible instance of an operation. It is clear that a single schema may define many specific state changes involving different before-states and after-states.

Operations involving no change of state

If an operation does not lead to a change of state then the values of the after-state components must be equal to the values of the before-state components. There is a convention within Z, similar to the Δ convention, by which if S is:

```
┌─ S ──────────────────────────────────────
│ s : ℙ ℤ
│ i : ℕ
├──────────────────────────────────────────
│ i = #s
└──────────────────────────────────────────
```

then ΞS is the schema:

```
┌─ S ──────────────────────────────────────
│ ΔS
├──────────────────────────────────────────
│ s = s'
│ i = i'
└──────────────────────────────────────────
```

In general, if S is any schema then ΞS is ΔS together with predicates that ensure that all the after-state components are equal to their corresponding before-state components.

A common misconception

If we interpret the schema definition for an operation from the point of view of a state-based model, it is natural to think of some state as the current state occupied by the model and to see the schema as a description of how the current state is modified. This is fine provided we understand that this is an interpretation of a Z description.

Readers who are familiar with computer programming will know that in a computer program, the programmer must describe exactly how a value for a variable is to be calculated. The emphasis in programming is in describing 'how' rather than 'what'. High-level languages attempt to insulate the programmer from some of the detail of how calculations are specified but a program is nonetheless a description of how a calculation will be performed. There is a danger that we may mistakenly attempt to understand Z descriptions as descriptions of calculations. For example, if we consider the predicate:

$$i' = i + \#s?$$

and try to interpret it as a description of a calculation we would probably interpret it as:

> To calculate the value of i', add the value of i to the number of elements in the set $s?$.

This sort of interpretation regards the predicate as something akin to an assignment statement in a programming language. And indeed, if we were to implement this operation in a procedural programming language we might well do so by overwriting the values of the state observations before the operation with the values after the operation. The assignment statement interpretation is particularly seductive because:

$$i' = i + \#s?$$

provides us with a very obvious clue about how to calculate the value of the integer state observation.

In reality, a formal specification is not at all a description of a calculation. A formal specification describes values rather than calculations. The expressions present in the predicate part of a schema are logical predicates. A logical predicate and an assignment statement in a programming language are two very different things. The fact that a predicate may provide a very obvious clue about how to give a description of a calculation does not mean that the predicate is actually a description of a calculation. We can see this quite clearly if we consider predicates that provide no clue about how to describe calculations. The following schema specifies an integer square root operation.

```
┌─ SquareRoot ──────────────────────────────────────────────
│  x? : ℤ
│  y! : ℕ
│ ─────────────────────────────────────────────────────────
│  y! * y! = x?
└───────────────────────────────────────────────────────────
```

6.6   The precondition for an operation: schema precondition

A state-based model is designed to participate in a sequential process in which it occupies a succession of states. According to this view, we often think of the particular after-state and output of an operation as being dependent on the before-state and the input. This process view implies that the model occupies the before-state before it occupies the after-state and indeed the terminology of before-state and after-state originates from this view. It would be in keeping with the process view to expect an answer to the question 'In what circumstances can an operation be performed?' in terms of conditions imposed on the before-state and the input. This condition is known as the precondition.

In terms of the state-based model, it might seem obvious that the precondition is predicated on the before-state and the input but we should not forget that within Z there is no statement that specifies that the before-state occurs before the after-state. This means that within Z, the question 'In what circumstances can an operation be performed?' could equally well be answered in terms of conditions on the after-state and output.

In the previous chapters, we have had to consider the circumstances in which an operation can be performed when determining subcase properties; we should therefore explain the relationship between the subcase property and what appears to be the very similar precondition. The subcase property is a property that is used to identify the restricted situations in which a partial operation can be performed but the property need not provide a complete characterization of those situations. In particular, the subcase property may exploit the fact that the before-state is specified to be in the state space by the state invariant. In contrast, the precondition of an operation is a property defined on all before-state and input combinations. For example, recall that in the car park example from Chapter 2, the operation *OrdinaryEntryOK* which allows a car into the car park is applicable in any state in which the car park is not full. This subcase property is an obvious consequence of the fact that the car park has a fixed capacity, that is, cars cannot enter the car park indefinitely, and it was specified using the predicate:

$$ordinaryCars < carParkCapacity$$

This predicate, however, cannot be the precondition because it is true when *ordinaryCars* is negative. In fact this predicate is implied by the state invariant and therefore logically redundant.

There are a number of reasons why precondition investigation is useful. Firstly, if we find that there are no states or inputs for which an operation is defined then we have clearly made a mistake in the definition of the operation. Secondly, we may wish to combine a number of partial operations to produce a total operation. In the car park example in Chapter 2, we took pains to ensure that all the possible subcases were considered so that we could define a total operation that was applicable in every situation. One way of doing this is to establish the situations in which each partial operation is defined and establish that they jointly cover every state and input situation.

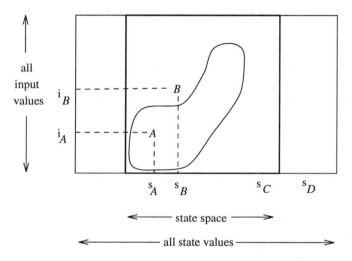

Figure 6.2: The precondition of a partial operation

An illustration of the precondition of a partial operation is given in Figure 6.2. Given that the effect of an operation depends on both the state and input, both of these are shown in the figure. The state space is a proper subset of the set of all possible states and the points within the closed curve represents bindings that satisfy the precondition. The situation labelled A satisfies the precondition for the operation because the state s_A is part of the state space and also satisfies the subcase property. The input i_A satisfies the subcase property. The operation is not defined for the situation labelled B and so this is not part of the precondition. Although the state s_B satisfies the subcase condition, the input i_B does not. The state s_C is within the state space but does not satisfy the precondition and state s_D in not within the state space.

The precondition of an operation is not always obvious from the schema defining the operation. Fortunately, for a given operation, there is a method by which a definition of the precondition property can be constructed. To explain the method, let us first take a simple case of an operation with no inputs or outputs. We will use a variation of the *OrdinaryEntryOK* operation that provides no output report.

```
┌─ OrdinaryEntryOK ─────────────────────────────────────
│ Δ CarPark
│ ─────────────────────────────────────
│ ordinaryCars' − ordinaryCars = 1
│ passesInUse' = passesInUse
└─────────────────────────────────────────────────────
```

We now wish to establish the circumstances in which the *OrdinaryEntryOK* operation can be performed by constructing a predicate on the before-state.

Let us consider an arbitrary before-state, A. This state can be represented with two values; let us name them $ordinaryCars_A$ and $passesInUse_A$. We know that the property of the above schema is true for some set of bindings and that each of these bindings represents a state change and thus has four components, $ordinaryCars$, $ordinaryCars'$, $passesInUse$ and $passesInUse'$. If in any of these bindings the $ordinaryCars$ and $passesInUse$ components have values $ordinaryCars_A$ and $passesInUse_A$ then the state A is a possible before-state. In other words, the state A satisfies the precondition. Notice that we are not concerned about which particular after-state results from the operation, we simply require that there is some after-state.

Properties on states can be defined using schemas (recall that this is what is done to specify the state space), so if we remove the after-state components from this schema and instead require only that some values for these variables exist, we obtain a schema that represents the precondition. In effect, we have a schema which is true of a state if there exists some other state that can be the after-state.

We thus normalize the *OrdinaryEntryOK* schema to expose all the predicates involving the components to be removed:

```
┌─ OrdinaryEntryOK ─────────────────────────────────────
│ ordinaryCars, ordinaryCars' : ℤ
│ passesInUse, passesInUse' : ℙ PASS
│ ─────────────────────────────────────
│ ordinaryCars ≥ 0
│ ordinaryCars ≤ carParkCapacity
│ ordinaryCars' ≥ 0
│ ordinaryCars' ≤ carParkCapacity
│ ordinaryCars' − ordinaryCars = 1
│ passesInUse' = passesInUse
└─────────────────────────────────────────────────────
```

We then remove the after-state variables as components of the schema and existentially quantify them to obtain a new schema which by convention has a name produced by adding the prefix *Pre* to the given schema name.

$$
\begin{array}{|l}
\_\, PreOrdinaryEntryOK \underline{\hspace{5cm}} \\
\; ordinaryCars : \mathbb{Z} \\
\; passesInUse : \mathbb{P}\, PASS \\
\hline
\; ordinaryCars \geq 0 \\
\; ordinaryCars \leq carParkCapacity \\
\; \exists\, ordinaryCars' : \mathbb{Z};\ passesInUse' : \mathbb{P}\, PASS \bullet \\
\qquad ordinaryCars' \geq 0 \wedge \\
\qquad ordinaryCars' \leq carParkCapacity \wedge \\
\qquad ordinaryCars' - ordinaryCars = 1 \wedge \\
\qquad passesInUse' = passesInUse
\end{array}
$$

This schema defines the precondition for the *OrdinaryEntryOK* operation. The precondition constructed in this way can usually be simplified. For example, in any situation in which *passesInUse* has a value:

$passesInUse' : \mathbb{P}\, PASS \bullet$

$\dots$

$passesInUse' = passesInUse$

will be true because *passesInUse'* will exist as the same value as *passesInUse*. Consequently, we remove this predicate from the predicate part to obtain:

$$
\begin{array}{|l}
\_\, PreOrdinaryEntryOK \underline{\hspace{5cm}} \\
\; ordinaryCars : \mathbb{Z} \\
\; passesInUse : \mathbb{P}\, PASS \\
\hline
\; ordinaryCars \geq 0 \\
\; ordinaryCars \leq carParkCapacity \\
\; \exists\, ordinaryCars' : \mathbb{Z} \bullet \\
\qquad ordinaryCars' \geq 0 \wedge \\
\qquad ordinaryCars' \leq carParkCapacity \wedge \\
\qquad ordinaryCars' - ordinaryCars = 1
\end{array}
$$

If we substitute for *ordinaryCars'* using the value *ordinaryCars* + 1 we can eliminate this variable to obtain:

$$
\begin{array}{|l}
\_\, PreOrdinaryEntryOK \underline{\hspace{5cm}} \\
\; ordinaryCars : \mathbb{Z} \\
\; passesInUse : \mathbb{P}\, PASS \\
\hline
\; ordinaryCars \geq 0 \\
\; ordinaryCars \leq carParkCapacity \\
\; ordinaryCars + 1 \geq 0 \\
\; ordinaryCars + 1 \leq carParkCapacity
\end{array}
$$

The predicate $ordinaryCars \geq 0$ implies $ordinaryCars + 1 \geq 0$ and so this latter
predicate is redundant. Also, the predicate $ordinaryCars + 1 \leq carParkCapacity$
implies $ordinaryCars \leq carParkCapacity$ and so this latter predicate is redundant. The final schema is thus:

```
┌─ PreOrdinaryEntryOK ──────────────────────────────────
│ ordinaryCars : Z
│ passesInUse : P PASS
├───────────────────────────────────────────────────────
│ ordinaryCars ≥ 0
│ ordinaryCars < carParkCapacity
└───────────────────────────────────────────────────────
```

To construct the precondition for an operation with inputs and outputs we
use the same approach. For a given operation, we wish to construct a predicate on the before-state and the input. This predicate should be true of any
before-state/input combination for which there exists some after-state/output
combination that satisfies the definition of the operation. For a given before-
state/input combination, if the precondition is true then that operation is applicable. The precondition is constructed by removing both the after-state and
output components from a schema and quantifying these variables existentially
in the predicate part of the schema.

Until now we have relied on an intuitive understanding of the meaning of
a partial or total operation. We can now give a more formal description. An
operation with a precondition that is satisfied by every state in the state space
and any input values is known as a total operation. If an operation is defined
for some but not all of the state space or for some but not all input values then
it is partial.

Z provides a precondition operator *pre* so that if S is a schema then:

  pre S

is the precondition for S.

To recap, there is no special significance, within the Z notation, attached
to predicates on the before-state and input variables as opposed to any other
components of a schema. From the state-based model point of view, however,
this is an interesting predicate since it describes when an operation can be
performed in terms of attributes that are known before the operation takes
place. Note that an operation with a false precondition implies an operation
defined with a schema which is satisfied by no bindings, and vice versa.

We have stressed the distinction between the Z notation view and the state-
based model view because this is a real source of confusion for students whose
background lies more in the computing sciences than in mathematics. Table 6.1
summarizes the differences between the two views.

Z notation view	State-based model view
The state space is a set of bindings.	The set of possible states is important; perhaps more important is the concept of the current state.
There is no Z description of the current state.	The state-based model is thought of as always occupying some state, the current state.
The existence of a state, known as the initial state, is demonstrated simply to establish that the state space is not inconsistent and therefore empty. The use of the term 'initial' should not be taken to mean that this state is the first state in some process of state changes. No such process is specified.	It is natural to think of a state-based model participating in a process of state changes. Many processes must begin in a specific state known as the initial state.
An operation is a set of bindings. The components of those bindings have decorated variables which conform to certain conventions.	An operation is the means by which inputs are received, outputs are produced and the current state is possibly modified.
The precondition of a partial operation is not satisfied by every state/input combination where the state is within the state space.	A partial operation cannot be applied in every state within the state space and under all input circumstances.
The precondition of an operation is the schema with the property formed by existentially quantifying the '' and '?' decorated components.	The precondition of an operation is normally expressed as a subcase property on the current state and the input.

Table 6.1: The relationship between the Z notation and state-based models

6.7 The scope of names

The scope of any name declared in the declaration part of a schema is the predicate part of the schema. In particular, the names declared in the predicate part cannot be used in the declaration part. For example, the following is illegal.

$$
\begin{array}{l}
\_\_IllegalSchema _____ \\
aSet : \mathbb{P}\, \mathbb{Z} \\
aNumber : aSet
\end{array}
$$

The correct way to write the above schema is:

```
┌─ LegalSchema ──────────────────────────────────────
│ aSet : ℙℤ
│ aNumber : ℤ
├────────────────────────────────────────────────────
│ aNumber ∈ aSet
└────────────────────────────────────────────────────
```

Non-global names are known as *local names*.

We have seen schemas that would appear to violate the scope rules for local variables; for example, declarations for s and s' do not appear in the following schema.

```
┌─ SetAndNumberStateChange ──────────────────────────
│ ΔSetAndNumber
│ s? : ℙℤ
├────────────────────────────────────────────────────
│ s' = s ∪ s?
└────────────────────────────────────────────────────
```

In fact s and s' are not global variables but are declared in the schema by virtue of the inclusion of the schema $\Delta SetAndNumber$.

The description of scope we have presented so far is too simplistic because it allows the possibility that the scopes of names can overlap without restriction. Consider the following example in which a name x is used as a global name:

```
│ x : ℤ
├──────────
│ x > 3
```

and also as a local name:

```
┌─ S ────────────────────────────────────────────────
│ x : ℤ × ℤ
├────────────────────────────────────────────────────
│ first(x) = 0
└────────────────────────────────────────────────────
```

The scope of the global name x would ordinarily include both the declarative part and the predicate part of the schema S. The use of x as a local name within S, however, introduces a potential ambiguity. The occurrence of x in $first(x) = 0$ may be an occurrence of the global x or it may be an occurrence of the local x. This ambiguity is resolved by adopting the rule that the scope of the local name is always removed from the scope of the global name. In other words, the local name has precedence and we say that the local name hides the global name. We are now in a position to revise our earlier statement concerning the scope of global names. Earlier we said that the scope of a global name extended from the point in the specification at which it was declared up to the end of the specification. In fact the scope of a name may contain 'holes' due to the declaration of a local name with the same identifier. It is of course possible to introduce a 'hole' in the scope of a local name by declaring some 'more local' name as in the example:

$$
\begin{array}{|l}
\hline
\!\!S \underline{} \\
x : \mathbb{Z} \times \mathbb{Z} \\
\hline
\mathit{first}(x) \in \{x : \mathbb{Z} \mid P\ x\} \\
\hline
\end{array}
$$

Such nested scopes were first described with respect to quantified variables in predicates: see §3.3.

We should point out that the global name x and the local name x may denote distinct values and this would seem to violate our assertion earlier that a name always denotes a specific value. The earlier assertion should therefore be qualified as follows: a name in a given scope always denotes a specific value. We can say that there should never be a name in any single scope that denotes more than one value.

Variables may be global or local depending on where they are declared. In contrast, the names of generic constants and schema names are always global. In the case of generic constants, the scope of the name may have a 'hole' in it, or equivalently we say the name may be hidden, if the same identifier is used in a local declaration. This local declaration may be a component of a schema or a variable declared within the predicate part of a schema. The name of a schema can never be hidden by a local declaration. A schema name will always denote the single schema in which that name was introduced.

6.8 Schema operations

In this section we will describe a number of operations that allow us to define new schemas by combining other schemas. By reusing schemas in this way, we can be considerably more productive in creating a specification. In addition, by factoring common parts of a specification into a single schema, the specification becomes easier to read and modify.

We first encountered schema operations in the car park example in Chapter 2. If there is space in the car park we allow a car to enter, otherwise entry is barred. To specify this operation we specified an operation for each of the two subcases and then combined these using schema disjunction ($\vee$). In this section we are going to look at this and similar operations in detail.

To provide some rationale for these operations, consider the following modelling situation. A broking firm maintains an individually tailored investment strategy for each of its private clients. Some clients prefer to bet on the fairly safe but unexciting prospects of large 'blue chip' companies; other clients will hanker after some exposure to the more volatile fortunes of small companies in emerging markets. We will use schemas to represent investment strategies, that is, conditions for investment in certain kinds of company.

The companies in which shares can be bought are represented by a given set *COMPANY*. Companies are grouped into a number of sets; we will employ just two of these sets as defined below.

$$
\begin{array}{l}
smallCompany : \mathbb{P}\ COMPANY \\
profitableCompany : \mathbb{P}\ COMPANY
\end{array}
$$

Using these sets, an investment strategy that picks out a small company can be represented by the schema:

$$
\begin{array}{|l}
\underline{\ SmallCompany\ } \\
c : COMPANY \\
\hline
c \in smallCompany
\end{array}
$$

The company denoted by c is in keeping with an investment strategy directed at small companies if the property of the *SmallCompany* schema holds for c. Similarly, an investment strategy that picks out a profitable company can be represented by the schema:

$$
\begin{array}{|l}
\underline{\ ProfitableCompany\ } \\
c : COMPANY \\
\hline
c \in profitableCompany
\end{array}
$$

Schema conjunction

Let us suppose that a particular private client wishes to invest in companies that are both small and profitable. A broker could of course construct a specific schema to represent this client's chosen strategy:

$$
\begin{array}{|l}
\underline{\ SmallAndProfitableCompany\ } \\
c : COMPANY \\
\hline
c \in smallCompany \\
c \in profitableCompany
\end{array}
$$

Notice that the predicate of *SmallAndProfitableCompany* is the conjunction of the predicates of *SmallCompany* and *ProfitableCompany*.

A simpler way of specifying the schema *SmallAndProfitableCompany* is to form the conjunction of the schemas *SmallCompany* and *ProfitableCompany*. Formally, the conjunction of two given schemas is a schema in which the declaration part is formed by merging the declaration parts of the given schemas. The property of the new schema is the conjunction of the properties of the given schemas. We specify the conjunction of two schemas in the following way:

$$
SmallAndProfitableCompany \ \widehat{=}\ SmallCompany \wedge ProfitableCompany
$$

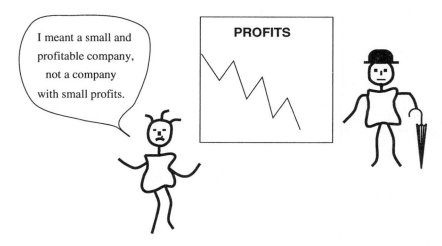

Figure 6.3: The importance of specifying investment strategy

The symbol used for schema conjunction is the same as that used for logi-cal conjunction but the operations are obviously not the same. The context is used to resolve any ambiguity. We need to be precise about what is meant by merging the variables declared in the declaration parts of the given schemas. Firstly, merging is not possible if the signatures of the given schemas contain a name clash, that is, a name declared with one type in one schema and the same name declared with a different type in the other schema. If the signatures of two schemas cannot be merged then it is not possible to conjoin the schemas. If there are no name clashes in the signatures then the signature of the conjoined schema is formed by taking every variable that occurs in either of the two sig-natures. All variables retain their types in the new signature. When conjoining the properties of two schemas we need to be careful to identify accurately the properties of the schemas involved.

It is possible to construct a schema which is the conjunction of two others as illustrated in the following example.

Example 6.1 Given the two schemas S and T below:

$$
\begin{array}{l}
\underline{\hspace{0.2cm}S\hspace{0.2cm}} \\
x : \mathbb{Z} \\
y : \mathbb{N} \\
\hline
x > y
\end{array}
$$

and:

$$
\begin{array}{|l}
\hline
\;T \underline{\hspace{7cm}} \\
\;\; y : \mathbb{Z} \\
\;\; s : \mathbb{P}\,\mathbb{Z} \\
\hline
\;\; y \in s \\
\;\; \exists\, x : \mathbb{P}\,\mathbb{Z} \bullet x \subset s \\
\hline
\end{array}
$$

(notice that x occurs bound in the predicate part of T but not in the signature of T) we can define the schema conjunction:

$SandT \mathrel{\widehat{=}} S \wedge T$

The construction of $S \wedge T$ proceeds with the following steps. The first step is to normalize S in order to identify the signature and property.

$$
\begin{array}{|l}
\hline
\;S \underline{\hspace{7cm}} \\
\;\; x : \mathbb{Z} \\
\;\; y : \mathbb{Z} \\
\hline
\;\; y \geq 0 \\
\;\; x > y \\
\hline
\end{array}
$$

T is normalized as given. We then check that any common variables in the signatures have the same type; in this case y is common and has the same type in both S and T. Notice that the variable x in T that does not occur in the signature of T is not a candidate for merging, it is simply part of the property (see scope of names §6.2 and §6.7). We can now construct $SandT$ by placing in the declarative part the merged variables from S and T and by placing in the predicate part the conjunction of the properties from S and T.

$$
\begin{array}{|l}
\hline
\;SandT \underline{\hspace{6cm}} \\
\;\; x : \mathbb{Z} \\
\;\; y : \mathbb{Z} \\
\;\; s : \mathbb{P}\,\mathbb{Z} \\
\hline
\;\; y \geq 0 \wedge x > y \\
\;\; \wedge \\
\;\; y \in s \wedge \exists\, x : \mathbb{P}\,\mathbb{Z} \bullet x \subset s \\
\hline
\end{array}
$$

It is conventional to write this schema as:

$$
\begin{array}{|l}
\hline
\;SandT \underline{\hspace{6cm}} \\
\;\; x, y : \mathbb{Z} \\
\;\; s : \mathbb{P}\,\mathbb{Z} \\
\hline
\;\; y \geq 0 \\
\;\; x > y \\
\;\; y \in s \\
\;\; \exists\, x : \mathbb{P}\,\mathbb{Z} \bullet x \subset s \\
\hline
\end{array}
$$

□

In the above discussion we have ignored the problem that arises if a global name that occurs in one schema also occurs as a component of the other. In this case the construction given above will not produce the required conjunction. This problem can be resolved by renaming the offending component to some suitable value. For example, given:

$$y == 5$$

and:

```
┌─ S ──────────────────────────────────────────
│  x : ℤ
│ ─────────────────────
│  x > y
└──────────────────────────────────────────────
```

and:

```
┌─ T ──────────────────────────────────────────
│  y : ℤ
│ ─────────────────────
│  y < 0
└──────────────────────────────────────────────
```

then if:

$$SandT \mathrel{\widehat{=}} S \wedge T$$

then $SandT$ does not satisfy the binding in which x has the value 4 and y has the value -1. If we naively attempt to construct $SandT$ then we suffer a *variable capture* problem in obtaining:

```
┌─ SandTIncorrect ─────────────────────────────
│  x : ℤ
│  y : ℤ
│ ─────────────────────
│  x > y
│  y < 0
└──────────────────────────────────────────────
```

which does indeed satisfy the binding in which x has the value 4 and y has the value -1. The problem is that the y in the predicate $x > y$ is captured by the local declaration. The solution is to rename the component y in T to some other unused name, say z.

The reader will have noticed a similarity between schema conjunction and schema inclusion and in some cases a schema conjunction can be constructed by the use of schema inclusion. The example of variable capture above illustrates that this is not always the case. Schema inclusion is a concise form of declaration and if as a result names are captured then this is presumably intended. Schema conjunction, however, is defined in terms of schema properties, distinct from schema predicates.

Schema disjunction

To explain the intuitive notion of schema disjunction, let us consider once again our broking firm which represents the investment strategies of its private clients using schemas. A certain client believes that small companies or profitable companies are equally good bets for investment. As before, a broker could of course construct a specific schema to represent this client's chosen strategy:

$$
\begin{array}{|l}
\hline \text{\_\_} SmallOrProfitableCompany \text{_____} \\
\quad c : COMPANY \\
\hline
\quad c \in smallCompany \lor c \in profitableCompany \\
\hline
\end{array}
$$

Given the schemas *SmallCompany* and *ProfitableCompany* as defined earlier, however, a more convenient definition of the required schema is the disjunction of these two schemas, that is:

$$SmallOrProfitableCompany \ \hat{=} \ SmallCompany \lor ProfitableCompany$$

The operation of schema disjunction is analogous to that of schema conjunction. The variables in the signatures of the schemas are merged in exactly the same way under the same restrictions, namely name clashes must be avoided. The property of the new schema, however, is the disjunction of the properties of the given schemas.

Example 6.2 If we construct the disjunction of S and T given above, taking care to normalize schemas where necessary, we obtain the schema:

$$
\begin{array}{|l}
\hline \text{\_\_} SorT \text{_____} \\
\quad x, y : \mathbb{Z} \\
\quad s : \mathbb{P}\,\mathbb{Z} \\
\hline
\quad y \geq 0 \land x > y \\
\quad \lor \\
\quad y \in s \land \exists x : \mathbb{P}\,\mathbb{Z} \bullet x \subset s \\
\hline
\end{array}
$$

□

Example 6.3 Given:

$$
\begin{array}{|l}
\hline \text{\_\_} OrdinaryEntryOK \text{_____} \\
\quad \Delta CarPark \\
\quad r! : REPORT \\
\hline
\quad ordinaryCars' - ordinaryCars = 1 \\
\quad passesInUse' = passesInUse \\
\quad r! = success \\
\hline
\end{array}
$$

and:

```
┌─ OrdinaryCarParkFull ──────────────────────────────
│ ΞCarPark
│ r! : REPORT
├────────────────────────────────────────────────────
│ ordinaryCars = carParkCapacity
│ r! = ordinaryCarParkFull
└────────────────────────────────────────────────────
```

we can explicitly construct:

$$OrdinaryEntry \mathrel{\widehat{=}} OrdinaryEntryOK \lor OrdinaryCarParkFull$$

as:

```
┌─ OrdinaryEntry ────────────────────────────────────
│ ΔCarPark
│ r! : REPORT
├────────────────────────────────────────────────────
│ (ordinaryCars' − ordinaryCars = 1 ∧
│  passesInUse' = passesInUse ∧
│  r! = success)
│ ∨
│ (ordinaryCars = carParkCapacity ∧
│  ordinaryCars' = ordinaryCars ∧
│  passesInUse' = passesInUse ∧
│  r! = ordinaryCarParkFull)
└────────────────────────────────────────────────────
```

□

Notice that the absence of $\Xi CarPark$ in *OrdinaryEntry* requires the two predicates:

$$ordinaryCars' = ordinaryCars$$
$$passesInUse' = passesInUse$$

Exercise 6.3 Explain why we cannot include $\Xi CarPark$ in *OrdinaryEntry* above. □

Schema implication

The reader who has read the descriptions of schema conjunction and disjunction will probably have a good idea of what to expect for the operation of schema implication. Let us nonetheless return to the representation of investment strategy in order to provide an intuitive justification for this operation. A certain client believes that small companies are a good bet for investment only if they are also profitable companies. If a small company is not profitable then this client does not wish to invest in it. The client is also willing to invest in companies other than small companies.

As before, a broker could of course construct a specific schema to represent this client's chosen strategy:

```
┌─ SmallImpliesProfitableCompany ──────────────────────────
│  c : COMPANY
├──────────────────────────────────────────────────────────
│  c ∈ smallCompany ⇒ c ∈ profitableCompany
└──────────────────────────────────────────────────────────
```

Exercise 6.4 Convince yourself that this schema specifies the client's chosen strategy by considering the value of the schema property when c is a small profitable company, when c is a small unprofitable company and when c is a large company.   □

Once again, given the schemas *SmallCompany* and *ProfitableCompany* as defined earlier, a more convenient definition of the required schema is the implication of these two schemas, that is:

$$SmallImpliesProfitableCompany \mathrel{\widehat{=}} SmallCompany \Rightarrow ProfitableCompany$$

The operation of schema implication is analogous to that of schema conjunction and disjunction except that in contrast:

$$Schema1 \Rightarrow Schema2$$

is not in general the same schema as:

$$Schema2 \Rightarrow Schema1$$

The variables in the signatures of the schemas are merged in exactly the same way under the same restrictions, namely that name clashes must be avoided. The property of the new schema, however, is the property obtained by forming the implication of the properties of the given schemas. The property of the schema to the left of the schema implication symbol ⇒ is the antecedent property in the implication of the properties and the property of the schema to the right of the schema implication symbol is the consequent property in the implication.

Example 6.4 If we construct the implication of T by S where S and T are as given earlier we obtain:

```
┌─ SimpliesT ──────────────────────────────────────────────
│  x, y : ℤ
│  s : ℙℤ
├──────────────────────────────────────────────────────────
│  (y ≥ 0 ∧ x > y) ⇒ (y ∈ s ∧ ∃x : ℙℤ • x ⊂ s)
└──────────────────────────────────────────────────────────
```

□

Schema negation

Let us once again return to the example concerning the representation of investment strategy in order to provide an intuitive justification for schema negation. A certain client wishes to invest in unprofitable companies because these have a low share price which will increase if the company returns to profitability. If the broker were to construct a schema explicitly to represent this strategy then the result would be:

```
┌─ UnprofitableCompany ─────────────────────────────
│  c : COMPANY
├───────────────────────────────────────────────────
│  ¬ c ∈ profitableCompany
└───────────────────────────────────────────────────
```

An alternative way of specifying *UnprofitableCompany* is to make use of the existing *ProfitableCompany* schema as follows:

$$UnprofitableCompany \mathrel{\widehat{=}} \neg\ ProfitableCompany$$

The negation of a given schema has the same signature as the given schema and a property which is the negation of the property of the given schema. Since the property includes any predicates introduced in the declarative part, this sometimes this leads to unexpected results. For example, consider the schema below which represents an investment strategy that specifies investment in a company with a profit of at least one million pounds.

```
┌─ VeryProfitableCompany ───────────────────────────
│  c : COMPANY
│  x : ℕ
├───────────────────────────────────────────────────
│  profit c = x
│  x ≥ 1000000
└───────────────────────────────────────────────────
```

If we now consider how we might use a schema to represent an investment strategy that specifies investment in companies that do not make a profit of at least one million pounds we might be tempted to negate the schema *VeryProfitableCompany*. If we do this, however, we do not get the result we expect. We first normalize *VeryProfitableCompany* to obtain:

```
┌─ VeryProfitableCompany ───────────────────────────
│  c : COMPANY
│  x : ℤ
├───────────────────────────────────────────────────
│  x ≥ 0
│  profit c = x
│  x ≥ 1000000
└───────────────────────────────────────────────────
```

and then the negation of *VeryProfitableCompany* is the schema:

```
┌─ NegatedVeryProfitableCompany ──────────────────────
│  c : COMPANY
│  x : ℤ
├──────────────────────
│  ¬ (x ≥ 0 ∧
│       profit  c = x ∧
│       x ≥ 1,000,000)
└──────────────────────
```

We can simplify the predicate part of this schema using De Morgan's Laws (see Chapter 3, page 57) to obtain:

$$\neg (x \geq 0) \vee \neg (\text{profit } c = x) \vee \neg (x \geq 1000000)$$

and simplify further to obtain:

$$x < 0 \vee \text{profit } c \neq x \vee x < 1000000$$

To investigate the meaning of *NegatedVeryProfitableCompany* we must consider the bindings that satisfy the property. By inspection of the simplified predicate it is clear that it is true of many bindings that were not intended. For example, the property is true of a company with a profit of two million pounds if x is a value other than two million.

Schema renaming

Schema renaming is something of a misnomer. It is not possible to change the name of a schema unless this is done systematically throughout the entire specification. This is because schema names must have global scope (see §6.2 and §6.7). The effect is as if the original name had never been used and this sort of renaming is not a formal operation but simply a presentation detail.

Schema renaming is in fact the renaming of one or more components of a schema. The need to rename a component generally arises from a need to avoid name clashes in the use of schema operations. For example, suppose that we take the schema representing small companies as given earlier:

```
┌─ SmallCompany ──────────────────────
│  c : COMPANY
├──────────────────────
│  c ∈ smallCompany
└──────────────────────
```

and a schema representing profitable companies as given earlier but where the component is named d rather than c:

```
┌─ ProfitableCompanyD ─────────────────────────────
│ d : COMPANY
├──────────────────────
│ d ∈ profitableCompany
└──────────────────────────────────────────────────
```

This latter schema has essentially the same meaning as a schema in which d is replaced by c or indeed any other suitable name. This does not mean, however, that this schema produces the same effect when combined with another schema. Consider for example the schema $SmallCompany \land ProfitableCompanyD$. Because c and d are not merged, we have:

```
┌─ SmallAndProfitableCompanyD ─────────────────────
│ c, d : COMPANY
├──────────────────────
│ c ∈ smallCompany
│ d ∈ profitableCompany
└──────────────────────────────────────────────────
```

We have not specified that the companies denoted by c and d should be equal and therefore the property of this schema is true for two distinct companies, one of which is small and the other profitable. This schema thus has a different meaning than the schema $SmallCompany \land ProfitableCompany$ given below in which both schemas include the single component c:

```
┌─ SmallAndProfitableCompany ──────────────────────
│ c : COMPANY
├──────────────────────
│ c ∈ smallCompany
│ c ∈ profitableCompany
└──────────────────────────────────────────────────
```

and where the property is true only for a small and profitable company.

In order to use $ProfitableCompanyD$ in a suitable schema conjunction expression, we must rename the component d to c. The expression:

$$ProfitableCompanyD[c/d]$$

is the schema $ProfitableCompanyD$ in which the component d has been replaced with the component c. The reader may find it useful to remember the expression $Schema[new/old]$ as an aid to learning the notation.

As a result of renaming, two or more components may have the same name and type and so can be merged. For example, $SmallAndProfitableCompanyD$ has two components but:

$$SmallAndProfitableCompanyD[c/d]$$

has only one. Every name declared in a schema must be declared to be of exactly one type and therefore we are not allowed to rename components in such a way that the same name is declared to be of two or more distinct types.

Note that there is a difference between renaming components and renaming all occurrences of a variable. In particular, bound variables in the predicate part are not components and so if T is the schema:

$$
\begin{array}{|l}
\hline
T \\
\hline
x : \mathbb{Z} \\
s : \mathbb{P}\,\mathbb{Z} \\
\hline
x \in s \\
\exists\, x : \mathbb{P}\,\mathbb{Z} \bullet x \subset s \\
\hline
\end{array}
$$

then $T[y/x]$ is the schema:

$$
\begin{array}{|l}
\hline
T \\
\hline
y : \mathbb{Z} \\
s : \mathbb{P}\,\mathbb{Z} \\
\hline
y \in s \\
\exists\, x : \mathbb{P}\,\mathbb{Z} \bullet x \subset s \\
\hline
\end{array}
$$

and the existentially quantified variable x is not renamed since it is not a component of the schema.

Schema hiding

Schema hiding, like schema renaming, is also something of a misnomer. Schema hiding is the operation of hiding or 'removing' components from a schema. If we can remove components from a schema then there is a greater potential for reusing schemas; the following example illustrates this. The broking firm introduced as an example earlier provides a dealing service for its private clients. Dealing instructions are represented as schemas. For example, the following schema is used to specify the instruction to buy shares in a given company provided the share price does not exceed a given value.

$$
\begin{array}{|l}
\hline
BuySubjectToPrice \\
\hline
c? : COMPANY \\
price? : \mathbb{N} \\
action! : ACTION \\
\hline
sharePrice\ c? \leq price? \\
action! = buy \\
\hline
\end{array}
$$

On rare occasions the market is so bullish[5] that investors will buy shares at any price. This potentially reckless instruction can be represented by the

---

[5] In a bull market share prices are expected to rise.

schema *BuySubjectToPrice* if we remove or hide the *price?* component and modify the property so that it is true irrespective of the price of the shares. The schema we require is:

```
┌─ BuyAtAnyPrice ──────────────────────────────────
│ c? : COMPANY
│ action! : ACTION
├──────────────────────────────────────────────────
│ ∃ price? : ℕ • sharePrice c? ≤ price?
│ action! = buy
│
└──────────────────────────────────────────────────
```

In effect we have specified that shares should be bought if there is some price that the shares do not exceed. This price can be any non-negative value.

Exercise 6.5 Suppose the existential quantifier ($\exists$) in the above schema is replaced by the universal quantifier ($\forall$). Describe in English the meaning of this modified schema. □

Using the notation for schema hiding, we can define *BuyAtAnyPrice* by reusing *BuySubjectToPrice*:

$$BuyAtAnyPrice \,\widehat{=}\, BuySubjectToPrice \setminus (price?)$$

In general, if a schema S contains the components $x_1, x_2, \ldots$ then the schema obtained from S by hiding the components $x_1, x_2, \ldots$ is denoted:

$$S \setminus (x_1, x_2, \ldots)$$

The components of this schema are those of S except for those that appear in the list $(x_1, x_2, \ldots)$ and the property of this schema is true for all bindings that are restrictions of the bindings that satisfy S. A restriction of a given binding is another binding in which some of the components of the given binding are ignored. If the property of S is true for a binding then the property of $S \setminus (x_1, x_2, \ldots)$ will also be true for that binding after excluding the components in the list $(x_1, x_2, \ldots)$.

Schema composition

Schema composition provides us with a means of combining two operations sequentially. Let us return to the example of the broking firm and suppose that certain companies are bought and sold in their entirety. In such circumstances, a portfolio of investments is a set of companies. The size of the portfolio is the number of companies held in the portfolio.

```
┌─ Portfolio ──────────────────────────────────────
│ portfolio : ℙ COMPANY
│ portfolioSize : ℤ
├──────────────────────────────────────────────────
│ portfolioSize = #portfolio
│
└──────────────────────────────────────────────────
```

The operation to sell a company requires that the company be in the portfolio (that is, be owned by the investor). Once a company is sold it is no longer part of the portfolio. The operation of selling a company can thus be represented by the following schema.

$$
\begin{array}{l}
\_SellCompany _____ \\
\Delta Portfolio \\
c? : COMPANY \\
\hline
c? \in portfolio \\
portfolio' = portfolio \setminus \{c?\} \\
\end{array}
$$

Notice that even though we expect the size of the portfolio to decrease by one after a sell operation we have not included the predicate:

$$portfolioSize' = portfolioSize - 1$$

since this predicate is implied by the predicates in the state invariant.

A company can be bought only if it is not in the portfolio (that is, not already owned); consequently, the operation to buy a company can be represented by the following schema.

$$
\begin{array}{l}
\_BuyCompany _____ \\
\Delta Portfolio \\
c? : COMPANY \\
\hline
c? \notin portfolio \\
portfolio' = portfolio \cup \{c?\} \\
\end{array}
$$

Given the sell and buy operations above, we now wish to specify an operation in which we sell a company and then immediately buy it back.[6] One way to achieve the effect of the sell and buy operation is to perform the sell operation given above and follow it immediately with the buy operation. We can exploit this fact and give a definition of the sell and buy operation by specifying that it is the composition of the sell operation followed by the buy operation. The notation for schema composition is given in the definition below.

$$SellAndBuyCompany \mathrel{\widehat{=}} SellCompany \mathbin{\raise.2ex\hbox{$\scriptstyle\S$}} BuyCompany$$

To introduce the definition of schema composition let us explicitly construct the *SellAndBuyCompany* schema from the two schemas *SellCompany* and *BuyCompany*. The use of these two schemas suggests the existence of three states as illustrated in Figure 6.4. These three states may not be distinct. We

---

[6]This sell and buy operation (performed to avoid capital gains tax) is known in stock market circles as a 'bed and breakfast' operation because in order to minimize price fluctuations, the sale is typically made just before close of business on one day and the purchase is made just after the commencement of business on the following day.

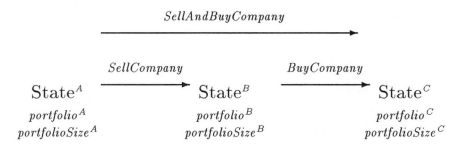

Figure 6.4: The states before and after the sell and buy operations

wish to define a schema that describes a particular relationship between the components of State^A and State^C. These relationships can be expressed using the schemas *SellCompany* and *BuyCompany* and an intermediate state State^B. For the purpose of exposition, we rename the components of these schemas to refer to the before and after states shown in Figure 6.4. After renaming, we obtain[7]:

```
┌─ SellCompany ──────────────────────────────────────
│  Portfolio^A
│  Portfolio^B
│  c? : COMPANY
├────────────────────────────────────────────────────
│  c? ∈ portfolio^A
│  portfolio^B = portfolio^A \ {c?}
└────────────────────────────────────────────────────
```

$$\begin{array}{l} \hline \textit{SellCompany} \\ \hline Portfolio^A \\ Portfolio^B \\ c? : COMPANY \\ \hline c? \in portfolio^A \\ portfolio^B = portfolio^A \setminus \{c?\} \\ \hline \end{array}$$

$$\begin{array}{l} \hline \textit{BuyCompany} \\ \hline Portfolio^B \\ Portfolio^C \\ c? : COMPANY \\ \hline c? \notin portfolio^B \\ portfolio^C = portfolio^B \cup \{c?\} \\ \hline \end{array}$$

In the state transition from State^A to State^C we require the properties of both of the above schemas to hold, so we form the conjunction of these two schemas.

---

[7]The proposed Z standard does not allow variable decoration with characters other than '''', '!'and '?'. We use *A* and *B* for explanatory purposes only.

$\_\_$ *SellCompanyAndBuyCompany* $_____$

$Portfolio^A$
$Portfolio^B$
$Portfolio^C$
$c? : COMPANY$

$c? \in portfolio^A$

$c? \notin portfolio^B$

$portfolio^B = portfolio^A \setminus \{c?\}$

$portfolio^C = portfolio^B \cup \{c?\}$

It is conventional not to decorate the before-state components and to decorate the after-state components with a "'". If we do this and use the $\Delta Portfolio$ convention for the inclusion of $Portfolio$ and $Portfolio'$, we obtain:

$\_\_$ *SellCompanyAndBuyCompany1* $_____$

$\Delta Portfolio$
$Portfolio^B$
$c? : COMPANY$

$c? \in portfolio$

$c? \notin portfolio^B$

$portfolio^B = portfolio \setminus \{c?\}$

$portfolio' = portfolio^B \cup \{c?\}$

There is no need for the components of $State^B$ to be components of the *SellAndBuyCompany* schema. The schema should specify relationships between components of $State^A$ and $State^C$ only, and we require no more than that there exists some state $State^B$. We thus hide the components of this state to obtain the definition of the *SellAndBuyCompany* operation.

$\_\_$ *SellAndBuyCompany* $_____$

$\Delta Portfolio$
$c? : COMPANY$

$\exists portfolio^B : \mathbb{P}\ COMPANY;\ portfolioSize^B : \mathbb{Z} \bullet$
$\quad c? \in portfolio \wedge$
$\quad c? \notin portfolio^B \wedge$
$\quad portfolio^B = portfolio \setminus \{c?\} \wedge$
$\quad portfolio' = portfolio^B \cup \{c?\}$

Exercise 6.6 * Define, using schema composition and schema renaming, a sell and buy operation in which the company bought need not be the same as the company sold.   □

Exercise 6.7 * Explicitly construct a schema defining a sell and buy operation in which the company bought need not be the same as the company sold. Do not simplify this schema. □

Exercise 6.8 * Simplify the schema defined in the previous exercise. □

If we generalize from the above example we can see that given any two schemas S and T which represent operations then the required steps to form $S \mathbin{\raise0.2ex\hbox{$\scriptstyle\circ$}}_9 T$ are:

1. Check that there is a one-to-one correspondence between the "′" decorated components of S (the after-state variables, say x_1', x_2', ...) and the undecorated components of T (the before-state variables, say x_1, x_2, ...) such that components with the same base name (the base name is the name stripped of any decoration) have the same type. In addition, the types of any common components must be the same. If these conditions are not satisfied then the composition operation is not defined.

2. Rename the after-state variables of S using names that do not appear in S or T, for example $S[x_1'/x_1'', x_2'/x_2'', \ldots]$.

3. Rename the before-state variables of T to the names used to rename the components of S in accordance with the one-to-one correspondence established in step 1 above, for example $T[x_1/x_1'', x_2/x_2'', \ldots]$.

4. Form the conjunction of the renamed schemas, that is:

$$S[x_1'/x_1'', x_2'/x_2'', \ldots] \wedge T[x_1/x_1'', x_2/x_2'', \ldots]$$

5. Hide all the renamed components since these refer to the intermediate state, that is:

$$(S[x_1'/x_1'', x_2'/x_2'', \ldots] \wedge T[x_1/x_1'', x_2/x_2'', \ldots]) \setminus (x_1'', x_2'', \ldots)$$

The schema explicitly constructed using these steps can usually be simplified. For example, given that $portfolio^B = portfolio \setminus \{c?\}$ implies $c? \notin portfolio^B$, the predicate $c? \notin portfolio^B$ can be dropped from the schema. We can also take the two predicates:

$$portfolio^B = portfolio \setminus \{c?\}$$
$$portfolio' = portfolio^B \cup \{c?\}$$

and substitute for $portfolio^B$ to obtain:

$$portfolio' = (portfolio \setminus \{c?\}) \cup \{c?\}$$

Given that the variable $portfolio^B$ no longer appears in the predicate part the existential quantification for this variable is redundant and can be removed. Using the fact that $c? \in portfolio$ we have:

$$portfolio' = portfolio$$

The resulting simplified schema is thus:

```
┌─ SellAndBuyCompany ─────────────────────────────────
│ ΔPortfolio
│ c? : COMPANY
├─────────────────────────────────────────────────────
│ c? ∈ portfolio
│ portfolio' = portfolio
│ portfolioSize' = portfolioSize
└─────────────────────────────────────────────────────
```

which specifies that the portfolio does not change, which is what we would expect. This schema is conventionally written as:

```
┌─ SellAndBuyCompany ─────────────────────────────────
│ ΞPortfolio
│ c? : COMPANY
├─────────────────────────────────────────────────────
│ c? ∈ portfolio
└─────────────────────────────────────────────────────
```

In this chapter we have introduced essentially all of the Z notation that we will use in this book. The remaining chapters are largely concerned with operations from the Z library.

Chapter 7

Functions

We first introduced functions in Chapter 3. In basic terms, a function is applied to a value in order to denote some value. In this chapter we will consider functions in some detail.

A function is a special kind of relation, namely a relation which is not of the one-to-many or many-to-many kind. Let us consider a simple example. As a lecturer, I frequently lend books to students and other lecturers and so I need a system to keep track of where my books are. Whenever I lend a book, I make a note of the title of the book, against which the borrower signs his or her name. My system is based on a relation:

$$borrowedBy : BOOKTITLE \leftrightarrow PERSON$$

There is a problem with this system because I have two books with the same title, *Mind Over Machine*. When both of these books are borrowed, I do not know who has borrowed my *Mind Over Machine*, a critique of artificial intelligence, and who has borrowed my *Mind Over Machine*, a study of Californian New Age cults. If we look at Figure 7.1, which illustrates a possible *borrowedBy* relation, we can see that the problem shows itself as a pair of arrows emanating from the single title *Mind Over Machine*. To overcome this problem, a library associates a class number with each book. Class numbers are unique and so a single class number is never associated with more than one book.[1] This means that my two books called *Mind Over Machine* would each have their own class number. It is this class number which is then associated with a borrower. Figure 7.2 illustrates a possible relation from *CLASSNUMBER* to *PERSON*. Notice the conspicuous absence of two or more arrows emanating from a single class number.

---

[1] A class number is not, strictly speaking, unique in itself. A Cutter number (after a Mr Cutter) is added to the end.

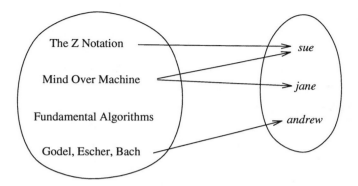

Figure 7.1: The title-borrower relation

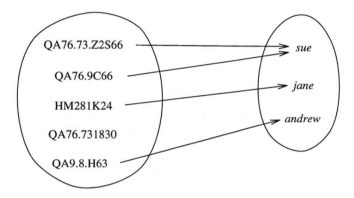

Figure 7.2: The class number-borrower relation

7.1   Partial function

If the relation *borrowedBy* is to usefully model the borrowers of my books then
no element of the source should be related to more than one element of the
target. Relations that have this property are called *partial functions*.

More formally, a partial function from X to Y is a relation from X to Y
such that each element x in X is related to at most one y in Y. The notation
for denoting the set of partial functions is shown in the definition below.

$$X \rightarrow Y == \{f : X \leftrightarrow Y \mid \forall x : X; \; y_1, y_2 : Y \bullet$$
$$x \mapsto y_1 \in f \wedge x \mapsto y_2 \in f \Rightarrow y_1 = y_2\}$$

This definition, generic in two parameters, X and Y, is based on the observation
that if a function maps an element x to y_1 and also to y_2 then since there cannot
be any one-to-many relationships, y_1 and y_2 must be the same element.

Exercise 7.1 Explain why the following definition of the set of partial functions is incorrect.

$$X \nrightarrow Y == \{f : X \leftrightarrow Y \mid \forall x : X; \exists_1 y : Y \bullet x \mapsto y \in f\}$$

Hint: construct a simple example partial function that violates the above definition. □

Example 7.1 No person can have more than one tax code, so the taxCode relation is thus a partial function.[2] If:

$$X == \{sue, theQueen, joy, jane, val\}$$

and:

$$Y == \{4521, 2330, 3445\}$$

then a possible partial function from X to Y, that is, a possible member of $X \nrightarrow Y$, is:

$$taxCode = \{sue \mapsto 2330, joy \mapsto 4521, jane \mapsto 4521, val \mapsto 3445\}$$

□

Notice that the Queen, who at the time of writing does not pay any tax, does not map to any element of the target and is thus not in the domain of the taxCode partial function.

7.2 Total function

A *total function* is a special kind of partial function. If every element of the source is mapped to some element of the target, we say that the partial function is a total function. For a given non-empty source and target, the total functions are thus a proper subset of the partial functions.

As an example of a total function, consider a relation that maps a person to that person's weight. The relation is a partial function because no person can have more than a single weight. The relation is also a total function because every person has a weight.

Formally, a total function from X to Y is a relation from X to Y such that each element x in X is related to exactly one y in Y. Alternatively, the domain of the total function must be equal to the source. The notation for denoting the set of total functions from X to Y is shown in the definition below.

$$X \rightarrow Y == \{f : X \nrightarrow Y \mid \text{dom } f = X\}$$

Notice that this definition is framed in terms of the set of partial functions.

---

[2] We exclude individuals who might have multiple tax codes as part of a tax evasion scheme.

Example 7.2 No person can have more than one age; the *ageOf* relation is thus a partial function but because each person (including the Queen) has an age the *ageOf* relation is also a total function. If $X == \{sue, joy, jane, val\}$ then a possible (not to mention flattering) total function from X to $\mathbb{N}$ is:

$$ageOf = \{sue \mapsto 30, joy \mapsto 21, jane \mapsto 21, val \mapsto 23\}$$

□

Terminology

The reader should note that the term 'function' is, strictly speaking, ambiguous between 'partial function' and 'total function'. The intended meaning is, however, usually clear from the context. The reader should be aware that some authors use the term 'partial function' where we would use the term 'non-total function'.

Exercise 7.2 Categorize each of the following relations as either a total function, a non-total function or a relation which is not a function.

i. *MuchLessThan* $== \{x, y : \mathbb{Z} \mid x < y - 99 \bullet x \mapsto y\}$

ii. The size of the population of each country of the world as a relation from countries of the world to the set of integers.

iii. The number of cars owned by a person as a relation from the set of people to $\mathbb{N}_1$ ($\mathbb{N}_1 == \mathbb{N} \setminus \{0\}$).

□

7.3   Declaring a function and its type

Although a function is a special kind of relation, there is no new function type. The type of a function from X to Y is the same as that of a relation from X to Y, that is, $\mathbb{P}(X \times Y)$. If we were to declare a function variable f as:

$f : \mathbb{P}(X \times Y)$

or as is more usual as:

$f : X \leftrightarrow Y$

then from this declaration we cannot determine that f is a function as opposed to an arbitrary relation. To overcome this problem, we exploit the fact that the value of a variable can be constrained to take a proper subset of the values of a type by adding a constraint at the point at which the variable is declared. We have already seen examples of this such as:

$$\boxed{\quad n : \mathbb{N} \quad}$$

This is really a more concise way of stating:

$$\boxed{\begin{array}{l} n : \mathbb{Z} \\ \hline x \geq 0 \end{array}}$$

Analogously, we can declare a function as:

$$\boxed{\quad f : X \nrightarrow Y \quad}$$

which is really a more concise way of stating:

$$\boxed{\begin{array}{l} f : X \leftrightarrow Y \\ \hline \forall\, x : X;\ y_1, y_2 : Y \bullet (x \mapsto y_1 \in f) \wedge (x \mapsto y_2 \in f) \Rightarrow y_1 = y_2 \} \end{array}}$$

Example 7.3 Consider the *double* function which maps each integer onto an integer twice its value. The type of *double* is the set of relations from $\mathbb{Z}$ to $\mathbb{Z}$. We can, however, declare the variable *double* to take values within only the set of total functions from $\mathbb{Z}$ to $\mathbb{Z}$:

$$double : \mathbb{Z} \rightarrow \mathbb{Z}$$

To ensure that the variable *double* is equal to exactly the function we intend, we constrain its value by using a suitable predicate. The complete definition is:

$$\boxed{\begin{array}{l} double : \mathbb{Z} \rightarrow \mathbb{Z} \\ \hline double = \{x : \mathbb{Z} \bullet x \mapsto 2 * x\} \end{array}}$$

$\square$

Example 7.4 An explicit definition of the inverse of the function *double*, *double*$^\sim$, is:

$$\boxed{\begin{array}{l} half : \mathbb{Z} \nrightarrow \mathbb{Z} \\ \hline half = \{x : \mathbb{Z} \bullet 2 * x \mapsto x\} \end{array}}$$

Notice that $2 * x \mapsto x$ does not provide an explicit formula by which values in the range can be constructed. We have, however, made our specification sufficiently precise to ensure that the values are uniquely determined. $\square$

Exercise 7.3 The Z library provides the integer division operation div which discards any remainder. Another attempt to define *half* might therefore be:

$$\boxed{\begin{array}{l} half : \mathbb{Z} \nrightarrow \mathbb{Z} \\ \hline half = \{x : \mathbb{Z} \bullet x \mapsto x \text{ div } 2\} \end{array}}$$

Explain why $half \neq double^\sim$. $\square$

7.4   Function application

A function may be applied to an element of the domain; this is an expression
with a value from the range of the function. For example, the application of
the function *double* to the value 3 is the value 6. The notation for function
application is illustrated in the examples below.

Example 7.5

> *double* 2 = 4
> *half* 6 = 3
> *ageOf jane* = 21
> $\{sue \mapsto 30, joy \mapsto 21, jane \mapsto 21, val \mapsto 23\}\ jane = 21$

□

Notice that, although meaningful, a function application in which the function
is defined by extension is probably not useful.

Formally, if $f : X \nrightarrow Y$, then the application of f to some element $x : X$ in
the domain of f is denoted $f\ x$ and is an expression with a value in the range
of f. If x is not in the domain of f then $f\ x$ is not defined.

Note that if f is a total function it is also a relation and therefore $f(\!|\{x\}|\!) = \{f\ x\}$.

Sometimes $f\ x$ will be written as $f(x)$. This is not really a different notation
because in Z we are allowed to surround any expression with '()'. We might
want to do this to make the expression easier to read but sometimes parentheses
are necessary to specify the structure of an expression. For example, function
application associates to the left, which means that an expression such as:

> *double ageOf val*

is the application of *double* to *ageOf* and the value of this expression should be
a function which is applied to *val*; in other words the expression is bracketed
to the left as in:

> (*double ageOf*) *val*

Clearly *ageOf* is not in the domain of *double* or even of the correct type and
so:

> *double ageOf*

is meaningless. In contrast, the function application:

> *double* (*ageOf val*)

is meaningful and has the value 46 because *val* is a young 23.

7.5 More complex function types

A function is a relation between sets and as such there is no restriction on the type of the sets involved. In particular, the sets can be sets of sets or product sets. If we return to the simple system for recording the people to whom I have lent books, we saw in that example that if two books have the same title then I must make an additional note of the author, say, in order to distinguish the two books. If I were do this consistently for all the books that I lend; then my record would essentially be a function with the type:

$$(BOOKTITLE \times AUTHOR) \leftrightarrow PERSON$$

Clearly, this technique of incorporating additional attributes can be applied in many situations.

Example 7.6 Consider the relation between some article and its price as sold in a number of shops. This relation is not in general a function because the same article can have more than one price depending on the shop in which it is sold. If we assume, however, that the combination of an article and a shop specifies no more than one price then we can declare a *price* function thus:

$$price : (SHOP \times ARTICLE) \nrightarrow \mathbb{N}$$

$\square$

Example 7.7 The Z library function $+$ has the type $\mathbb{P}((\mathbb{Z} \times \mathbb{Z}) \times \mathbb{Z})$ although it would be declared as $\_ + \_ : (\mathbb{Z} \times \mathbb{Z}) \to \mathbb{Z}$. $\square$

Example 7.8 The Z library function *min*, which maps sets of integers to the smallest member, has the type $\mathbb{P}\,\mathbb{Z} \leftrightarrow \mathbb{Z}$ although it would be declared:

$$min : \mathbb{P}_1\,\mathbb{Z} \nrightarrow \mathbb{Z}$$

where $\mathbb{P}_1\,X == \{S : \mathbb{P}\,X \mid S \neq \varnothing\}$. The function *min* is clearly not a total function because there is no smallest integer in some infinite subsets of the integers. $\square$

We have seen examples of the use of product sets and power set types as the source of a function. These types can also be used as the target of a function.

Example 7.9 We know that an article on sale in a number of shops will not in general have the same price in all the shops, that is, we have a relation:

$price : ARTICLE \leftrightarrow \mathbb{Z}$

$price = \{beans \mapsto 32, beans \mapsto 29, peas \mapsto 89, bread \mapsto 65, bread \mapsto 68\}$

Given a specific article, say *beans*, we might want to know the set of prices for this article. This is the value of a relational image expression, that is:

$$price(\!|beans|\!) = \{32, 29\}$$

A consumer organization publishes a list of articles and against each article is a list of the prices for that article. This information can be modelled by the *price* relation above but sometimes a more natural model is a function in which we map each article to a set. This set contains all the prices for which the article is on sale. If an article is not on sale it is mapped to the empty set.

$$priceSet : ARTICLE \rightarrow \mathbb{P}\,\mathbb{Z}$$

$$priceSet = \{beans \mapsto \{32, 29\}, peas \mapsto \{89\}, bread \mapsto \{65, 68\}\}$$

□

The *priceSet* function is simply an alternative way of structuring the information present in the *price* relation. This 'restructuring' technique is, of course, generally applicable and can be used to define a function from any relation $R : X \leftrightarrow Y$. We take each element x of X and map this element to the set of elements in Y that x relates to through R. If x is in the domain of R then x maps to a non-empty set, otherwise x maps to an empty set. Indeed we can even define a function that maps any relation to the function corresponding to the relation.

This function is illustrated in Figure 7.3 and, although it looks rather daunting, can be easily specified in Z as follows.

$$=[X, Y]============$$
$$relationToFunction : (X \leftrightarrow Y) \rightarrow (X \rightarrow \mathbb{P}\,Y)$$
$$\forall R : X \leftrightarrow Y \bullet$$
$$relationToFunction = \{x : X \bullet x \mapsto \{y : Y \mid x \mapsto y \in R\}\}$$

Notice that the definition is generic because it is applicable to any sets X and Y. In the definition, the set comprehension:

$$\{y : Y \mid x \mapsto y \in R\}$$

identifies the set of elements in Y that x relates to through R. For every relation we can define just one corresponding function, and so *relationToFunction* is a function.

We can now define *priceSet* as:

$$priceSet == relationToFunction\; price$$

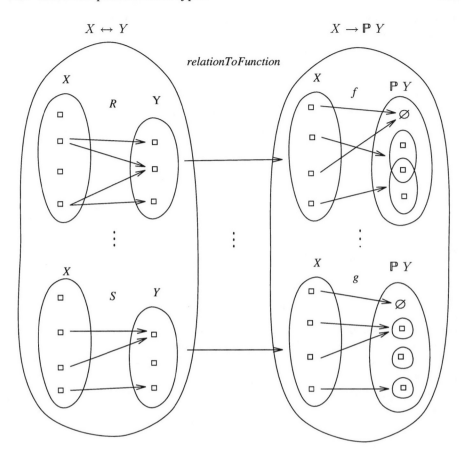

Figure 7.3: A function that maps a relation to a function

Example 7.10 A consumer protection organization wishes to produce a price list that associates each item on sale in any shop with the lowest price for which that item is available. This price list is clearly a partial function. For example:

$$min(priceSet\ beans)$$

is the lowest price for which *beans* are on sale. The required price list is thus the function:

$$minPrice : ARTICLE \nrightarrow \mathbb{Z}$$
$$minPrice = \{x : ARTICLE \mid priceSet\ x \neq \emptyset \bullet x \mapsto min(priceSet\ x)\}$$

$\square$

Example 7.11 The set operations of union, intersection and difference each associate a pair of sets with a single set. These operations are defined in the Z library as generic functions.

$$
\begin{array}{l}
=[X]= \\
\hline
\_\cup\_,\_\cap\_,\_\setminus\_:(\mathbb{P}\,X \times \mathbb{P}\,X) \to \mathbb{P}\,X \\
\hline
\forall\, S, T : \mathbb{P}\,X \bullet \\
\quad S \cup T = \{x : X \mid x \in S \lor x \in T\}\ \land \\
\quad S \cap T = \{x : X \mid x \in S \land x \in T\}\ \land \\
\quad S \setminus T = \{x : X \mid x \in S \land x \notin T\}
\end{array}
$$

$\square$

7.6 Further kinds of function

Surjective functions

Consider the set of teams taking part in the Formula 1 Grand Prix. We can define a function from *CAR* to *TEAM* which maps a racing car to the team to which it belongs. The relation is a function because no car can belong to more than one team. In addition, every team must have at least one racing car. The function from *CAR* to *TEAM* therefore maps a racing car to every team in the target *TEAM*. Since every element of the target is mapped to, we say the function is surjective. Figure 7.4 illustrates surjective and non-surjective functions.

Formally, if f is a partial function from X to Y and the range of f is equal to Y then f is a partial surjection. The notation for denoting the set of partial surjections is shown in the definition below.

$$X \twoheadrightarrow Y == \{f : X \nrightarrow Y \mid \text{ran } f = Y\}$$

The set of total surjections can be similarly defined.

$$X \twoheadrightarrow Y == \{f : X \to Y \mid \text{ran } f = Y\}$$

Example 7.12 Suppose we have a set of lecturers *LECTURER* and a set of courses *COURSE* which are taught by the lecturers. Lecturers are too busy to teach more than one course. Suppose further that we wish to specify that there is at least one lecturer teaching each course. A simple way to do this would be to specify a partial surjective function *teaches* as follows:

$$teaches : LECTURER \twoheadrightarrow COURSE$$

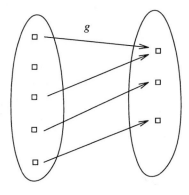
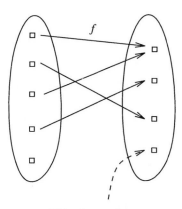

g is a surjection because
every element of the target
is in the range of g

This element is
outside the range of *f* and
so *f* is not a surjection

Figure 7.4: An illustration of surjective and non-surjective functions

The declaration of *teaches* does not tell us which lecturer is teaching which course; to do that we would probably give an extensional definition in which we listed the maplets. If we wanted to specify in addition that every lecturer must teach a course then we could declare *teaches* as a total surjection. □

Exercise 7.4 Give a concise English description of the following set.

$$(X \twoheadrightarrow Y) \cap (X \to Y)$$

□

Injective function

In many situations there is a need to model one-to-one relationships. For example, when allocating national insurance (or social security) numbers to citizens, it is important that each citizen has only one number and that no two citizens have the same number. This situation can be modelled by imposing conditions on a relation from *CITIZEN* to *NUMBER*. Firstly, this relation is a function because a citizen can have only one number. Secondly, this relation never maps two or more citizens to any single number. A function in which every element of the range is mapped to by only one element of the domain is called an injective function. In Figure 7.5 we illustrate injective and non-injective functions.

Formally, if *f* is a partial function from X to Y and *f* maps distinct elements in the domain to distinct elements in the range then *f* is a partial injection.

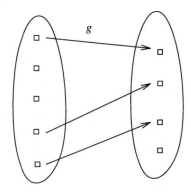 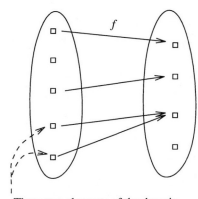

g is an injection because distinct   These two elements of the domain
elements in the domain map to   map to the same element in the
distinct elements in the range   range and so *f* is not an injection

Figure 7.5: An illustration of injective and non-injective functions

The notation for denoting the set of partial injections is shown in the definition below.

$$X \rightarrowtail\!\!\!\rightarrow Y == \{f : X \nrightarrow Y \mid \forall x_1, x_2 : \text{dom } f \bullet f(x_1) = f(x_2) \Rightarrow x_1 = x_2\}$$

The set of total injections can be similarly defined.

$$X \rightarrowtail Y == \{f : X \rightarrow Y \mid \forall x_1, x_2 : \text{dom } f \bullet f(x_1) = f(x_2) \Rightarrow x_1 = x_2\}$$

Example 7.13 Let us suppose that we can model marriage relationships using a function from the set of men to the set of women. We want to specify that no wife has more than one husband. (That no man is married to more than one wife is implicit in the use of a function rather than a relation.) A simple way to model this restriction is to use a partial injective function *marriedTo* as follows:

$$marriedTo : MEN \rightarrowtail\!\!\!\rightarrow WOMEN$$

Again, this declaration does not tell us who is married to whom; it simply specifies a particular moral code.   □

Exercise 7.5 How would you declare the *marriedTo* function above to specify that every man is married?   □

Exercise 7.6 Give a concise English description of the following set.

$$(X \rightarrowtail\!\!\!\rightarrow Y) \cap (X \rightarrow Y)$$

                                                                              □

Bijective function

A function can be surjective independently of whether or not it is an injection. This means that it is possible for a function to be both surjective and injective and such functions are called bijective. Such a function is illustrated in Figure 7.6.

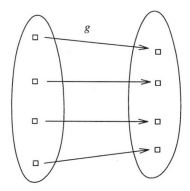

Figure 7.6: An illustration of a bijective function

Formally, if f from X to Y is both a total surjection and a total injection then f is bijective. The notation for denoting the set of bijections is shown in the definition below.

$$X \rightarrowtail\!\!\!\rightarrow Y == (X \twoheadrightarrow Y) \cap (X \rightarrowtail Y)$$

Exercise 7.7 * In each of the following example relations, the source and target is the set $\{a, b, c, d\}$. For each example, state if the relation is a function and if so what specific kind of function.

   i. $\{a \mapsto a, b \mapsto a, c \mapsto a, d \mapsto a\}$

  ii. $\{a \mapsto b, b \mapsto c, c \mapsto d, d \mapsto a\}$

 iii. $\{a \mapsto b, b \mapsto c, c \mapsto d\}$

 iv. $\{a \mapsto b, a \mapsto c, c \mapsto d, d \mapsto a\}$

□

Finite functions

A finite function contains a finite number of maplets. The set of finite partial functions from X to Y is denoted $X \nrightarrow\!\!\!+ Y$ and can be specified as:

$$X \nrightarrow\!\!\!+ Y == \{f : X \nrightarrow Y \mid \operatorname{dom} f \in \mathbb{F} X\}$$

Exercise 7.8 * Justify the following statements. To ensure that a function is finite, it is sufficient to specify that the domain of the function is finite. The same cannot be said of a relation.   □

Exercise 7.9 * Give an example to show that $X \twoheadrightarrow Y$ is not necessarily finite. □

7.7   Operations on functions

Up to this point in the chapter, we have described various kinds of function without saying very much about how to define or use functions. The following operations are useful for defining functions from existing functions.

Inverse of a function

You will recall that given a relation we can define the inverse relation as the relation obtained by swapping the source and target sets and including in the inverse relation the maplet $y \mapsto x$ for every maplet $x \mapsto y$ in the original relation. Since a function is a relation we can define the inverse of a function without introducing anything new.

We must take care, however, because although the inverse of a relation is always a relation, the inverse of a function is not always a function. For example, given the function:

$$ageOf = \{sue \mapsto 30, joy \mapsto 21, jane \mapsto 21, val \mapsto 29\}$$

the inverse of $ageOf$ is written $ageOf^\sim$ and:

$$ageOf^\sim = \{30 \mapsto sue, 21 \mapsto joy, 21 \mapsto jane, 29 \mapsto val\}$$

and since the element 21 is mapped to more than one element of the range, $ageOf^\sim$ is not a function.

Exercise 7.10 If f is a bijection, describe the kind of function that is the inverse of f.   □

Exercise 7.11 * If f is a total injection, describe the kind of function that is the inverse of f.   □

Function composition

Function composition is simply relation composition (see §5.4) where the relations involved happen to be functions. Although the inverse of a function need not be a function, the composition of two functions is always a function. The composition of two functions is illustrated in Figure 7.7.

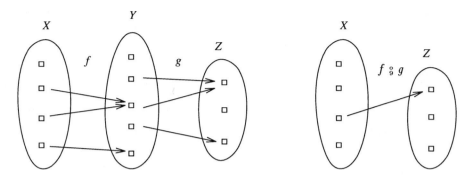

Figure 7.7: An illustration of function composition

Exercise 7.12 * Argue that the composition of two functions is a function. Hint: take functions declared as $f : X \nrightarrow Y$ and $g : Y \nrightarrow Z$ and by using the property that each of f and g is a function, show that $f \,\mathring{,}\, g$ also has this property.   □

Function override

Suppose we decide to model the share price of companies listed on the stock exchange as a function from the set $COMPANY$ to the set $\mathbb{N}$. If:

$$COMPANY == \{bt, ici, glaxo, shell\}$$

then the *sharePrices* function might be:

$$sharePrices = \{bt \mapsto 130, ici \mapsto 221, glaxo \mapsto 121, shell \mapsto 119\}$$

As a result of an investigation by a regulatory commission, bt are barred from providing entertainment services via its phone lines. The share price consequently drops to 76. It would be convenient if we could define the new *sharePrices* function by simply taking the old function and specifying that the new function is just like the old function except for the new maplet:

$$bt \mapsto 76$$

which should replace whatever maplet involves the element bt. This would be convenient because with functions that are defined by extension we would avoid respecifying many maplets that have already been specified.

One way to set about doing this is to define the function that does not contain the maplet involving bt, that is:

$$sharePrices \setminus \{bt \mapsto 130\}$$

In fact we are not interested in the old price of *bt* shares and so it might be more convenient to remove the maplet without specifying the old price, as in:

$$sharePrices \setminus \{bt \mapsto sharePrices\ bt\}$$

Using this function, we can specify the function containing the new maplet as the union of two functions:

$$(sharePrices \setminus \{bt \mapsto sharePrices\ bt\}) \cup \{bt \mapsto 76\}$$

The Z library provides a function override operation (denoted as $\oplus$) for combining functions in this way. Using $\oplus$ the *newSharePrices* function would be specified as:

$$newSharePrices = sharePrices \oplus \{bt \mapsto 76\}$$

The *newSharePrices* function agrees with the *sharePrices* function except where a domain element is present in the function $\{bt \mapsto 76\}$. In this case, we take the maplet from the function $\{bt \mapsto 76\}$ and discard the maplet in the *sharePrices* function.

Example 7.14 The override operation can be used to double the *bt* share price.

$$newSharePrices = sharePrices \oplus \{bt \mapsto double(sharePrices\ bt)\}$$

□

An error that is sometimes made is to specify the overriding of a function by specifying only the new maplet, for example by specifying:

$$newSharePrices\ bt = 76$$

This specifies the new share price of the *bt* shares but says nothing about the price of any other shares and as such it is not a full specification of *newSharePrices*.

To give a specification of the $\oplus$ operator we need to consider some other basic operations on relations. These operations are, however, useful in their own right for creating new relations which are subsets of existing relations and so it is worth spending some time understanding them.

7.8   Specifying subsets of a relation

We are going to describe four related operations. To provide some rationale for the operations consider the following modelling situation. A mail order music company maintains a customer database of the musical tastes of each of its customers. This information can be modelled as a relation:

$$musicalTaste : CUSTOMER \leftrightarrow MUSIC$$

where:

$$MUSIC ::= rock \mid blues \mid jazz \mid classical \mid pop \mid country$$

This relation is unlikely to be a function because a single person may like both *rock* and *blues*, say. We will use this relation to construct a new relation, one for each of the four operations described below.

Domain restriction

The mail order music company, which is based in Hull in the north of England, decides to set up a regional office in London. This regional office will copy a portion of the customer database and hold it locally, the portion that contains the customers who live in the south of England. Given that we are modelling the database as a relation:

$$musicalTaste : CUSTOMER \leftrightarrow MUSIC$$

we would like to model the portion of the database that should be copied to the regional office. The relation we require is a subset of the *musicalTaste* relation, and has a domain that is equal to the set of customers who live in the south of England. We can use the domain restriction operation to specify the required relation by using this subset of customers. Figure 7.8 illustrates the domain restriction operation.

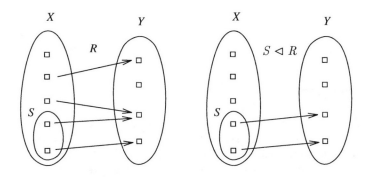

Figure 7.8: An illustration of domain restriction

Formally, if R is a relation from X to Y and S is a subset of X then the expression:

$$S \lhd R$$

denotes the relation consisting of the set of pairs in R whose first members are also members of S. The definition of the $\lhd$ operation is as follows.

$$
\begin{array}{l}
\underline{\quad[X, Y]\quad} \\
\hline
\_ \lhd \_ : (\mathbb{P}\, X \times (X \leftrightarrow Y)) \to (X \leftrightarrow Y) \\
\hline
\forall S : \mathbb{P}\, X; \ R : X \leftrightarrow Y \ \bullet \\
\qquad S \lhd R = \{x : X; \ y : Y \mid x \mapsto y \wedge x \in S \in R \bullet x \mapsto y\}
\end{array}
$$

Notice that this definition employs a generic schema since the $\lhd$ operation is independent of the type of the relation involved. If we look at the declaration of $\_ \lhd \_$ we can see that it is a total function. The crucial part of the definition is the predicate $x \in S$ in the set comprehension. This limits the pairs defined by the set comprehension to be those that have a first element in S.

Example 7.15 Consider a relation that models the index of a book on formal specification.

$$
\begin{array}{l}
index : SUBJECT \leftrightarrow \mathbb{N} \\
\hline
index = \{bag \mapsto 225,\, div \mapsto 193,\, formal \mapsto 75,\, name \mapsto 146\}
\end{array}
$$

If we are interested in only some of the subjects in the book, that is, the subjects of interest belong to a set *interestingSubject* and this set is a subset of *SUBJECT*:

$$
interestingSubject == \{formal, name\}
$$

then the subset of the index that is of interest to us is:

$$
interestingSubject \lhd index = \{formal \mapsto 75,\, name \mapsto 146\}
$$

$\square$

Range restriction

The mail order music company is currently gripped by the latest business fad which involves splitting up organizations into smaller competing businesses. As a result the mail order music company is split into a number of smaller companies, each dealing with only a few specific tastes in music. Each of these companies requires a portion of the original company database. The rock and pop mail order music company, for example, requires the details only of customers who like rock or pop. To model the rock and pop database we can define a subset of the original relation which contains only those pairs that have a second element in the set:

$$
\{rock, pop\}
$$

which is a subset of the target of the *musicTaste* relation. This is called *range restriction*. Figure 7.9 illustrates the range restriction operation.

Formally, if R is a relation from X to Y and T is a subset of Y then the expression:

$$R \triangleright T$$

denotes the relation consisting of the set of pairs in R whose second members are also members of T. The definition of the $\triangleright$ operation is as follows.

$$
\begin{array}{l}
\llbracket X, Y \rrbracket \\
\hline
\_ \triangleright \_ : ((X \leftrightarrow Y) \times \mathbb{P}\, Y) \to (X \leftrightarrow Y) \\
\hline
\forall R : X \leftrightarrow Y; \ T : \mathbb{P}\, Y \bullet \\
\quad R \triangleright T = \{x : X; \ y : Y \mid x \mapsto y \in R \wedge y \in T \bullet x \mapsto y\}
\end{array}
$$

This definition is very similar to the definition of domain restriction. Compare the role of the predicate $y \in T$ in this definition with the role of the predicate $x \in S$ in the definition of the domain restriction.

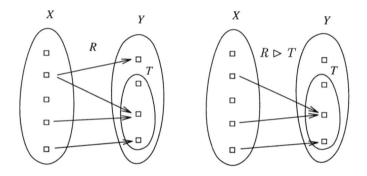

Figure 7.9: An illustration of range restriction

Example 7.16 Consider a relation:

$$
\begin{array}{l}
pointsTable : \mathbb{N} \leftrightarrow DRIVER \\
\hline
pointsTable = \{81 \mapsto senna, 71 \mapsto prost, 79 \mapsto mansell, 59 \mapsto hill\}
\end{array}
$$

that records the points of each driver in the Formula 1 championship. If we are interested in the points of the British drivers only:

$$britishDriver == \{mansell, hill\}$$

then we can construct the relation:

$$pointsTable \triangleright britishDriver = \{79 \mapsto mansell, 59 \mapsto hill\}$$

$\square$

Domain subtraction

An alternative way of restricting the domain or range of a relation is to specify
what is not in the domain or range. This is useful if it is easier to specify what
is not required than it is to specify what is required.

The mail order music company decides that it is spending too much money
on its computer systems and that the customer database is proving to be very
expensive. The cost of the database could be reduced if the amount of data was
reduced. The proposal is to delete all customers who have not placed an order in
the past two years. To model the new smaller database we need to construct a
relation with a domain that does not include any of these infrequent customers.
The required relation is a subset of the original formed by not including these
customers. Figure 7.10 illustrates the domain subtraction operation.

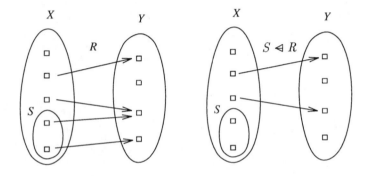

Figure 7.10: An illustration of domain subtraction

Formally, if R is a relation from X to Y and S is a subset of X then the
expression:

$$S \lhd R$$

denotes the relation consisting of the set of pairs in R whose first members are
not members of S. The definition of the $\lhd$ operation is as follows.

$$
\begin{array}{l}
\underline{\underline{[X, Y]}} \\
\hline
\_ \lhd \_ : (\mathbb{P}\, X \times (X \leftrightarrow Y)) \to (X \leftrightarrow Y) \\
\hline
\forall S : \mathbb{P}\, X;\ R : X \leftrightarrow Y \bullet \\
\qquad S \lhd R = \{x : X;\ y : Y \mid x \mapsto y \in R \wedge x \notin S \bullet x \mapsto y\}
\end{array}
$$

Notice how this definition differs from the definition of domain restriction by
the inclusion of the predicate $x \notin S$ in place of $x \in S$.

Example 7.17 A restaurant specializing in exotic foreign dishes wishes to include the ingredients of each dish on the menu. The required information can be modelled as a relation:

$$ingredient : FOODSTUFF \leftrightarrow DISH$$
$$ingredient = \{beef \mapsto steaknChips, e223 \mapsto steaknChips\}$$

that relates a foodstuff to a dish if that foodstuff is present in that dish. The chef is reluctant to supply all of this information because many dishes contain secret ingredients. These are specified below.

$$secretFoodstuff : \mathbb{P}\, FOODSTUFF$$
$$secretFoodstuff = \{e402, e223, e113, e338, e765, e225, e772, e342\}$$

It is decided to produce a menu listing the ingredients of each dish apart from the secret ingredients. The ingredient information in the menu could be modelled as a subset of the *ingredient* relation. The required relation is:

$$secretFoodstuff \lhd ingredient$$

□

Range subtraction

The mail order music company has now been established for a number of years. Over time the management have awarded themselves big pay rises and become rather lazy. The company continues to make a profit but in the opinion of a predatory entrepreneur, it is underperforming. This entrepreneur buys the mail order company, sacks the management and disposes of the unprofitable sections of the business, those dealing with classical music and jazz. As a result a smaller database is required. To model the new smaller database we need to construct a relation, which is a subset of the full relation, with a range that does not include classical music or jazz. Figure 7.11 illustrates the range subtraction operation.

Formally, if R is a relation from X to Y and T is a subset of Y then the expression:

$$R \rhd T$$

denotes the relation consisting of the set of pairs in R whose second members are not members of T. The definition of the $\rhd$ operation is as follows.

$$
\begin{array}{l}
=\![X, Y]\!=\!= \\
\_\,\rhd\,\_ : ((X \leftrightarrow Y) \times \mathbb{P}\, Y) \to (X \leftrightarrow Y) \\
\hline
\forall R : X \leftrightarrow Y;\ T : \mathbb{P}\, Y \bullet \\
\quad R \rhd T = \{x : X;\ y : Y \mid x \mapsto y \in R \land y \notin T \bullet x \mapsto y\}
\end{array}
$$

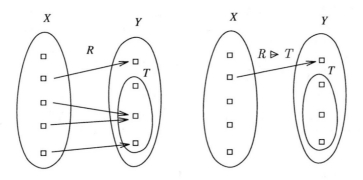

Figure 7.11: An illustration of range subtraction

Again, notice how this definition differs from the definition of range restriction by the inclusion of the predicate $y \notin T$ in place of $y \in T$.

Example 7.18 A directory that lists chemist shops and the days on which they are open can be modelled as a relation from a set of shops to a set comprising the seven days of the week. A directory of chemists open at the weekends can be modelled as a relation constructed from the full relation by a range subtraction operation. We would subtract the five weekdays from the range of the full relation.   □

Function override definition

Now that we have defined a number of relation operations, we are in a position to use these operations to give a concise specification of the function override operation first discussed in §7.7. Informally, to override f with g, we subtract from f the part of f that 'overlaps' with g and then form the union of this restricted f and g. The formal definition is given in the generic schema below.

$$
\begin{array}{l}
=[X, Y]\!=\!=\!=\!=\!=\!=\!=\!=\!=\!=\!=\!=\!=\!=\!=\!=\!=\!=\!= \\
\underline{} \oplus \underline{} : (X \nrightarrow Y) \times (X \nrightarrow Y) \to (X \nrightarrow Y) \\
\hline
\forall f, g : X \nrightarrow Y \bullet \\
\qquad f \oplus g = ((\mathrm{dom}\ g) \vartriangleleft f) \cup g
\end{array}
$$

Exercise 7.13 * Explain, using an example, why:

$$f \oplus g \neq (f \setminus g) \cup g$$

for all f and g in $X \nrightarrow Y$.   □

7.9 Specification of a simple library system

The following simple example illustrates a number of the function and relational operations introduced in this chapter. The system specified allows members of a library to borrow and return books. In order to concentrate on the operations used in the specification, we will present a simple model as a fait accompli. The required operations are presented in Table 7.1. Notice that the operations are incomplete since, for example, we have not mentioned cases such as a member who tries to borrow a book that is not in the library.

Operation	Input	Subcase property
Borrow book	Member, book	Book in library
Return book	Member, book	Book on loan to member

Table 7.1: The operations of a simple library system

Given sets

The specification has the following given sets:

$$[BOOK, CLASSNUMBER, MEMBER]$$

The set *BOOK* represents physical books, some of which are lying on the library shelves.

Each book is associated with a unique class number.

$$catalogue : BOOK \rightarrowtail CLASSNUMBER$$

catalogue is total because every book has a class number, and an injection because no two books share the same class number.

Exercise 7.14 What would be the consequences of defining *catalogue* as:

$$catalogue : BOOK \rightarrowtail\!\!\!\to CLASSNUMBER$$

□

Exercise 7.15 How can the problem alluded to in the previous exercise be overcome? □

State

When a book is borrowed it is the responsibility of a single member of the library until the book is returned. We record the fact that a member has borrowed a book by associating the class number for that book with the member. The association should be modelled by a function because a class number can be associated with only one member. The function is not total because not every book will necessarily be on loan.

$$onLoan : CLASSNUMBER \nrightarrow MEMBER$$

To specify the state space we should consider the acceptable values of *onLoan*. In particular, we should ensure that if a class number is associated with a member then there is some book in the catalogue with that class number. The allowable states of the library system are specified in the schema:

```
┌─ SimpleLibrary ───────────────────────────────────
│  onLoan : CLASSNUMBER ⇸ MEMBER
├───────────────────────────────────────────────────
│  ∀ c : CLASSNUMBER;  m : MEMBER •
│      onLoan c = m ⇒ ∃ b : BOOK • catalogue b = c
└───────────────────────────────────────────────────
```

Initial state

In the initial state, no member has a book on loan.

```
┌─ InitSimpleLibrary ───────────────────────────────
│  SimpleLibrary'
├───────────────────────────────────────────────────
│  onLoan' = ∅
└───────────────────────────────────────────────────
```

Borrowing a book

To borrow a book we must ensure that the book is not already on loan. We establish the class number of the book using the *catalogue* function:

$$catalogue \; book?$$

and specify that this number is not associated with any member in the *onLoan* relation.

$$catalogue \; book? \notin \mathrm{dom} \; onLoan$$

The complete schema is given below:

```
┌─ BorrowBook ──────────────────────────────────────────
│ ΔSimpleLibrary
│ book? : BOOK
│ member? : MEMBER
├───────────────────────────────────────────────────────
│ catalogue book? ∉ dom onLoan
│ onLoan' = onLoan ⊕ {catalogue book? ↦ member?}
└───────────────────────────────────────────────────────
```

Exercise 7.16 Can we replace ⊕ by ∪ in *BorrowBook* without changing its meaning? □

Returning a book

A member can return a book only if that book is on loan to that member. To check this, we again establish the class number of the book being returned using the *catalogue* function and also check that this class number is associated with the member returning the book, that is:

$$catalogue \; book? \mapsto member? \in onLoan$$

The complete schema is given below:

```
┌─ ReturnBook ──────────────────────────────────────────
│ ΔSimpleLibrary
│ book? : BOOK
│ member? : MEMBER
├───────────────────────────────────────────────────────
│ catalogue book? ↦ member? ∈ onLoan
│ onLoan' = onLoan \ {catalogue book? ↦ member?}
└───────────────────────────────────────────────────────
```

Exercise 7.17 ** Rewrite the above specification using a *catalogue* function from *CLASSNUMBER* to *BOOK* rather than *BOOK* to *CLASSNUMBER* and comment on the clarity of the two specifications. □

Chapter 8

Extended Example: Hiring Sports Equipment

In this chapter we build a specification for a system which, although relatively simple, has sufficient complexity to justify the explicit development of a mathematical model.

8.1 Informal description of an equipment hire system

A system is required to keep track of the sports equipment hired by customers at a sports centre. Each customer can hire several items of equipment. Whenever a customer hires some equipment we must make a record of the equipment hired. We need to note not only, for example, that a racket was hired but also which specific racket. One reason for doing this is to ensure that if all the equipment is not returned then the sports centre has a record of which customer to pursue. In general, the customer hiring the equipment is held responsible for it until it is returned. To avoid any dispute about who exactly is responsible for any hired equipment, any item of equipment can be on hire to only one customer at any one time. In brief, the operations the system must support are:

Hire: A customer hires some items of sports equipment.

Return: A customer returns some items of sports equipment.

Enquire: Show the items of equipment on hire to a specific customer.

Let us consider each of these operations in more detail. The hire operation must take account of the availability of equipment. In fact, this operation should succeed only if all the requested items are available. In all other cases it should fail and no item of equipment should be hired to the customer. In particular, this means that a customer who requests a bat and ball when there are no bats available will receive no bat and no ball. There is, of course, nothing to stop the customer making a second request for the ball only.

The return operation should allow a customer to return some and not all of the equipment hired by that customer. We would expect the outstanding equipment to be returned at some later time. Notice that if we took an 'all or nothing' approach with the return of equipment then, in contrast to the hire operation, we might be in a situation in which a customer who had lost his ball would not be allowed to return his bat. When equipment is returned, the system must indicate whether the customer has returned all the items he or she has on hire.

8.2   Developing the model

A specification consists of a mathematical model expressed in a formal notation. We will develop the model first and then express it in Z. The process of developing the model is seldom straightforward. We will often be faced with a number of alternatives. For example, having decided to employ a relation in our model, we must decide whether that relation should be a function and if so which particular kind of function. These decisions usually require careful thought and often a fair amount of work is required before we are in a position to make the best choice. Sometimes, an option may be explored at length before deciding that it is unsuitable, a 'dead end' so to speak.

Requirements as operations

A good starting point for the development of the model is to describe the required operations in terms of input, output and subcase conditions. We do this without too much concern for how the operations will be specified. The result is shown in Table 8.1.

The act of completing the table ensures that for each operation we identify the input and the output. In addition, it is useful to consider the subcase properties for each operation. This will help us check that we can distinguish the various outcomes of a given operation. For example, the hire operation has two possible outcomes: the requested equipment is hired or no equipment is hired. Ultimately, we will want to check that the various subcases for an operation are exhaustive. If this is so, the operation is well defined in all appropriate states and inputs. We do this by considering the preconditions for each subcase of an operation.

Operation	Input	Subcase property	Output
Hire equipment	Customer, equipment set	All equipment available	Success
		Some equipment unavailable	Fail
Return equipment	Customer, equipment set	All outstanding equipment returned	Success
		Not all outstanding equipment returned	Equipment outstanding
Enquire	Customer	*None*	Equipment set

Table 8.1: The formulation of the requirements

Developing the state

Having expressed the required operations in terms of input, output and subcase condition, we are ready to proceed to develop the state of the model. Two essential given sets seem to be:

$$[CUSTOMER, \ EQUIP]$$

The fact that we need to associate a customer with several items of equipment suggests that one possibility is to base the model on a function from $CUSTOMER$ to sets of $EQUIP$. In this function, a customer would be mapped onto the set of equipment hired by that customer. Another possibility is a relation with the given sets as candidates for the source and target of the relation. In what follows, we assess each of these alternatives by establishing in general terms how each of the operations listed in Table 8.1 could be specified. We will initially consider only the specification of the new state and any important outputs. If no clear winner emerges, we will go on to consider the specification of the subcase properties and following that, the state space invariants. This particular ordering of concerns represents our view of a sensible way of developing a model but it is not always the best ordering.

Consider first the use of a function with the type:

$$CUSTOMER \nrightarrow \mathbb{P} \ EQUIP$$

and how we might specify the change of state required for the hire operation. When a customer hires some items of equipment, those items should be added to the set of items on hire to that customer. The function override operation would be useful in specifying the new function. In order to describe in more detail how this might be done, let us give a name to the function we are considering:

$$onHire : CUSTOMER \nrightarrow \mathbb{P}\, EQUIP$$

The equipment currently on hire to *jane* is *onHire jane*, so if *jane* hires a bat and a ball we have:

$$onHire' = onHire \oplus \{jane \mapsto ((onHire\ jane) \cup \{bat, ball\})\}$$

The return operation for a given customer will lead to the removal of elements from the set of equipment on hire to that customer. Again, the function override operation would be useful in specifying the new function. The set difference operation, however, would be used in place of set union. The enquire operation is very easily specified. Given the use of a function of the type described above, the specification of the required operations seems feasible. Before we adopt this function to specify the state, we should consider the alternative, namely the use of a relation.

We can assess the suitability of a relation as the basis of the state by once more considering how each operation might be specified. We know that the relation will involve the two sets *CUSTOMER* and *EQUIP* but we have not decided which of these sets should be the source and which the target. Nevertheless, even before we make this decision, it is worthwhile considering the specification of the required operations.

If we consider the hire operation, this will have the effect of adding elements to the relation. We know that a relation is a set of pairs and so the set union operation can be used to extend the relation. The return operation will conversely lead to the removal of elements from the relation. The set difference operation could be used here. The enquire operation will require us to identify all the items related to a particular customer. Again, this should not present problems since this is exactly the sort of information ideally modelled by a relation. At this stage, there seems to be a potential route by which we can specify the required operations and so the choice of a relation also looks promising.

In the above consideration of the required operations we did not consider how we might specify the subcase properties. Let us do that now for each alternative model.

Equipment can be hired only if it is not already on hire to some customer. We thus need some means of specifying the equipment that is currently on hire. The range of the function *onHire* is a set of sets of equipment, that is, it has the type $\mathbb{P}(\mathbb{P}\, EQUIP)$. The set of equipment that is on hire will have the type $\mathbb{P}\, EQUIP$. In fact the union of the elements of ran *onHire* is the entire set of equipment on hire. The set of equipment requested by any customer in a hire operation must not intersect the set of equipment on hire.

We must detect the case where a customer has returned all the equipment on hire to that customer. To specify this subcase condition we need specify only that the customer has no items on hire after the completion of the return operation. We have already established the feasibility of determining the set of items on hire to a customer in considering the enquiry operation.

We consider now the specification of the subcase properties given the use of a relation. For the hire operation, we must identify the set of equipment on hire to some customer. This is the set of elements of the equipment set that take part in the relation. In other words, depending on the type of the relation, it is the domain or the range. The specification of the hire subcase condition thus seems straightforward.

In order to detect the case in which the customer has returned all the equipment he or she has hired, we need specify only that the customer has no items on hire after the completion of the return operation. Once again, we have already established the feasibility of determining the set of items on hire to a customer in considering the enquiry operation.

Having investigated both alternatives with respect to specifying the required operations, we should now consider the results of our investigations. Each alternative is feasible. The relation is marginally the preferred choice at this stage because of the simplicity with which the subcase properties can be specified. Rather than make a decision at this stage, let us continue assessing the two alternatives in terms of expressing the state invariant.

The basic state invariant is that no item of equipment must be on hire to more than one customer. If we represent the state as a function:

$$onHire : CUSTOMER \nrightarrow \mathbb{P}\ EQUIP$$

then for any two customers c_1, c_2, we require:

$$onHire\ c_1 \cap onHire\ c_2 = \varnothing$$

If we represent the state as a relation which allows many-to-many relationships, some states would inevitably represent a situation in which many customers were hiring a single item of equipment. One form of this unacceptable situation is illustrated in Figure 8.1.

The necessary condition for the state invariant may be conveniently imposed if it can be done by insisting that the relation is a function, say. In order to explore this possibility in detail, we must decide on a type for the relation. There are two alternatives, $CUSTOMER \leftrightarrow EQUIP$ or $EQUIP \leftrightarrow CUSTOMER$. The number of alternatives under consideration for representing the state is growing. Before we move on to consider each in turn let us summarize the existing status of our alternatives, which are illustrated in Figure 8.2.

Let us continue now by considering the possibility of using a relation of the type:

$$CUSTOMER \leftrightarrow EQUIP$$

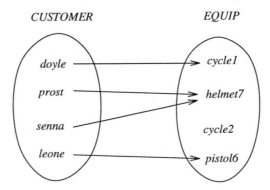

Figure 8.1: An unacceptable situation in which some items of equipment are on hire to more than one customer

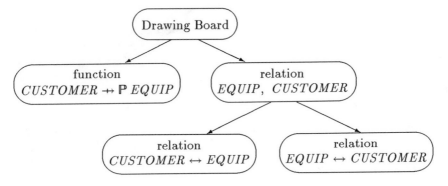

Figure 8.2: The initial exploration of the alternatives for specifying the state

A relation of this type would allow states in which several customers hired the same item of equipment. If we were to use a function to disallow many-to-one relationships we would need to insist that the relation be an injective function. Unfortunately, this is too strong a restriction because it would also outlaw one-to-many relationships and we must allow a customer to hire more than one item of equipment. We can therefore conclude that there does not seem to be a 'ready-made' relation (that is, a kind of function) that conforms to the constraints that we require. We could of course formulate our own constraint but we do not want to work any harder than necessary.

Let us now consider the alternative, that is, a relation of the type:

$$EQUIP \leftrightarrow CUSTOMER$$

Again, we must not allow an item of equipment to be hired to more than one customer, which means that we cannot allow one-to-many relationships. We can impose this constraint conveniently by specifying that the relation is a function. This normally gives us an additional benefit since usually, the more specialized a relation, the easier it is to work with in building a model. This alternative seems to be the more promising of the two relations.

We are probably now in a position to choose between the various models for representing the state. The investigations involved in the development of the model are summarized in Figure 8.3.

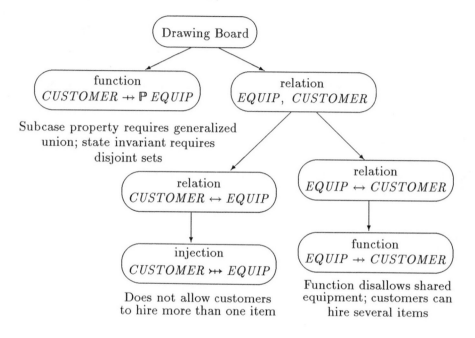

Figure 8.3: The exploration of alternatives in the development the state

Because of the simplicity with which the subcase properties and the state invariant can be specified, a relation of the type:

$$EQUIP \twoheadrightarrow CUSTOMER$$

is the most suitable for our model. Having chosen a model for the state, we should refine our description of the required operations given in Table 8.1. This is done in Table 8.2.

8.3   The specification

We are now in a position where we can begin to formalize the model. Let us begin as usual by specifying the given sets.

Operation	Input	Subcase property	State change
Hire equipment	Customer, equipment set	Equipment, domain of *onHire* disjoint	Add to *onHire*
		Equipment, domain of *onHire* not disjoint	*None*
Return equipment	Customer, equipment set	All outstanding equipment returned	Remove equipment from *onHire*
		Not all outstanding equipment returned	Remove equipment from *onHire*
Enquire	Customer	*None*	*None*

Table 8.2: The operations of the model given a state specified in terms of a relation

Basic types

We have a set of customers and a set of items of equipment.

$$[CUSTOMER, EQUIP]$$

The reports are defined below.

$$REPORT ::= success \mid fail \mid equipOutstanding$$

State

The state will include the *onHire* function. In addition, we have chosen to name explicitly the set of equipment that is presently available for hire, *free*. We have done this, even though it can always be calculated as the difference of two sets, to simplify the specification of hire and return operations.

```
┌─ SportsHire ──────────────────────────────
│ onHire : EQUIP ⇸ CUSTOMER
│ free : ℙ EQUIP
├───────────────────────────────────────────
│ free = EQUIP \ dom onHire
└───────────────────────────────────────────
```

Initial state

The initial state can be the state in which no equipment is hired out to any customer.

```
┌─ InitSportsHire ──────────────────────────────────
│ SportsHire'
│ ─────────────────
│ onHire' = ∅
└────────────────────────────────────────────────────
```

We have not given a value for the component *free* since from the state invariant we have:

$$free' = EQUIP \setminus \text{dom } onHire'$$

and if *onHire'* is the empty function then dom *onHire'* is empty and it follows that $free' = EQUIP$.

The fact that we can find values for the state components in the initial state shows that the initial state is possible, that is, it exists. The following is a specification for the initial state that cannot be satisfied.

```
┌─ InitSportsHireIncorrect ─────────────────────────
│ SportsHire'
│ ─────────────────
│ onHire' = {ball ↦ jane}
│ free' = EQUIP
└────────────────────────────────────────────────────
```

We specified in the state invariant that:

$$free' = EQUIP \setminus \text{dom } onHire'$$

which must be consistent with the value for *free* given in the initial state, that is:

$$free' = EQUIP$$

We know that this is not the case because:

$$EQUIP \setminus \text{dom } onHire' = EQUIP$$

is true only if $EQUIP \cap \text{dom } onHire' = \varnothing$; but:

$$\text{dom}\{ball \mapsto jane\} = \{ball\}$$

and since the source of *onHire'* is *EQUIP*, we have $\{ball\} \subseteq EQUIP$.

Operations

Hire operation

We can now consider the operation of hiring some items of equipment to a customer. The operation requires the items of equipment and the customer as input. The operation should succeed only if the equipment is free. If the equipment is free then each item is associated with the customer and added to the *onHire* function.

HireSuccess
$\Delta SportsHire$
$c? : CUSTOMER$
$e? : \mathbb{P}\, EQUIP$
$r! : REPORT$

$e? \subseteq free$
$onHire' = onHire \cup \{i : EQUIP \mid i \in e? \bullet i \mapsto c?\}$
$r! = success$

The set comprehension:

$$\{i : EQUIP \mid i \in e? \bullet i \mapsto c?\}$$

is the set of maplets that map each item of hired equipment to the customer hiring the items.

The precondition of *HireSuccess* is:

PreHireSuccess
$onHire : EQUIP \nrightarrow CUSTOMER$
$free : \mathbb{P}\, EQUIP$
$c? : CUSTOMER$
$e? : \mathbb{P}\, EQUIP$

$free = EQUIP \setminus \mathrm{dom}\, onHire$

$e? \subseteq free$

$\exists\, onHire' : EQUIP \nrightarrow CUSTOMER;\ free' : \mathbb{P}\, EQUIP;\ r! : REPORT \bullet$
$\quad onHire' = onHire \cup \{i : EQUIP \mid i \in e? \bullet i \mapsto c?\} \wedge$
$\quad free' = EQUIP \setminus \mathrm{dom}\, onHire' \wedge$
$\quad r! = success$

Clearly, *onHire'* exists, it is the function:

$$onHire \cup \{i : EQUIP \mid i \in e? \bullet i \mapsto c?\}$$

We may thus substitute this expression for *onHire'* and since *onHire'* no longer appears in the predicate, the existential quantification of *onHire'* can be removed (see page 70) to obtain:

$free' : \mathbb{P}\, EQUIP;\ r! : REPORT \bullet$
$\quad free' = EQUIP \setminus \mathrm{dom}(onHire \cup \{i : EQUIP \mid i \in e? \bullet i \mapsto c?\}) \wedge$
$\quad r! = success$

Similarly, it is clear that *free'* and *r*! exist and so the precondition is:

```
┌─ PreHireSuccess ─────────────────────────────────
│ onHire : EQUIP ⇸ CUSTOMER
│ free : ℙ EQUIP
│ c? : CUSTOMER
│ e? : ℙ EQUIP
├──────────────────────────────────────────────────
│ free = EQUIP \ dom onHire
│ e? ⊆ free
└──────────────────────────────────────────────────
```

which is what we would expect.

The hire operation will fail if some item requested is not free.

```
┌─ HireFail ───────────────────────────────────────
│ ΞSportsHire
│ c? : CUSTOMER
│ e? : ℙ EQUIP
│ r! : REPORT
├──────────────────────────────────────────────────
│ e? ⊄ free
│ r! = fail
└──────────────────────────────────────────────────
```

Exercise 8.1 * Define an operation similar to *HireFail* that provides a more informative report. The operation should output a set containing exactly the items that were requested but not available. □

The precondition construction and simplification for *HireFail* is similar to that for *HireSuccess* and so we will simply state it.

```
┌─ PreHireFail ────────────────────────────────────
│ onHire : EQUIP ⇸ CUSTOMER
│ free : ℙ EQUIP
│ c? : CUSTOMER
│ e? : ℙ EQUIP
├──────────────────────────────────────────────────
│ free = EQUIP \ dom onHire
│ e? ⊄ free
└──────────────────────────────────────────────────
```

The reader is advised, however, to explicitly construct and simplify preconditions of all operations as it provides a useful check that an operation is defined correctly.

Both *HireSuccess* and *HireFail* are partial operations, which means that they are not applicable in all possible inputs and states in the state space. By forming the disjunction of *HireSuccess* and *HireFail*, however, we claim to define a total operation, that is, an operation that is applicable in all states in the state space. To justify this claim consider that the property of *PreHireSuccess* is:

$$free = EQUIP \setminus \text{dom } onHire \wedge e? \subseteq free$$

and the property of *PreHireFail* is:

$$free = EQUIP \setminus \text{dom } onHire \wedge e? \not\subseteq free$$

The disjunction of these two properties is:

$$free = EQUIP \setminus \text{dom } onHire \wedge (e? \subseteq free \vee e? \not\subseteq free)$$

which is equivalent to the state invariant. We can now define an operation which we know is total:

$$Hire \stackrel{\frown}{=} HireSuccess \vee HireFail$$

Enquire operation

For a given customer, we must identify all the items of equipment that are related to that customer by the *onHire* function.

```
┌─ Enquire ──────────────────────────────
│ ΞSportsHire
│ c? : CUSTOMER
│ e! : ℙ EQUIP
├─────────────────────────────────────────
│ e! = onHire~(|{c?}|)
└─────────────────────────────────────────
```

Return operation

When some items of sports equipment are returned by a customer, we must check that the customer is not returning equipment hired out to someone else, since a customer can return equipment only if he or she has hired it. Only those items that have been hired by the customer will be accepted and made available for hire again. We refuse any equipment that does not belong to the customer.

The equipment on hire to a customer *c?* is:

$$onHire^{\sim}(\!|\{c?\}|\!)$$

If the customer returns the equipment set *e?* then the subset of *e?* that is hired to customer *c?* is:

$$e? \cap onHire^{\sim}(\!|\{c?\}|\!)$$

This subset must be removed from the domain of *onHire*; hence the following schema defines how the state should be modified when equipment is returned.

```
┌─ ReturnSome ──────────────────────────────────────────
│ ΔSportsHire
│ c? : CUSTOMER
│ e? : ℙ EQUIP
├───────────────────────────────────────────────────────
│ onHire' = (e? ∩ onHire~(|{c?}|)) ◁ onHire
└───────────────────────────────────────────────────────
```

Independently of what equipment is returned, we report success when the customer has returned all the equipment on hire to him or her.

```
┌─ Success ─────────────────────────────────────────────
│ SportsHire'
│ c? : CUSTOMER
│ r! : REPORT
├───────────────────────────────────────────────────────
│ onHire' ~(|{c?}|) = ∅
│ r! = success
└───────────────────────────────────────────────────────
```

We report that some items are outstanding if the customer has not returned all the equipment hired.

```
┌─ Outstanding ─────────────────────────────────────────
│ SportsHire'
│ c? : CUSTOMER
│ r! : REPORT
├───────────────────────────────────────────────────────
│ onHire' ~(|{c?}|) ≠ ∅
│ r! = equipOutstanding
└───────────────────────────────────────────────────────
```

We can now define the return operation as:

$$Return \,\widehat{=}\, (ReturnSome \wedge Success) \vee (ReturnSome \wedge Outstanding)$$

8.4 Enhancing the sports hire system

The material in the remaining part of this chapter is more advanced than that presented so far and can be omitted on a first reading. We wish now to enhance the specification given above to take account of the complications that arise with the introduction of safety regulations designed to ensure that sportsmen and sportswomen are adequately equipped. Two example regulations are shown below.

Any customer who hires a cycle must also hire or have already hired
a helmet and gloves.

Any customer who hires a helmet must also hire or have already
hired a balaclava.

In general, for each item of equipment, there are a number of associated
safety items which must also be hired. For the purpose of this example, we
will assume that safety items need be hired once only. So for example, a
customer who hires two cycles need hire only one helmet. Notice that in order to
determine the entire set of safety items required for a given item it is necessary,
in general, to consult several regulations, as in the example above. In other
words, the regulations state direct but not indirect relationships.

The regulations will affect our specification in that they constrain the state
space. They also modify the operations. A customer who requests a given set
of items may need to hire several more. In accordance with standard trad-
ing practice, however, we will not hire equipment to customers who have not
requested it and so customers must request safety equipment. If a request
contravenes the regulations, no equipment is hired but we output the safety
items required. The return and enquire operations are not affected by the new
regulations. The subcases of the hire operation are shown in Table 8.3.

Operation	Input	Subcase property	Output
Hire equipment	Customer, equipment set	All equipment available and safety regulations satisfied	Success
		Some equipment un-available and safety reg-ulations satisfied	Fail
		Safety regulations not satisfied	Required safety items

Table 8.3: The formulation of the requirements

The regulations impose a constraint on the possible values of the state
component that records the equipment on hire to each customer. The state
specification must therefore be modified.

We need to model the regulations as a mathematical object which we can
use to express the additional conditions on the state space. The regulations
appear to state relationships between items of equipment but there is of course
no mention of specific items of equipment, that is, specific cycles or helmets. A
first attempt at modelling the regulations might be a relation in which items
are associated as in the regulations. For example, each cycle is related to every
helmet and pair of gloves, every helmet is related to every balaclava and so on.

$$\begin{array}{|l}
\hline
safetyRegs : EQUIP \leftrightarrow EQUIP \\
\hline
safetyRegs = \{\, cycle1 \mapsto helmet1, cycle1 \mapsto helmet2, \ldots \} \\
\hline
\end{array}$$

Notice that the *safetyRegs* relation does not change from state to state and so should be a global constant.

A first attempt at using this relation to constrain the state space might be the condition:

> If a customer is hiring an item of equipment and *safetyRegs* relates this item to some other item of equipment then the customer must also hire this other item.

Unfortunately, this is too restrictive, since it implies that the customer who hires a cycle must hire every helmet. We cannot easily solve this problem by specifying that the customer should hire just one of the items related to the cycle, because if helmets and gloves are both related to the cycle then the customer must hire a helmet and gloves. In general, a customer must hire an item from each of the various kinds of safety equipment.

This leads us to treat different kinds of equipment separately. One way to do this is to group items of the same kind into subsets. These subsets would be disjoint. Alternatively, we can introduce an additional basic type to model the kinds of equipment. Indeed, this is implicit in the regulations since they are phrased in terms of kinds of equipment in general rather than specific items. A helmet must be hired whenever a cycle is hired but we do not care which specific helmet or which specific cycle.

We thus introduce an additional basic type of generic items of equipment, which we call *EQUIPGENERIC*. A generic bicycle in *EQUIPGENERIC* represents all specific bicycles in the *EQUIP* type. The safety relation should therefore be defined as:

$$\begin{array}{|l}
\hline
safetyRegs : EQUIPGENERIC \leftrightarrow EQUIPGENERIC \\
\hline
safetyRegs = \{\, cycle \mapsto helmet, helmet \mapsto balaclava, \ldots \} \\
\hline
\end{array}$$

We can now use this relation to describe the constraint we require.

> Any customer who hires a specific item of equipment, where that specific item is an instance of a generic item of equipment which is related to some other generic item of equipment by the relation *safetyRegs*, should also hire a specific instance of that other generic item of equipment.

In Figure 8.4, which illustrates the relationships involved, we can see that a customer has hired *cycle*1 and has therefore hired a cycle which requires a

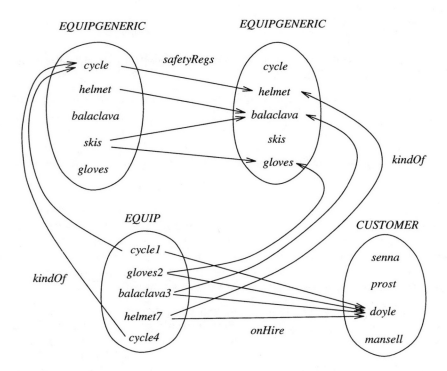

Figure 8.4: The relation that models safety regulations is concerned with equipment in general

helmet and so the customer has hired *helmet*7. Notice that the regulations also state that anyone who hires a helmet must hire a balaclava and so our customer has hired *balaclava*3.

We have not said how a specific item of equipment should be associated to its generic counterpart. In other words, how are we to know that some arbitrary element from the *EQUIP* set, say *cycle*1, is in fact a cycle and should therefore be associated with the element in *EQUIPGENERIC* which represents all specific cycles. Specific objects and their generic counterparts can also be related through a relation. Since each specific item of equipment can be an instance of only one generic item, the relation will be a function. Moreover, since all specific items must be instances of some generic item, the required function is total.

$$kindOf : EQUIP \rightarrow EQUIPGENERIC$$
$$kindOf = \{cycle1 \mapsto cycle, cycle2 \mapsto cycle, ...\}$$

Figure 8.4 can be used as a guide to formulating the new invariant which will ensure that all customers hire the prescribed equipment. If customer *c* hires item i_1:

$$onHire \ i_1 = c$$

and item i_1 is an instance of generic item g_1:

$$kindOf \ i_1 = g_1$$

and any customer who hires an instance of g_1 must also hire an instance of g_2:

$$g_1 \mapsto g_2 \in safetyRegs$$

then there exists an instance of g_2, call it i_2:

$$kindOf \ i_2 = g_2$$

and customer c is also hiring i_2:

$$onHire \ i_2 = c$$

This implication must be true for all customers and all items of equipment and all generic items of equipment. Bringing all this together and adding quantifiers we have:

$$\forall \ c : CUSTOMER; \ \forall \ i_1, \exists \ i_2 : EQUIP; \ \forall \ g_1, g_2 : EQUIPGENERIC \ \bullet$$
$$onHire \ i_1 = c \ \wedge$$
$$kindOf \ i_1 = g_1 \ \wedge$$
$$g_1 \mapsto g_2 \in safetyRegs$$
$$\Rightarrow kindOf \ i_2 = g_2 \ \wedge \ onHire \ i_2 = c$$

Notice that indirect relationships between items of generic equipment are not ignored. Confident that we can express the state invariant we can proceed with the specification.

Basic types

We should add the new basic type:

$$[CUSTOMER, EQUIP, EQUIPGENERIC]$$

State

We incorporate the new constraint into the state space description.

SportsHireSafety _____
$onHire : EQUIP \nrightarrow CUSTOMER$
$free : \mathbb{P} \, EQUIP$

$\forall \, c : CUSTOMER; \; \forall \, i_1, \exists \, i_2 : EQUIP; \; \forall \, g_1, g_2 : EQUIPGENERIC \bullet$
    $onHire \; i_1 = c \; \wedge$
    $kindOf \; i_1 = g_1 \; \wedge$
    $g_1 \mapsto g_2 \in safetyRegs$
        $\Rightarrow kindOf \; i_2 = g_2 \wedge onHire \; i_2 = c$
$free = EQUIP \setminus \mathrm{dom} \, onHire$

Initial state

The initial state does not require modification since it is consistent with the new invariant.

Operations

We can now reconsider the hire operation. In the former hire operation, a set of items could be hired if they were all free. We need to supplement this condition. The first step is to establish the set of safety items required for an arbitrary set of equipment.

First we identify the set of generic items corresponding to a set of specific items. We do this by defining a function similar to *kindOf* but for sets. If a customer c requests a set of items $e?$ then the generic items requested by customer c is:

    $kindsOf \; e?$

where:

$kindsOf : \mathbb{P} \, EQUIP \rightarrow \mathbb{P} \, EQUIPGENERIC$

$kindsOf = \{ e : \mathbb{P} \, EQUIP \bullet e \mapsto \{ i : EQUIP \mid i \in e \bullet kindOf \; i \} \}$

For a customer requesting a set of items $e?$, the safety regulations require the following generic items to be hired or on hire:

    $safetyRegs^{+} (\!| \{ kindsOf \; e? \} |\!)$

Note the use of the transitive closure operation to ensure that we identify all the indirectly related items.

The generic items already on hire for customer $c?$ are:

    $kindsOf(onHire^{\sim} (\!| \{ c? \} |\!))$

This set, together with the generic items requested, is subtracted from the set of all safety items required due to the equipment $e?$ to obtain the set of outstanding safety items.

$$safetyRegs^+ (\!|\{kindsOf\ e?\}\!|) \setminus (kindsOf(onHire^\sim (\!|\{c?\}\!|)) \cup kindsOf\ e?)$$

If this set is empty then the hire operation can proceed, otherwise it cannot.

SafetySuccess
SportsHireSafety
$c? : CUSTOMER$
$e? : \mathbb{P}\ EQUIP$

$\exists s : \mathbb{P}\ EQUIPGENERIC \bullet$
    $s = kindsOf\ e? \wedge$
    $\varnothing = safetyRegs^+ (\!|s|\!) \setminus (kindsOf(onHire^\sim (\!|\{c?\}\!|)) \cup s)$

Notice that we cannot use schema negation to define the situation in which *SafetySuccess* does not apply because insufficient equipment has been requested. Schema negation negates the entire property including the state invariant. We thus define:

SafetyFail
SportsHireSafety
$c? : CUSTOMER$
$e?, req! : \mathbb{P}\ EQUIP$

$\exists s : \mathbb{P}\ EQUIPGENERIC \bullet$
    $s = kindsOf\ e? \wedge$
    $req! = safetyRegs^+ (\!|s|\!) \setminus (kindsOf(onHire^\sim (\!|\{c?\}\!|)) \cup s)$
$\varnothing \neq req!$

We can now define a total operation:

$$HireSafety \ \widehat{=}\ (HireSuccess \wedge SafetySuccess) \vee HireFail \vee SafetyFail$$

Notice that the use of schema operations allows the reuse of the specification of *HireSuccess* and *HireFail*.

Exercise 8.2 ** We have assumed that the safety regulations can be modelled as a relation of the type:

$$EQUIPGENERIC \leftrightarrow EQUIPGENERIC$$

This relation may not be a suitable model if we must also model regulations such as:

Anyone who hires a cycle should also hire either a helmet or stabilizers.

Consider how the specification must be amended in order to model this kind of regulation.   □

Exercise 8.3 ** We have assumed that the safety regulations are constant and do not change during the life of the system. Modify the example so that there are operations for adding and deleting regulations. If you insist that the regulations can be changed only when the hire function is empty then this is not a difficult exercise. You may like to deal with the complications that arise if the regulations may change at the same time as customers have equipment on hire. You may wish to identify all the customers who must hire additional equipment and provide an operation to allow them to hire precisely the required items if they are available.   □

8.5   Summary

Modelling

Important steps in the development of a specification are:

1. Clarify the requirements by formulating them as operations, each with an input, an output and subcases if any.

2. Identify the objects at the core of the model: given sets, relations, functions, and so on. This identification can be quite tentative. Concentrate on gathering together all the alternatives before investigating any in depth.

3. Investigate the various alternatives from the previous step by considering the feasibility of specifying the required operations and the state invariant.

It is often useful to place all the alternatives explored on a single diagram to provide an overview of the main decisions made during the development of the model.

Chapter 9

Sequences

We have used sets to model collections of objects in which order is not important. There are many modelling situations, however, in which we wish to model a set of objects arranged in a specific order, in which case sets are inadequate. For example, let us consider how we might model the queue at a supermarket delicatessen counter. As customers arrive, the queue grows; once customers have been served, they leave the queue. This suggests that we need two operations, join the queue and leave the queue. Supermarket queues are normally 'fair' in the sense that people leave the queue in the same order in which they arrive; in other words, no one pushes in ahead of anyone else.

If we were to use a set to model the members of a queue, we would expect to specify the operation of joining a queue using set union and the operation of leaving a queue using set difference. If the queue is fair, however, the members of the queue should be removed in the order in which they were added. By considering the customers in the queue to be simply members of a set, however, we have no way of modelling the position of a customer in the queue and we do not know which customer should leave the queue first.

One way in which we could order the elements of a set is to use a numbering system to mark the position of each element. Many supermarkets operate such a scheme at the delicatessen counter. As customers arrive they pick up a numbered ticket. These tickets are part of a large roll from which they are dispensed in numerical order and customers are served in this order. What we are doing here is exploiting the fact that the numbers are themselves ordered.

If we accept that our model of a supermarket queue will require us to associate customers to numbers then we require some sort of relation involving the two sets:

$$CUSTOMER, \ \mathbb{Z}$$

A crucial decision we must make is the direction of the relation; is it to be $\mathbb{Z} \leftrightarrow CUSTOMER$ or $CUSTOMER \leftrightarrow \mathbb{Z}$?

Let us consider the first option, that is, that the relation has the type:

$\mathbb{Z} \leftrightarrow CUSTOMER$

Whenever we are considering the suitability of a relation for use in a model we should always consider whether the requirements for the model impose any special restrictions on the relation. A relation models many-to-many relationships, is this suitable as a model of a queue? If the model is based on the relation shown in Figure 9.1 then both *giusy* and *jane* are at the front of the queue.

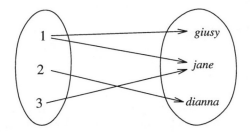

Figure 9.1: A possible member of $\mathbb{Z} \leftrightarrow CUSTOMER$

There can be only one person at the front of the queue and so an unrestricted relation is not a suitable model (Figure 9.2).

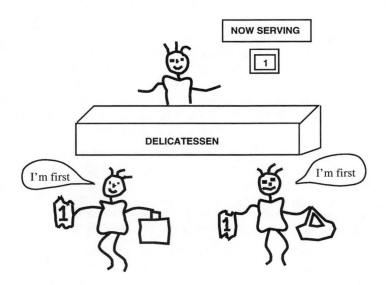

Figure 9.2: Something is wrong with the model

We can easily ensure that our relation does not include any one-to-many relationships by specifying that the relation should be a function.

If we look again at Figure 9.1 we notice that *jane* is occupying both the first and third position in the queue. The general question we must consider is whether we want to model one person in two positions in the queue. There are circumstances in which we might want to do this. Suppose *jane* picks a second ticket from the roll when she sees her friend approaching the delicatessen counter. By virtue of holding the two tickets, *jane* is occupying two places in the queue and if she does not give the second ticket to her friend she will have the opportunity of being served twice.

Let us now consider the alternative, that the relation has the type:

$$CUSTOMER \leftrightarrow \mathbb{Z}$$

Figure 9.3 illustrates a possible relation of this type.

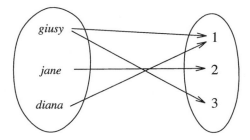

Figure 9.3: A possible member of $CUSTOMER \leftrightarrow \mathbb{Z}$

We can immediately see a problem at the front of the queue with both *giusy* and *dianna* claiming first place. To disallow the offending many-to-one relationships we would need to specify that the relation was an injective function. An injective function, however, cannot model any customer holding two or more places in the queue. If we want to keep this option open we should opt for the type $\mathbb{Z} \leftrightarrow CUSTOMER$. In fact, any relation of this type can easily be employed to model a queue in which no customer holds two places by specifying it to be an injective function. Figure 9.4 summarizes the choices we have considered in the development of our model of the queue. On balance, it would seem that the best model for a queue should be a partial function from the integers to whatever set of elements we use to model the objects in the queue.

The following is an example function which could be the model of a queue.

$$\{1 \mapsto giusy, 2 \mapsto jane, 3 \mapsto dianna\}$$

Functions of this kind are called sequences. Sequences can be represented using a notation that is more compact than listing the set of maplets. For example, $\{1 \mapsto giusy, 2 \mapsto jane, 3 \mapsto dianna\}$ is represented as:

$$\langle giusy, \ jane, \ dianna \rangle$$

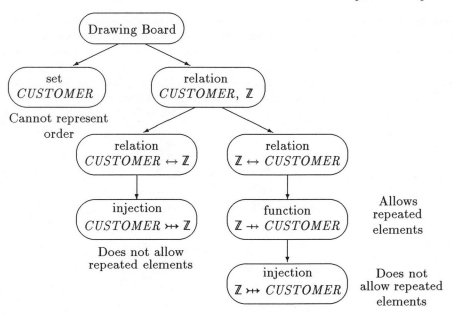

Figure 9.4: The exploration of alternatives in the development of a model of a queue

The elements of the sequence are listed between angle brackets in the order in which they occur in the sequence. The empty sequence is denoted $\langle\rangle$.

To generalize, we can model a queue or any ordered collection by constructing a function with a domain that consists of a subrange of the integers. The range should start at 1 and proceed up to the length of the queue or list. A sequence of n elements will thus have a domain of $1 \ldots n$. Furthermore, any function with a domain $1 \ldots n$ and target X will be a sequence over X of length n.

9.1   Sequence definition

The set of all finite sequences over a set X is defined as the set of finite partial functions from $\mathbb{N}$ to X where the domain of the function consists of consecutive numbers starting from 1 and proceeding up to some finite number.

$$\operatorname{seq} X == \{f : \mathbb{N} \nrightarrow X \mid \operatorname{dom} f = 1 \ldots \#f\}$$

The predicate $\operatorname{dom} f = 1 \ldots \#f$ may seem a little strange since it appears to define the domain of f in terms of the size of f and one might imagine that we would need to know the domain of f in order to determine the number of maplets in f. We can avoid this potential confusion if we remember that the predicate is a condition that is true if and only if f is a sequence and $1 .. \#f$ is not a formula by which we can calculate $\operatorname{dom} f$. Notice that the definition of seq is generic in the parameter X which stands for a set which is often a type. So for example, the set of sequences of integers is $\operatorname{seq} \mathbb{Z}$ and the set of sequences of natural numbers is $\operatorname{seq} \mathbb{N}$. The definition specifies that sequences are finite. Finite sequences have some useful properties not shared by infinite sequences; for example, a finite sequence always has a well-defined last element.

Example 9.1 A list of directions to the train station might be:

> 1st on the right
> 2nd on the left
> 1st on the right
> 3rd on the left

This list of directions cannot be modelled as a set. Firstly, the order of the directions is important and secondly, one direction:

> 1st on the right

is present twice, in the first and third positions. The list can, however, be modelled as a sequence. □

Exercise 9.1 Write the following using sequence notation.

i. $\{3 \mapsto fran, 1 \mapsto margaret, 2 \mapsto dorrie, 4 \mapsto janet\}$

ii. $\{4 \mapsto jane, 3 \mapsto niah, 1 \mapsto niah, 2 \mapsto vicki\}$

iii. $\{x : \mathbb{N} \mid x \leq 6 \bullet x + 1 \mapsto 6 - x\}$

□

Exercise 9.2 Explain why $\{4 \mapsto jane, 5 \mapsto chris, 1 \mapsto niah, 2 \mapsto vicki\}$ is not a sequence. □

Exercise 9.3 If the sequence s represents a queue of customers, give an expression equal to the set of customers in the queue. □

9.2 Sequence operations

Recall that when we studied operations on functions in Chapter 7, the point was made that a function is a relation and therefore all the operations that can be applied to relations can also be applied to functions. Given that a sequence is a function, it follows, by the same reasoning, that all relation and function operations are applicable to sequences.

Indexing

Since a sequence is a function, it is possible to index an item of the sequence by function application. For example, if:

$$s = \langle fran, margaret, dorrie, linda \rangle$$

then:

$$s\ 1 = fran$$
$$s\ 3 = dorrie$$

In general, the ith item of the sequence s is $s\ i$. Obviously $s\ i$ is defined only if $i \in \text{dom}\ s$, which is to say $i \in 1 \mathrel{..} \#s$.

Length

The length of a sequence is the number of elements it contains. For example, the length of:

$$\langle fran, margaret, dorrie, linda \rangle$$

is four and the length of $\langle \rangle$ is zero.

Given that a sequence is a function in which each element is a maplet, we can count the elements of the sequence by counting the maplets in the function. But a function is simply a set of maplets and so the number of maplets is in fact the cardinality of the set. The operation that provides the cardinality of a set is $\#$ and so the length of the sequence s is:

$$\#s$$

Head and tail

To motivate the *head* and *tail* operations let us return to the problem of modelling the supermarket queue. If we model the queue as a sequence s then the customer at the front or head of the queue is $s\ 1$ and *head s* means precisely $s\ 1$.

To complement the *head* operation, we define an operation *tail* that specifies the queue remaining once the first customer has left. Again, if the sequence s models the queue then *tail s* is simply the sequence without the first element.

In order to define *tail* we might reason along the following lines. A sequence is a set of maplets and so we can use the set difference operation to define the set of maplets except for the first maplet. For example, given:

$$s = \{1 \mapsto michele, 2 \mapsto lynne, 3 \mapsto barbara, 4 \mapsto derryn\}$$

then:

$$s \setminus \{1 \mapsto michele\} = \{2 \mapsto lynne, 3 \mapsto barbara, 4 \mapsto derryn\}$$

The example clearly shows the problem with this line of reasoning:

$$\{2 \mapsto lynne, 3 \mapsto barbara, 4 \mapsto derryn\}$$

is not a sequence because the domain is not the set $1 \mathbin{..} n$ for some n. We must construct a sequence from s by taking the successive elements of s starting from the second element. In other words, we require the sequence:

$$\{1 \mapsto lynne, 2 \mapsto barbara, 3 \mapsto derryn\}$$

which is the sequence:

$$\{1 \mapsto s(2), 2 \mapsto s(3), 3 \mapsto s(4)\}$$

The ith element of the required sequence is $i \mapsto s(i+1)$, where $i \in \#s - 1$.

Exercise 9.4 Give an example of a sequence from which a first element cannot be removed. □

We now give the formal definitions of the *head* and *tail* operations. Since these operations are defined only for non-empty sequences, it is convenient to define this set.

$$\mathrm{seq}_1 X == \mathrm{seq}\, X \setminus \{\langle\rangle\}$$

The definitions are:

$$
\begin{array}{l}
\boxed{\begin{array}{l}
[X] \\
\hline
head : \mathrm{seq}_1\ X \ \rightarrow\ X \\
tail : \mathrm{seq}_1\ X \ \rightarrow\ \mathrm{seq}\ X \\
\hline
\forall\ s : \mathrm{seq}_1\ X \bullet \\
\quad head\ s\ =\ s\ 1\ \wedge \\
\quad tail\ s\ =\ \{n : \mathbb{Z} \mid n \in 1 \mathbin{..} \#s - 1 \bullet n \ \mapsto s(n+1)\}
\end{array}}
\end{array}
$$

Notice that these operations are generic and so are defined for sequences over a set of any type.

Example 9.2 Programmers will be familiar with the stack data structure. A stack is essentially a first in, last out (FILO) queue in which the elements in the queue are items of data. We have used sequences to model supermarket queues which have a FIFO (first in, first out) discipline but we can also use sequences to model queues with a FILO discipline. A simple way to do this is to add elements to the front of the sequence and remove them also from the front. This will ensure that items are removed in the reverse order in which they were added.

A stack that is designed to be stored in a computer's finite memory will have a maximum length. If the stack has reached its maximum length then no new items of data can be added to it. An attempt to add an additional item to such a stack leads to a stack overflow error.

Of course a stack may be empty, in which case it is an error to attempt to remove an item from it. This error condition is known as stack underflow. Let us model a stack on which we can perform the removal and addition operations just described. It is customary to call them pop and push respectively.

Pop: Remove an item from the stack and output this item. Fail if the stack is empty and report an error message.

Push: Add an item to the stack. Fail if the stack is full and report an error message.

We will model the stack as a sequence on a given set:

$[DATA]$

We have a set of reports:

$REPORT ::= success \mid stackUnderflow \mid stackOverflow$

and the maximum length for a stack is:

$\mid \quad stackLimit : \mathbb{N}$

Every stack will have a length which is less than or equal to this number.

$$
\begin{array}{|l}
\hline
\_Stack \underline{\hspace{6cm}} \\
stack : \text{seq } DATA \\
\hline
\#stack \leq stackLimit \\
\hline
\end{array}
$$

If the stack is not empty then we remove the item at the front.

$$
\begin{array}{|l}
\hline
\_RemoveItem \underline{\hspace{5cm}} \\
\Delta Stack \\
item! : DATA \\
r! : REPORT \\
\hline
stack \neq \langle \rangle \\
stack' = tail\ stack \\
item! = head\ stack \\
r! = success \\
\hline
\end{array}
$$

The reader should establish that the precondition for *RemoveItem* contains the predicates:

$$stack \neq \langle\rangle \land$$
$$\#stack \leq stackLimit$$

An attempt to remove an item from an empty stack produces an error report.

```
┌─ StackEmpty ────────────────────────────
│ ΞStack
│ r! : REPORT
├─────────────────────────────────────────
│ stack = ⟨⟩
│ r! = stackUnderflow
└─────────────────────────────────────────
```

The pop operation can be defined as:

$$Pop \; \hat{=} \; RemoveItem \lor StackEmpty$$

$\square$

We have not yet covered the sequence operation that will allow us to define *push* and so we define *push* later.

Exercise 9.5 * Define the operations *last* and *front*, analogous to *head* and *tail* respectively. $\square$

Reverse

The reverse of a sequence is formed by taking the elements of a sequence in reverse order. For example:

$$rev \; \langle fran, pam, dorrie, barbara \rangle \; = \; \langle barbara, dorrie, pam, fran \rangle$$

The reverse of an empty sequence is the empty sequence.

To introduce the formal definition of reverse, consider the following example. If:

$$s = \langle fran, pam, dorrie, barbara \rangle$$

then:

$$rev \; s = \{1 \mapsto barbara, 2 \mapsto dorrie, 3 \mapsto pam, 4 \mapsto fran\}$$
$$= \{1 \mapsto s(4), 2 \mapsto s(3), 3 \mapsto s(2), 4 \mapsto s(1)\}$$
$$= \{1 \mapsto s(\#s), 2 \mapsto s(\#s - 1), 3 \mapsto s(\#s - 2), 4 \mapsto s(\#s - 3)\}$$

The ith element of the reverse of s is $i \mapsto s(\#s - i + 1)$, where $i \in 1 .. \#s$.

The following is the formal definition of the reverse operation.

$$
\begin{array}{|l}
\hline
\;[X]\!= \\
\;rev : \text{seq } X \;\rightarrow\; \text{seq } X \\
\hline
\;\forall\; s : \text{seq } X \;\bullet\; rev\; s \;=\; \{i : \mathbb{Z} \mid i \in 1 \mathinner{..} \#s \bullet i \;\mapsto\; s(\#s - i + 1)\} \\
\hline
\end{array}
$$

Exercise 9.6 Give alternative definitions for the operations *last* and *front* from the previous exercise, this time using only the operations *rev*, *head* and *tail*.   □

Concatenation

Concatenation is the operation of joining two sequences end to end to form a single sequence. If we wanted to define the concatenation operation we might be tempted to think along the following lines. Given that a sequence is a set of maplets, all of the set operations can be applied to sequences. In particular we can take the union of two sequences; for example, given:

$$s = \langle giusy, dorrie, linda \rangle$$
$$t = \langle giusy, linda \rangle$$

then:

$$s \cup t = \{1 \mapsto giusy, 2 \mapsto dorrie, 2 \mapsto linda, 3 \mapsto linda\}$$

Clearly $s \cup t$ is not a sequence because the number 2 is mapped to both *dorrie* and *linda* which in fact means that $s \cup t$ is not even a function. This example illustrates why the union of two sequences is not necessarily a sequence.

Exercise 9.7 * Describe the circumstances in which the union of two sequences is a sequence and the intersection of two sequences is a sequence.
□

The concatenation of two sequences s and t is written as:

$$s \frown t$$

Returning to our example sequences:

$$s \frown t = \langle giusy, dorrie, linda, giusy, linda \rangle$$

In maplet form:

$$
\begin{aligned}
s \frown t &= \{1 \mapsto giusy, 2 \mapsto dorrie, 3 \mapsto linda, 4 \mapsto giusy, 5 \mapsto linda\} \\
&= \{1 \mapsto s(1), 2 \mapsto s(2), 3 \mapsto s(3), 4 \mapsto t(1), 5 \mapsto t(2)\} \\
&= s \cup \{4 \mapsto t(1), 5 \mapsto t(2)\} \\
&= s \cup \{(1 + \#s) \mapsto t(1), (2 + \#s) \mapsto t(2)\}
\end{aligned}
$$

The reader should now be able to understand the formal definition of the concatenation operation given below.

$$
\begin{array}{|l}
\underline{}[X]\underline{} \\
\hline
\_ \frown \_ : \operatorname{seq} X \times \operatorname{seq} X \rightarrow \operatorname{seq} X \\
\hline
\forall \; s, t : \operatorname{seq} X \; \bullet \; s \frown t = s \cup \{ n : \mathbb{Z} \mid n \in 1 \,..\, \#t \bullet (n + \#s) \mapsto t \; n \}
\end{array}
$$

Notice that both of the sequences to be concatenated must be over the same set.

Example 9.3 Now that we have covered concatenation we can use this operation to complete our data stack of Example 9.2. We have yet to define the push operation for adding an item of data to the stack. Our stack is modelled as a sequence and we use the concatenation operation to describe the sequence that models the stack after an item has been added to the front.

$$
\begin{array}{|l}
\underline{}AddItem\underline{} \\
\Delta Stack \\
item? : DATA \\
r! : REPORT \\
\hline
stack' = \langle item? \rangle \frown stack \\
r! = success
\end{array}
$$

An item can be added only if the stack has not reached the maximum length, but notice that the subcase property:

$$\#stack < stackLimit$$

is implied by the state invariant on the after-state and so is not explicitly written in the schema. The reader should check the precondition of *AddItem* to confirm the presence of the subcase property.

An attempt to add an item to a full stack produces an error report.

$$
\begin{array}{|l}
\underline{}StackFull\underline{} \\
\Xi Stack \\
r! : REPORT \\
\hline
\#stack = stackLimit \\
r! = stackOverflow
\end{array}
$$

Again, the reader should check the precondition of *StackFull* and confirm the presence of $\#stack = stackLimit$. We can now define the push operation.

$$Push \mathrel{\widehat{=}} AddItem \lor StackFull$$

□

Exercise 9.8 Give a concise description of $\langle head\ s\rangle \frown tail\ s$ where s is a non-empty sequence.   □

Exercise 9.9 * Define a generic operation to remove the ith and all successive elements from a sequence.   □

Exercise 9.10 * Define a generic operation to remove the ith element from a sequence.   □

9.3   Example: queues at the airport

The following example illustrates the use of sequences for modelling passenger queues.

Informal description

On alighting from the aircraft, international passengers must queue at passport control and then at customs before entering the country. Each queue has a FIFO (first in, first out) discipline. The queues follow each other in the sense that each passenger must pass through the passport queue before joining the customs queue. We wish to specify the process of entering the country by specifying how passengers move through the two queues. In brief, the operations the specification must define are:

> **Join passport queue:** A passenger joins the passport control queue at the end.
>
> **Leave customs:** A passenger leaves the customs queue from the front.
>
> **Move from passport control to customs:** The passenger at the front of the passport control queue leaves to join the end of the customs queue.

There is no single operation by which a passenger can move from the customs queue back to the passport queue. We do not want to specify that this can never happen, as it might happen through a succession of operations, but we are not going to model this movement as a single operation. Table 9.1 describes the required operations in terms of input, output and subcase properties. In addition to a report, two operations output a passenger. The output is not defined in some cases.

Operation	Input	Subcase property	Output	Report
Join passport queue	Passenger	Passenger not in a queue	*None*	Success
		Passenger in passport queue	*None*	In passport
		Passenger in customs queue	*None*	In customs
Leave customs	*None*	Customs queue not empty	Passenger	Success
		Customs queue empty	*Undef*	Empty customs
Move from passport control to customs	*none*	Passport queue not empty	Passenger	Success
		Passport queue empty	*Undef*	Empty passport

Table 9.1: The required operations in terms of input, output and subcase condition

Developing the state

Given that we have two queues to model, it would seem sensible to define a state consisting of two sequences. The elements of each sequence will consist of passengers. As sensible as our decision seems, we should nonetheless take a moment to consider whether a state consisting of two sequences will be an adequate model for the operations we require. In particular, we should study Table 9.1 to reassure ourselves that we can specify the subcase properties and outputs of each operation and perform an appropriate state change. In addition, we should convince ourselves that we can express the state invariant.

Some subcases require that we specify an empty queue and this can be specified as an empty sequence. Other subcases require that we specify that a given passenger is not in either queue. An element is a member of a sequence if it is in the range of the sequence. Two operations must output a passenger. In each case the required passenger is easily obtained because the passenger is at the front of a queue. In the model, we simply output the head of the appropriate sequence. When a passenger joins a queue, we can add that passenger to the end of the corresponding sequence using the concatenation operation. When a passenger leaves a queue we can define the remaining queue as the tail of the corresponding sequence. These initial design decisions should be recorded, and we have done so in Table 9.2.

A model consisting of two sequences seems to be a sensible choice but we should also check that we can restrict the possible values of the state in the

Operation	Input	Subcase property	State change	Output
Join passport queue	Passenger	Passenger not in a queue	Add to sequence end	*None*
		Passenger in passport queue	*None*	*None*
		Passenger in customs queue	*None*	*None*
Leave customs	*None*	Customs queue not empty	Tail sequence	Passenger at head of sequence
		Customs queue empty	*None*	*Undef*
Move from passport control to customs	*None*	Passport queue not empty	Add to sequence end, tail sequence	Passenger at head of sequence
		Passport queue empty	*None*	*Undef*

Table 9.2: The required operations in terms of input, output, subcase conditions and state change

model to those that represent possible states of passenger queues at the airport. For example, a sequence may contain a single element repeated at different positions. An airport queue, however, will not contain any passenger more than once. In fact we can disallow repeated elements by specifying that the sequence is an injective function. We must also specify that any passenger who is in one sequence is not in the other, that is, that the ranges of the sequences are disjoint.

The specification

Basic types and global variables

We require a set to model passengers. The two queues will be modelled as sequences of elements from this set:

[*PASSENGER*]

Operations that provide reports will provide an element from the following set:

$$REPORT ::= success$$
$$\mid \quad inPassport$$
$$\mid \quad inCustoms$$
$$\mid \quad emptyPassport$$
$$\mid \quad emptyCustoms$$

State of the system

We need a sequence to model the queue for passport control and another for customs. The sequence definition is generic and so we must instantiate the definition with the type of the elements to be used to model the queue.

$$passportQueue : \text{seq } PASSENGER$$
$$customsQueue : \text{seq } PASSENGER$$

No passenger can appear in any queue more than once. A sequence which is also an injective function contains no repeated elements.

$$passportQueue \in \mathbb{Z} \rightarrowtail PASSENGER$$
$$customsQueue \in \mathbb{Z} \rightarrowtail PASSENGER$$

It is convenient to define injective sequences generically. The Z library provides:

$$\text{iseq } X == \text{seq } X \cap (\mathbb{N} \rightarrowtail X)$$

hence we will declare the state components as:

$$passportQueue : \text{iseq } PASSENGER$$
$$customsQueue : \text{iseq } PASSENGER$$

No passenger is in both queues.

$$\text{ran } passportQueue \cap \text{ran } customsQueue = \varnothing$$

The state is thus:

```
┌─ AirportQueues ──────────────────────────────
│ passportQueue : iseq PASSENGER
│ customsQueue : iseq PASSENGER
├──────────────────────────────────────────────
│ ran passportQueue ∩ ran customsQueue = ∅
└──────────────────────────────────────────────
```

Initial state

The initial state is two empty queues.

```
┌─ InitAirportQueues ─────────────────────────────────────
│ AirportQueues'
├─────────────────────────────────────────────────────────
│ passportQueue' = ⟨⟩
│ customsQueue' = ⟨⟩
└─────────────────────────────────────────────────────────
```

We must check that this state is possible, that is, that it satisfies the state invariant. An empty sequence is a member of the partial injective sequences and the intersection of two empty sets is empty, so there is no problem here.

Operations

A passenger can join the passport queue if that passenger is not already in either queue.

```
┌─ JoinPassportOK ────────────────────────────────────────
│ ΔAirportQueues
│ p? : PASSENGER
│ r! : REPORT
├─────────────────────────────────────────────────────────
│ p? ∉ ran passportQueue ∪ ran customsQueue
│ passportQueue' = passportQueue ⌢ ⟨p?⟩
│ customsQueue' = customsQueue
│ r! = success
└─────────────────────────────────────────────────────────
```

Exercise 9.11 * Can we replace the predicate $p? \notin$ ran $passportQueue \cup$ ran $customsQueue$ with $p? \notin$ ran $passportQueue$ and preserve the meaning of $JoinPassportOK$?   □

A passenger cannot join the passport queue if that passenger is already in the passport queue or the customs queue. We distinguish between these two cases.

```
┌─ InPassportQueue ───────────────────────────────────────
│ ΞAirportQueues
│ p? : PASSENGER
│ r! : REPORT
├─────────────────────────────────────────────────────────
│ p? ∈ ran passportQueue
│ r! = inPassport
└─────────────────────────────────────────────────────────
```

The precondition of this partial operation clearly contains:

$$p? \in \text{ran } passportQueue$$

and the precondition of:

_InCustomsQueue_____
$\Xi AirportQueues$
$p? : PASSENGER$
$r! : REPORT$

$p? \in \mathrm{ran}\ customsQueue$
$r! = inCustoms$

---

contains:

$$p? \in \mathrm{ran}\ customsQueue$$

We can define the operation of joining the passport queue as:

$$JoinPassport \;\hat{=}\; JoinPassportOK \vee InPassportQueue \vee InCustomsQueue$$

By explicitly constructing the precondition, the reader should check our intuition that because a passenger is either in one queue or no queue then *JoinPassport* is total.

The partial operations for leaving the customs queue are similar to the operations for joining the passport queue just defined. A passenger may leave the customs queue if that passenger is at the front of the customs queue.

_LeaveCustomsOK_____
$\Delta AirportQueues$
$p! : PASSENGER$
$r! : REPORT$

$\langle p!\rangle \frown customsQueue' = customsQueue$
$passportQueue' = passportQueue$
$r! = success$

Notice that $p!$ must be at the front of *customsQueue* because this queue is equal to $\langle p!\rangle \frown customsQueue'$. If we had used the more obvious predicate *head customsQueue* $= p!$ we would require additional predicates to specify that *customsQueue* is not empty and to specify the value of *customsQueue'*.

The precondition of this partial operation contains the predicate:

$$\exists\, customsQueue' : \mathrm{iseq}\ PASSENGER;\ p! : PASSENGER \bullet$$
$$\langle p!\rangle \frown customsQueue' = customsQueue$$

which is equivalent to *customsQueue* $\neq \langle\rangle$ because there is no constraint on the value of $p!$.

Of course, no one can leave the customs queue if it is empty.

```
┌─ CustomsEmptyQueue ──────────────────────────────────
│  ΞAirportQueues
│  r! : REPORT
├──────────────────────────────────────────────────────
│  customsQueue = ⟨⟩
│  r! = emptyCustoms
└──────────────────────────────────────────────────────
```

We can define the operation to leave the customs queue as:

$$LeaveCustoms \ \widehat{=}\ LeaveCustomsOK \ \lor \ CustomsEmptyQueue$$

and since *LeaveCustoms* is total with no inputs, we would expect the precondition to be the state invariant.

The third operation required must model the movement of a passenger from passport control to customs. Anyone leaving the passport queue must join the customs queue. If we think about this state change in operational terms, which is to say in terms of how the state change is composed from smaller state changes, then we would proceed along the following lines. Firstly, we would identify the passenger at the front of the passport queue in the state before the operation, first checking of course that the passport queue is not empty.

$$\exists\, p : PASSENGER \bullet$$
$$passportQueue \neq \langle\rangle \land p = head\ passportQueue$$

Secondly, we would specify that in the state after the operation, this passenger is at the end of the customs queue.

$$customsQueue' = customsQueue \frown \langle p \rangle$$

This operational way of thinking about state change comes naturally to computer programmers who are familiar with procedural languages. The technique of solving a problem by breaking it down into subproblems is a sensible one to use when writing command sequences to control a machine. In writing logical predicates, however, we are concerned only with the way in which they constrain the values of variables. If we are biased to see a specification problem in operational terms we may fail to see the simple solution.

For example, let us reconsider the problem of moving a passenger from the front of the passport queue to the end of the customs queue. This movement means that passengers essentially move through each queue in turn, in effect as if they were moving through a single long queue. In fact, the concatenation of the two queues remains constant. The relative size of each queue, however, is affected. The passport queue size decreases by one and the customs queue increases by one. This provides us with an elegant way of specifying the transfer of a passenger from one queue to another.

```
┌─ PassportToCustomsOK ────────────────────────────────────
│ ΔAirportQueues
│ r! : Report
├──────────────────────────────────────────────────────────
│ customsQueue' ⌢ passportQueue' = customsQueue ⌢ passportQueue
│ #passportQueue − #passportQueue' = 1
│ r! = success
└──────────────────────────────────────────────────────────
```

Notice that $passportQueue \neq \langle \rangle$ is implicit in the above schema because the property cannot be true when $\#passportQueue = 0$.

No passenger can move from the passport queue to the customs queue if the passport queue is empty.

```
┌─ PassportQueueEmpty ─────────────────────────────────────
│ ΞAirportQueues
│ r! : Report
├──────────────────────────────────────────────────────────
│ passportQueue = ⟨⟩
│ r! = emptyPassport
└──────────────────────────────────────────────────────────
```

The operation to move from the passport queue to the customs queue is thus:

$$PassportToCustoms \; \widehat{=} \; PassportToCustomsOK \lor PassportQueueEmpty$$

and this operation is clearly total.

Exercise 9.12 ** Extend the example to include passengers leaving the aircraft and joining the queue at passport control. □

Exercise 9.13 ** Extend the example to specify two queues at the customs, a green 'nothing to declare' queue and a red 'something to declare' queue. Once a passenger has joined one of these queues, he or she cannot move to the other queue. □

Exercise 9.14 ** Extend the example to allow a passenger to leave either queue without having passed to the front. A passenger can thus leave the queue from the middle, and rejoin the same or some other queue at the end. You will find the result of Exercise 9.10 useful. □

Chapter 10

Bags

In many modelling situations there is a need to model collections of elements in which a given element may appear several times. We know that repeated elements are not possible in a set but are possible in a sequence. The elements of a sequence are ordered but this is not always required. For example, consider a basket of groceries which contains, for the sake of argument, a loaf of bread, three eggs, two bottles of wine and two tubs of yogurt. We know that if we attempt to model this basket of groceries as a set expression, that is:

$$\{bread, egg, egg, egg, wine, wine, yogurt, yogurt\}$$

then we 'lose' any repeated elements and the above set is in fact equal to the set:

$$\{bread, egg, wine, yogurt\}$$

If we decide to model the basket of groceries using a sequence then we might have the sequence:

$$\langle bread, egg, egg, egg, wine, wine, yogurt, yogurt\rangle$$

and although in this model we do not 'lose' any repeated elements, this model does impose an order on the grocery items which is not present in the real basket of groceries.

We might wonder if there is any harm in imposing an order on an unordered collection. After all, the sequence model can be used to answer questions about which items are in the basket of groceries and how many items the basket contains. The sequence model would not be very convenient, however, for testing whether two grocery baskets contained the same items since the same basket might be represented by different sequences. Recall the discussion concerning the advantages of simplicity in the model in §1.4. This is not to say that models that contain information not present in the subject of the specification cannot serve a useful purpose; see §12.2 for an example where sequences are used to model sets.

253

10.1   Description and definition

The Z library provides a means by which unordered collections with repeated elements can be modelled; such collections are called bags. The basket of groceries given above could be modelled as the bag:

$$[\![bread, egg, egg, egg, wine, wine, yogurt, yogurt]\!]$$

where the elements of the bag are enclosed between $[\![\;]\!]$. Obviously, the order in which the items of the bag are listed is not important and so the bag modelling the grocery basket could equally well have been written as:

$$[\![yogurt, bread, wine, egg, wine, egg, yogurt, egg]\!]$$

The empty bag is written as $[\![\;]\!]$.

A bag is not a new type but is a specific kind of function. In this respect a bag is like a sequence in that it too is not a type but a special kind of function. An obvious way of using a function to model an unordered collection of possibly repeated elements is to associate each element with a number representing the number of times that element is repeated in the collection. This association is best modelled as a function since for each element we associate at most a single number. The bag:

$$[\![bread, egg, egg, egg, wine, wine, yogurt, yogurt]\!]$$

is thus the function:

$$\{ bread \mapsto 1, egg \mapsto 3, wine \mapsto 2, yogurt \mapsto 2 \}$$

If we assume that there is some given set $GROCERY$ then a bag of elements from this set is a partial function from $GROCERY$ to the positive numbers. In other words, the set of all bags of elements from the set $GROCERY$ is the set of all partial functions from $GROCERY$ to $\mathbb{N}_1$. The notation for declaring bags is given in the definition below:

$$\text{bag } GROCERY == GROCERY \nrightarrow \mathbb{N}_1$$

and generically, bags can be defined as:

$$\text{bag } X == X \nrightarrow \mathbb{N}_1$$

where X is a generic parameter which stands for a set of elements.

Exercise 10.1 Write the following using bag notation:

   i. $\{ beans \mapsto 3, pasta \mapsto 1, cheese \mapsto 2 \}$

   ii. $\{ x : \mathbb{N} \mid x \leq 4 \bullet x \mapsto x + 1 \}$

□

Exercise 10.2 Write the following bags using maplet notation:

   i. $[\![milk, bun, milk, bun, apple]\!]$

  ii. $[\![3, 3, 0, 4, 2, 2, 1, 3, 2, 1, 4, 0]\!]$

□

Exercise 10.3 * Write the following bags using set comprehension notation:

   i. $[\![1, 1, 2, 2, 2, 3, 3, 3, 3]\!]$

  ii. $[\![3, 3, 0, 4, 2, 2, 1, 1, 2, 1, 1, 0, 0, 0, 0]\!]$

□

10.2 Bag operations

Bag membership

Bag membership is the analogue of set membership. An element that is a member of a bag appears in the bag one or more times. The notation for bag membership is shown in the example below:

$$wine \text{ in } [\![bread, egg, egg, egg, wine, wine, yogurt, yogurt]\!]$$

Note that:

$$wine \in \{bread \mapsto 1, egg \mapsto 3, wine \mapsto 2, yogurt \mapsto 2\}$$

is undefined because bag membership is not the same as set membership and this leads to a type error. The definition of bag membership is given in the generic definition below.

$$
\begin{array}{l}
\hline
[X] \\
\hline
\_ \text{ in } \_ : X \leftrightarrow \text{bag } X \\
\hline
\forall x : X;\ B : \text{bag } X \bullet \\
\qquad (x \text{ in } B \Leftrightarrow x \in \text{dom } B) \\
\hline
\end{array}
$$

The relation _ in _ contains the pair (x, B) if x is an element in the bag B, which is to say a member of the domain of the function B.

Bag element count

In addition to knowing whether an element occurs in a bag, it is obviously useful to be able to determine how many times an element is repeated in a bag. If the element is a member of the bag then we can simply apply the bag function to the element so, for example:

$$[\![bread, wine, wine, yogurt, yogurt]\!]\ wine = 2$$

If the element is not a member of the bag then the application of the bag to that element will be undefined, for example:

$$[\![bread, wine, wine, yogurt, yogurt]\!]\ egg \qquad\qquad - \text{ is undefined}$$

because *egg* is not in the domain of the bag. This suggests that it might be useful to have a different definition of a bag. Perhaps a bag should be a total function from some given set to $\mathbb{N}$ and any elements that are not in the bag should be mapped to zero. This alternative definition could be adopted but it would mean that a bag of elements from an infinite set would necessarily be an infinite function even though the bag might contain one member. Infinite sets are generally more difficult to work with since our intuition about the way in which sets behave is generally applicable only to finite sets.

The solution is to retain the standard bag definition but to provide a means to extend the bag function in the way described above. The function *count*, defined generically below, maps a bag to the required total function.

$$
\begin{array}{|l}
\underline{[X]} \\
\quad count : \mathrm{bag}\,X \rightarrowtail\!\!\!\rightarrow (X \rightarrow \mathbb{N}) \\
\hline
\quad \forall\, B : \mathrm{bag}\,X \bullet \\
\qquad count\ B = \{x : X \bullet x \mapsto 0\} \oplus B \\
\end{array}
$$

If:

$$GROCERY ::= egg \mid bread \mid wine \mid yogurt$$

then an example of the use of *count* is:

$$
\begin{aligned}
count\ &[\![bread, wine, wine, yogurt]\!] = \\
&\{egg \mapsto 0, bread \mapsto 1, wine \mapsto 2, yogurt \mapsto 1\}
\end{aligned}
$$

The function produced by *count* is normally applied to an element of the bag, for example:

$$count\ [\![bread, wine, wine, yogurt]\!]\ egg = 0$$

Recall from Chapter 7 that function application associates to the left and so the above example is in fact:

$$(count\ [\![bread, wine, wine, yogurt, yogurt]\!])\ egg = 0$$

Bag union

The union of two bags is the bag that contains every element that is a member of either bag. Moreover, the number of times the element occurs in the union is equal to the sum of the number of occurrences in each bag. The notation for bag union is shown in the following example:

$$[\![bread, wine, yogurt, yogurt]\!] \uplus [\![bread, wine, egg]\!] =$$
$$[\![bread, wine, yogurt, yogurt, bread, wine, egg]\!]$$

Notice that bag union behaves differently from set union. In particular, if L is a set and $x \in L$ then:

$$L \cup \{x\} = L$$

whereas if B is a bag and x in B then:

$$B \uplus [\![x]\!] \neq B$$

The definition of bag union is given in the generic definition below.

$$
\begin{array}{l}
\underline{[X]} \\
\_ \uplus \_ : \text{bag } X \times \text{bag } X \to \text{bag } X \\
\hline
\forall B, C : \text{bag } X;\ x : X \bullet \\
\quad count\ (B \uplus C)\ x = count\ B\ x + count\ C\ x
\end{array}
$$

The bag $B \uplus C$ is that bag in which the count of every element is equal to the sum of the counts of that element in each of the bags B and C.

Total number of elements in a bag

The size of a bag depends not only on the number of distinct elements it contains but also on the number of times each element is repeated. Let us consider some simple examples.

$$size[\![\ ]\!] = 0$$
$$size[\![bread, wine, wine, yogurt]\!] = 4$$

The size of the bag is in fact the sum of the numbers in the range of the bag. Given that the plus function can be applied to only a pair of numbers, we must find a way of successively applying the plus function to pairs of numbers drawn from the range of the bag. This suggests that a recursive definition is required. The base case is $size[\![\ ]\!] = 0$. In the general case, a number from the range is added to the sum of the remaining numbers, and we thus have:

$$
\begin{array}{l}
\underline{\hspace{0.5em}[X]}\\
\quad size : \text{bag } X \rightarrow \mathbb{N}\\
\hline
\quad \forall\, x : X;\ n : \mathbb{N};\ b : \text{bag } X \;\bullet\\
\qquad \text{dom } b \in \mathbb{F}\, X \;\wedge\\
\qquad size[\![\,]\!] = 0 \;\wedge\\
\qquad size(\{x \mapsto n\} \uplus b) = n + (size\ b)
\end{array}
$$

To ensure that this definition makes sense we must ensure that the bag does not contain an infinite number of different elements, because the total number of elements in an infinite set is not finite, that is, not a member of $\mathbb{N}$, (see §4.5).

Defining a bag from a sequence

We mentioned at the start of this chapter that a sequence was an example of a collection which allowed repeated elements. Unlike a bag, the elements of a sequence are ordered. If we take a sequence and discard the order of the elements then we have a bag. The Z library contains a function *items* which maps a sequence onto the bag of elements it contains, so for example:

$$
\begin{array}{l}
items\langle bread,\ bread,\ wine,\ wine,\ yogurt,\ yogurt\rangle =\\
\quad [\![bread,\ bread,\ wine,\ wine,\ yogurt,\ yogurt]\!]
\end{array}
$$

In order to define the function *items*, we must determine the number of times each element occurs in any given sequence. For each occurrence of an element x in a sequence there corresponds a maplet which maps a number to x; it is therefore sufficient to count these maplets. For a given sequence s and element x, this number can be expressed as:

$$
\#(s \rhd \{x\})
$$

or as:

$$
\#\{i : \text{dom } s \mid s\ i = x\}
$$

The definition of *items* is given in the generic definition below.

$$
\begin{array}{l}
\underline{\hspace{0.5em}[X]}\\
\quad items : \text{seq } X \rightarrow \text{bag } X\\
\hline
\quad \forall\, s : \text{seq } S;\ x : X \;\bullet\\
\qquad count\ (items\ s)\ x = \#\{i : \text{dom } s \mid s\ i = x\}
\end{array}
$$

10.3 Example: stock control system

Informal description

A specification is required for a system to control the levels of stock kept in a warehouse. Stock leaves the warehouse in response to requests for single items but new stock arrives in bulk in response to an order. There are two methods by which the warehouse can order new stock to replenish its stores. Every month a large order is produced which includes every item in the warehouse with a stock level below the specific minimum level for that item. The amount ordered for each item is twice the minimum level for that item.

The expectation is that the items ordered each month will accommodate all the requests that are made within a month. In practice, however, requests for items cannot be accurately predicted and sometimes the warehouse runs out of a particular item. There is thus a second method by which the warehouse can order items. Each day, the warehouse has the opportunity to make one order. The number of single items that can be ordered in this way is restricted because of transport logistics. The number of items must lie between two limits that are supplied to the warehouse at the time the order is placed. This means that the warehouse does not know from one day to the next how many items can be placed on a daily order.

The warehouse makes use of the daily ordering scheme to order requested items that it has not been able to supply. During the day, each unfulfilled request is placed on a queue. When a daily order is made, the requests at the front of the queue are dealt with first. Remaining requests are held over to the next day.

The specification should include the following operations:

Request item: Request a single item from the warehouse. This request may be denied if the item is not available, in which case the request is placed on the end of the daily order queue.

Daily order: The size of the order must lie between two given limits. If the queue of outstanding requests is not sufficiently large to achieve the minimum order level then no order is placed.

Monthly order: The size of the monthly order is determined by the number of items that have dropped below their reorder levels.

Stock arrival: New items are delivered to the warehouse. These items must be added to the stock and any requests on the order queue that can now be satisfied are removed. We assume that the timing of orders and deliveries is outside the scope of this specification.

Developing the model

A bag of items is an obvious way of modelling the stock level of each item held in the warehouse. We can use the operation of bag membership to specify that an item is present in the warehouse. Bag union can be used to define the operation for accepting new stock. The bag union operation can also be used to specify the removal of an item from the store since the union of the stock without the item and the bag containing the item is equal to the stock before the item is removed.

The queue of requests for unavailable items can be modelled as a sequence of items. To model the reorder levels we must associate a number with each distinct item of stock; a total function would be an obvious choice. The operations are described in Table 10.1.

Operation	Input	Subcase property	State change	Output	Report
Request item	An item	Item available	Remove item from store	*None*	*Undef*
		Item not available	Add item to order queue	*None*	Item to order
Daily order	Minimum, maximum order levels	Order queue too short	*None*	*Undef*	No order
		Order queue long enough	Order queue reduced	Items ordered	*Undef*
Monthly order	*None*	*None*	*None*	Bag of items to be ordered	*None*
Stock arrival	Bag of items	*None*	Items added to store; order queue purged	Bag of items removed from queue	*None*

Table 10.1: The operations including state change descriptions

The state invariant is that the queue of requests cannot contain a request for an item that is present in the warehouse.

Given sets and global variables

Each item held in the warehouse is a member of a given set:

$[ITEM]$

The reports required by some operations are:

$REPORT ::= noOrder \mid itemToOrder$

For each item there is a reorder level, the number below which an order for that item must be included in the monthly order. When an item is discontinued, the reorder level for that item will be zero.

$$\mid \; ReOrderLevel : ITEM \rightarrow \mathbb{N}$$

The state

The state consists of two observations: the stock held, modelled by a bag of *ITEM*, and the queue of requests for unavailable items, modelled by a sequence of *ITEM*. The state invariant that the queue of requests cannot contain a request for an item that is present in the warehouse is specified by stating that the set of items in the queue and the set in the warehouse have an empty intersection.

```
┌─ Warehouse ──────────────────────────
│ toOrder : seq ITEM
│ store : bag ITEM
├──────────────────────────────────────
│ ran toOrder ∩ dom store = ∅
└──────────────────────────────────────
```

The initial state is one in which the warehouse and the queue of requested items is empty.

```
┌─ InitWarehouse ──────────────────────
│ Warehouse'
├──────────────────────────────────────
│ toOrder = ⟨⟩
│ store = [[ ]]
└──────────────────────────────────────
```

Operations

Request item

If a request is made for an item that is in the store then the request is satisfied. Note the specification for the after-state value of the store as that bag which

when used to form the bag union with the requested item produces a bag
equal to the before-state value of the store. Note that this predicate implies
$i?$ in *store*.

$$
\begin{array}{l}
\rule{0pt}{1em}\\
\textit{RequestOK}\\[-0.3em]
\hline
\Delta\,\textit{Warehouse}\\
i? : \textit{ITEM}\\
\hline
store' \uplus [\![i?]\!] = store\\
toOrder' = toOrder
\end{array}
$$

We should construct the precondition for this operation to check that it
contains the expected predicate $i?$ in *store*. The precondition schema is:

$$
\begin{array}{l}
\textit{PreRequestOK}\\[-0.3em]
\hline
toOrder : \operatorname{seq} \textit{ITEM}\\
store : \operatorname{bag} \textit{ITEM}\\
i? : \textit{ITEM}\\
\hline
\operatorname{ran} toOrder \cap \operatorname{dom} store = \varnothing\\
\exists\, toOrder' : \operatorname{seq} \textit{ITEM};\ store' : \operatorname{bag} \textit{ITEM} \bullet\\
\quad \operatorname{ran} toOrder' \cap \operatorname{dom} store' = \varnothing \wedge\\
\quad store' \uplus [\![i?]\!] = store \wedge\\
\quad toOrder' = toOrder
\end{array}
$$

This can be simplified. By substituting *toOrder* for *toOrder'* we obtain:

$$
\begin{array}{l}
\textit{PreRequestOK}\\[-0.3em]
\hline
toOrder : \operatorname{seq} \textit{ITEM}\\
store : \operatorname{bag} \textit{ITEM}\\
i? : \textit{ITEM}\\
\hline
\operatorname{ran} toOrder \cap \operatorname{dom} store = \varnothing\\
\exists\, store' : \operatorname{bag} \textit{ITEM} \bullet\\
\quad \operatorname{ran} toOrder \cap \operatorname{dom} store' = \varnothing \wedge\\
\quad store' \uplus [\![i?]\!] = store
\end{array}
$$

The set dom *store'* must be a subset of dom *store* because $store' \uplus [\![i?]\!] = store$.
This means that:

$$(\operatorname{ran} toOrder \cap \operatorname{dom} store = \varnothing) \Rightarrow (\operatorname{ran} toOrder \cap \operatorname{dom} store' = \varnothing)$$

which means that the consequent can be removed since the antecedent is
present. If the bag *store'* exists then *store* is that bag with $i?$ included and so
$i?$ is in *store*. If $i?$ is in *store* then *store'* exists because it is the bag obtained
be removing $i?$ from *store*. The precondition is thus:

```
 ___ PreRequestOK _____
  toOrder : seq ITEM
  store : bag ITEM
  i? : ITEM
 _____
  ran toOrder ∩ dom store = ∅
  i? in store
```

which is what we would expect.

If the requested item is not in the store then it is added to the queue of items to order. The item is added to the end of the queue. We will ensure a first-in, first-out queue discipline by removing items from the front of the queue.

```
 ___ RequestToOrder _____
  Δ Warehouse
  i? : ITEM
  r! : REPORT
 _____
  toOrder' = toOrder ⌢ ⟨i?⟩
  store' = store
  r! = itemToOrder
```

The expected subcase property ¬ *i? in store* is implied by the state invariant which specifies that no item can be both in the order queue and in the store.

We will not construct the precondition for this operation since the exercise is very similar to that for *RequestOK*. In fact we will not construct the preconditions of any of the remaining operations since it would illustrate nothing new. The reader and anyone constructing a specification, however, is strongly encouraged to construct and simplify the preconditions of each operation defined.

The request operation can now be defined as:

$$Request \cong RequestOK \lor RequestToOrder$$

Daily order

Each day there is an opportunity to place an order for a number of items where the number must lie between two given numbers. The minimum order level is at least zero and the maximum order level must be higher than or equal to the minimum. Items for this order are taken from the queue of unfulfilled requests. If there are insufficient requests then an order is not placed.

```
┌─ OrderBelowMin ──────────────────────────────
│ Ξ Warehouse
│ minOrderLevel? : ℕ
│ maxOrderLevel? : ℕ
│ r! : REPORT
├──────────────────────────────────────────────
│ minOrderLevel? ≤ maxOrderLevel?
│ #toOrder < minOrderLevel?
│ r! = noOrdersTaken
└──────────────────────────────────────────────
```

The case in which there are sufficient orders in the queue is specified below.

```
┌─ OrderOK ─────────────────────────────────────
│ Δ Warehouse
│ minOrderLevel? : ℕ
│ maxOrderLevel? : ℕ
│ orders! : bag ITEM
├───────────────────────────────────────────────
│ minOrderLevel? ≤ maxOrderLevel?
│ #toOrder ≥ minOrderLevel?
│ ∃ toOrderSub : seq ITEM •
│      toOrderSub ⌢ toOrder' = toOrder ∧
│      #toOrderSub = min{#toOrder, maxOrderLevel?} ∧
│      orders! = items toOrderSub
│ store' = store
└───────────────────────────────────────────────
```

we thus have the operation:

$$DailyOrder \mathrel{\widehat{=}} OrderBelowMin \lor OrderOK$$

Exercise 10.4 * Investigate the precondition of the *DailyOrder* operation. □

Monthly order

Each month every item with a stock level below the reorder level is placed on an order. The number ordered of each such item is twice the reorder level.

```
┌─ MonthlyOrder ────────────────────────────────
│ Ξ Warehouse
│ orders! : bag ITEM
├───────────────────────────────────────────────
│ orders! = {i : ITEM | count store i < ReOrderLevel i •
│                          i ↦ 2 * (ReOrderLevel i)}
└───────────────────────────────────────────────
```

Delivery

The arrival of new stock can occur at any time. New stock is added to the store and any requests on the order queue for items that are now in the store are removed. Recall that the state invariant specifies that items in the store are not in the *toOrder* queue. We might thus specify:

```
┌─ Delivery ──────────────────────────────────────────
│ Δ Warehouse
│ delivery? : bag ITEM
├──────────────────────────────────────────────────────
│ store' = store ⊎ delivery?
└──────────────────────────────────────────────────────
```

in which case the value of *toOrder'* is any queue that satisfies the state invariant, perhaps the empty queue. This is unsatisfactory since we may lose orders for which no item exists in the warehouse. We must specify additional constraints on the value of *toOrder'*.

Items in the delivery are either entered into the store or output to satisfy a request on the *toOrder* queue. Items on the *toOrder* queue which are output are removed from this queue. The correct definition of *Delivery* is therefore:

```
┌─ Delivery ──────────────────────────────────────────
│ Δ Warehouse
│ delivery? : bag ITEM
│ orders! : bag ITEM
├──────────────────────────────────────────────────────
│ store ⊎ delivery? = store' ⊎ orders!
│ toOrder = toOrder' ⊎ orders!
└──────────────────────────────────────────────────────
```

Exercise 10.5 ** It seems a pity to not make use of the opportunity of a daily order simply because there have been insufficient requests for out-of-stock items. Think of a rational scheme for adding requests to the queue of outstanding requests in order to make the most of the daily order and respecify the stock control system. Note that the state invariant will require modification.
□

Chapter 11

Extended Example: Photocopier

The purpose of this chapter is to give another illustration of how the mathematical theory and the Z notation presented in the previous chapters can be applied in the development of a formal specification. We have chosen to specify a photocopier because it is a familiar machine for which a state-based model appears to be an intuitive choice. As usual we will describe the development of the model before formalizing it in the Z notation. The example is in two parts, the second being more challenging than the first.

A specification that captures the functionality of a basic photocopier is required. The specification should describe what the copier can do but should not be concerned with how the copier works or the specific way in which a user interacts with the copier. This kind of specification might be used in the early stages of the design of a photocopier.

11.1 Informal description of a photocopier

The copier accepts a single original document, up to A3 in size, and some money and produces a given number of copies. It is possible to set the number of copies required and to load the copier with paper. There is one size of paper tray, A4. There is a fixed price for each copy which may be zero, that is, copies may be free. The copier accepts money only if it consists of coins of given denominations and the copier attempts to give a refund for any unused money.

The copier has enlargement and reduction facilities. The enlargement facility requires the user to enter a percentage between 101% and 200%. The reduction facility is similar and the user is required to enter a percentage between 99% and 50%. In addition to these facilities, the user can control the scaling ratio by specifying the size of the original document to be either A4 or A3 (irrespective of the true size of the original). If the original document is specified to be A4 then the ratio is 100%, otherwise it is 71%.

The straightforward operation of the copier is simple enough but there are a number of boundary conditions to consider. If insufficient money has been inserted into the machine for the selected number of copies then the number of copies actually produced corresponds to the money inserted. In any case, the number of copies produced is always limited to the number of blank sheets held in the copier. It is possible to load paper into the copier but there is a maximum amount of paper that can be held. There is a limit to the amount of money that the copier can hold and excess coins, together with defective coins, are rejected.

11.2   Developing the model

As usual we will develop the model of the photocopier by a process of exploration. We will start with a very basic idea of what is required and then refine this idea until we have a model that is sufficiently developed for it to be formalized in the Z notation in a straightforward way.

Identifying the operations

Using the description given above we might begin the development of a state-based model by identifying the following activities as candidates for operations.

Load original: Present a document to the copier.

Set size of original: The size can be set to A4 or to A3.

Set copy number: Set the number of copies to be made from the original.

Enlarge: Set the scaling ratio between 101% and 200%.

Reduce: Set the scaling ratio between 99% and 50%.

Insert money: Coins are inserted into the copier; some or all of the coins may be rejected if they are defective or the copier is full.

Print: Produce the selected number of copies of some original.

Load paper: Load a given number of sheets of paper into the copier.

Refund money: Unused money is returned.

The operations listed above arise from thinking about how someone uses the copier but the purpose of the specification should dictate the operations the specification defines. Our purpose is to specify the functionality of the copier rather than how it is used and so we should use the above list as no more than a guide to identifying operations. Notice, for example, that there are a number of operations that enlarge or reduce the image. Given that our specification must describe the functionality of the copier, we need not concern ourselves with the variety of ways in which this function can be performed. The enlarge and reduce operations differ only in the value of their parameters and so these can be subsumed under a single operation which has a single parameter in the range 50% to 200%. Similarly, the operation to set the size of the original serves no function other than to provide input for the calculation of the scaling ratio. This suggests that we should subsume these various operations under a single operation to set the scaling ratio.

Moving on to consider the other operations, we would expect the money refund operation to be performed automatically and immediately after the print operation. Generally, when specifying operations in Z we specify what the operation does but not when the operation should be applied. If we want to specify that any refund is always given immediately after the print operation then one way to do this is to incorporate the refund into the print operation.

By reviewing our initial list of operations from the point of view of the functionality of the copier we have arrived at a collection of operations which are in keeping with the purpose of the specification.

Load original: Present a document to the copier.

Set copy number: Set the number of copies to be made from the original.

Set scale: Set the scaling ratio between 50% and 200%.

Insert money: Coins are inserted into the copier; some or all of the coins may be rejected.

Print: Produce a given number of scaled copies of some original, and refund any unused money.

Load paper: Load a given number of sheets of paper into the copier.

Refining the operations

Once an operation has been identified, the next step is to determine the input, output and subcase properties. We do this as usual without too much concern for how the operations will be specified. The print operation has possibly the most complex subcase properties, so let us consider this operation first. The number of copies produced by the print operation depends on the number

Subcase property	Excess money inserted	Exact money inserted	Insufficient money inserted
Sufficient paper	Print requested copies; give refund	Print requested copies	Print copies paid for
Insufficient paper	Print copies allowed by paper; give refund	Print copies allowed by paper; give refund	Print copies paid for or allowed by paper; refund, whichever is lower

Table 11.1: Analysing the subcases of the print operation

requested, the amount of blank paper in the machine and the money inserted. If there is enough paper and enough money we obtain the requested number of copies. If either of these two conditions is not met, however, we will receive fewer copies.

In Table 11.1 we have broken down the print operation into six subcases by taking each of two possibilities for the amount of paper present with each of three possibilities for the money inserted. From the table it can be seen that the most complex subcase occurs when there is both insufficient paper and insufficient money for the requested copies. In this situation we must determine the maximum number of copies that can be produced with the remaining paper, and bought with the money inserted, and pick the lower of these two numbers.

The case in which there is insufficient money but sufficient paper is a special case of the subcase just described. In this case, there is no harm in also determining the maximum that can be printed with the available paper. Thus we can treat these two subcases as one. In fact we can determine the number of copies in each of the six cases by always taking the minimum of three numbers: number of requested copies, number of sheets of copy paper and number of copies paid for.

The operation to load paper into the copier is complicated by the fact that there is a maximum amount of paper that can be held in the copier. Let us assume that the load paper operation has an input representing the number of sheets to be loaded. If there is not enough room to load all these sheets then we fill the paper tray and discard any excess sheets. It thus appears that there are two subcases to consider. We can, however, generalize them to a single case in which the amount of paper added is the minimum of the number of sheets input and the number of sheets required to fill the paper tray. Table 11.2 summarizes the operations that should be specified.

This brings us to the general issue of what exactly constitutes a subcase. An important point to bear in mind is that we should not equate the subcases identified in an analysis of an operation with the subcases we wish to specify, as there is no reason why they should be the same. In general, we can say that

Operation	Input	Subcase property	Output
Load original	An original	*None*	*None*
Set number of copies	Number of copies	*None*	*None*
Scale	A percentage	*None*	*None*
Insert money	Amount of money	*None*	Reject coins
Print	*None*	*None*	Number of scaled copies; refund
Load paper	Number of sheets	*None*	*None*

Table 11.2: The operations in terms of input, output and subcase properties

subcases are worth distinguishing when they are specified in very different ways with possibly different outputs. If, however, the specification of a number of subcases involves the use of very similar predicates then the specification may be simplified by treating these subcases as a single case.

When tackling a complex specification it is often helpful if the specification can be divided into a number of parts. In the case of the photocopier we notice that the reduction and enlargement facilities are largely independent of the other features provided. We will exploit this natural division to develop the specification in two parts. This will make the presentation clearer and allow us to illustrate the use of some of the schema operations described in Chapter 6. In the following sections we develop the specification for the part of the copier not concerned with scaling; this facility will be specified later.

Developing the state

Having expressed the required operations in terms of input, output and subcase condition, we are ready to develop the state of the model excluding the scaling facility. In contrast to the sports equipment example from Chapter 8, the copier does not provide any obvious clues as to the required given sets such as *CUSTOMER* or *EQUIP*. In the sports equipment example it was fairly obvious that the state should record the hiring of equipment; in the copier, however, it is not so obvious what the role of the state should be.

One approach to developing the state is to focus on the subject we are modelling (the copier), knowledge of which may suggest some obvious state observations. For example, the state might record the amount of paper in the machine. Examination of the subject to be specified is often a useful approach to take but it should not be regarded as definitive. We must bear in mind that the observations of the state provide the information with which operations

Operation	Input	State change	Output
Set number of copies	Number of copies	Define value of state variable	*None*
Insert money	Amount of money	Define value of state variable	Reject coins
Print	*None*	Subtract paper consumed and add money inserted minus refund	Number of copies; refund
Load paper	number of sheets	Add paper loaded subject to limit	*None*

Table 11.3: The operations including state change descriptions.

can be defined. State observations that do not play any useful part in the definition of any operation are redundant. Let us therefore develop the state by considering how the operations might be defined.

Consider the print operation. This operation requires several items of information including the required number of copies, the amount of copy paper present and the money inserted. None of these items are provided as input to the print operation, so they must be available from the state.

The observations of the required number of copies and the amount of paper present can each be modelled by integers. We know that any money inserted must consist of coins of given denominations. In a collection of coins, any coin can be repeated and so this suggests the use of a bag of coins. We must also introduce a set of coin denominations that can be inserted into the copier.

Inserted money, once it is used to pay for copies, is accumulated within the copier and so the total money held in the copier is also a necessary state observation. Overall, this suggests that the state should be represented by the following observations:

- the amount of paper available, an integer;

- the number of copies requested, an integer;

- the money previously paid into the copier, a bag of coins;

- the money credited for the next printing operation, a bag of coins.

Having decided on the necessary state observations and chosen a type for each, we should refine our description of the required operations given in Table 11.2. This is done in Table 11.3.

If we consider how each of the state changes listed in Table 11.3 can be specified we notice that in the print operation we must be able to calculate the number of copies bought with a given bag of coins. In the insert money operation, coins will be rejected if the money box is full and this implies we must be able to count coins. Let us therefore develop a model for coins.

One way of modelling coin denominations is to use numbers, each coin represented by its monetary value. This would not be a wise choice because a type checker could not detect meaningless expressions in which one coin is multiplied by another, say (see §1.5 and §6.1). We thus choose to use a given set *COIN*. We will, nonetheless, want to determine the monetary value of a bag of coins, which means that we must be able to determine the monetary value of each coin. We could do this by defining a function $COIN \rightarrow \mathbb{N}$.

At this point we might notice that once coins have been inserted into the copier and any defective coins rejected, the important state observation from the point of view of the print operation is the monetary value of the coins rather than the individual coins themselves. The coins can be added to the copier's coin box and are available if a refund is necessary. If the money credited for the next printing operation is represented as a number, the size of the state space will be reduced since many different bags of coins have the same monetary value. In general, we want to abstract away from any irrelevant information in building our model and we therefore change our earlier decision to model the money credited for the next print operation as a bag and use a number instead.

11.3 The specification

We are now in a position where we can begin to formalize the model and give a specification of the copier excluding the scaling facility.

Given sets

An amount of money is modelled as a bag of *COIN*.

$$COIN ::= \textit{five} \mid \textit{ten} \mid \textit{twenty}$$

Global variables

$$\textit{FullPaperTray} == 500$$

The price of a single copy is:

$$\mid \textit{Price} : \mathbb{N}$$

We have allowed the possibility that the price of a copy is zero pence. The money box is full when it holds 1000 coins.

$$\textit{FullCoinBox} == 1000$$

The following function determines the monetary value of each coin.

$$worth : COIN \rightarrow \mathbb{N}$$
$$worth = \{five \mapsto 5, ten \mapsto 10, twenty \mapsto 20\}$$

General theory

The function *size* defined in §10.2 can be used to count the number of coins in a bag. We require a function that determines the monetary value of a bag of coins. This function is similar to *size*:

$$value : \text{bag } COIN \rightarrow \mathbb{N}$$

$$\forall\, c : COIN;\ n : \mathbb{N};\ b : \text{bag } COIN \bullet$$
$$value\ [\![\ ]\!] = 0 \land$$
$$value(\{c \mapsto n\} \uplus b) = (worth\ c) * n + (value\ b)$$

Notice that we do not need to specify that infinite bags are excluded from the domain of *value* because *COIN* is finite.

The discussion of the print operation in §11.2 assumes that it is possible to establish the maximum number of copies that can be printed from a given credit. Essentially, this number can be found by dividing the credit by the price per copy but we must take care, given that the price can be zero. This number is given by the following function.

$$copiesBought : \mathbb{N} \rightarrow \mathbb{N}$$

$$copiesBought =$$
$$\{credit, copies : \mathbb{N} \mid$$
$$(\exists\, refund : \mathbb{N} \bullet$$
$$credit = Price * copies + refund \land refund < Price)$$
$$\lor$$
$$(Price = 0 \land copies = FullPaperTray)$$
$$\bullet\ credit \mapsto copies\}$$

The predicate:

$$\exists\, refund : \mathbb{N} \bullet$$
$$credit = Price * copies + refund \land refund < Price$$

is false when *Price* = 0 because there does not exist a suitable value for *refund* that will satisfy the predicate *refund* < *Price*. We have decided that the number of copies that have been paid for when the price per copy is zero should be the maximum number of copies that the copier can produce.

State

The state observations are the components of the schema below. The money available to pay for copies is represented by *credit*.

```
┌─ Copier ─────────────────────────────────────────────
│ paper : ℕ
│ requiredCopies : ℕ
│ money : bag COIN
│ credit : ℕ
├──────────────────────────────────────────────────────
│ paper ≤ FullPaperTray
│ requiredCopies > 0
│ size money ≤ FullCoinBox
└──────────────────────────────────────────────────────
```

The state invariant specifies that the paper tray holds a limited amount of paper, that the user cannot request a zero number of copies and that the total number of coins held in the copier is limited.

Initial state

For the initial state we can take a copier state in which no paper is loaded, no money held and the required number of copies is set to one.

```
┌─ InitCopier ─────────────────────────────────────────
│ Copier′
├──────────────────────────────────────────────────────
│ paper′ = 0
│ requiredCopies′ = 1
│ money′ = ⟦ ⟧
│ credit′ = 0
└──────────────────────────────────────────────────────
```

We must show, as always, that there exists a state that satisfies *InitCopier*. We have given the explicit values of the components of the initial state and we must therefore demonstrate that a state with these values satisfies the state invariant. Let us take the component *paper′*. The state invariant constrains the value of this component through the predicates:

$$paper′ \geq 0 \qquad \text{– from the declaration } paper′ : ℕ$$
$$paper′ \leq FullPaperTray$$

and it is clear that these are both true when $paper′ = 0$. The values of the remaining components of *InitCopier* can be checked in a similar manner.

Operations

Load paper

This operation loads a specific number of sheets of blank paper into the copier paper tray. The number of sheets is given by the input.

```
┌─ LoadPaper ─────────────────────────────────────────────────
│ Δ Copier
│ paperOffered? : ℕ
├─────────────────────────────────────────────────────────────
│ paper' = min {FullPaperTray, paper + paperOffered?}
│ requiredCopies' = requiredCopies
│ money' = money
│ credit' = credit
└─────────────────────────────────────────────────────────────
```

Note that there are no changes to any state observation other than the amount of paper loaded.

Intuitively, the *LoadPaper* operation appears to be total but we must take account of constraints on the input value. We construct the precondition schema in the usual way by hiding the after-state and output components of the *LoadPaper* schema to obtain:

```
┌─ PreLoadPaper ──────────────────────────────────────────────
│ paper : ℕ
│ requiredCopies : ℕ
│ money : bag COIN
│ credit : ℕ
│ paperOffered? : ℕ
├─────────────────────────────────────────────────────────────
│ paper ≤ FullPaperTray
│ requiredCopies > 0
│ size money ≤ FullCoinBox
│ ∃ paper', requiredCopies', credit' : ℕ;  money' : bag COIN •
│       paper' ≤ FullPaperTray ∧
│       requiredCopies' > 0 ∧
│       size money' ≤ FullCoinBox ∧
│       requiredCopies' = requiredCopies ∧
│       money' = money ∧
│       credit' = credit ∧
│       paper' = min {FullPaperTray, paper + paperOffered?}
└─────────────────────────────────────────────────────────────
```

We can simplify this schema considerably. For example, the predicate:

$$\exists\ requiredCopies' : \mathbb{N} \bullet$$
$$requiredCopies' > 0 \land$$
$$requiredCopies' = requiredCopies$$

is clearly true because *requiredCopies'* can be any positive number, so let it be *requiredCopies* which is greater than 0. This predicate can therefore be deleted because it is implied by *requiredCopies* > 0. From a state-based model viewpoint, we can argue that the need to establish a value for the number of required copies is no impediment to the *LoadPaper* operation because this observation simply retains its former value.

Similarly, we can simplify the following predicate:

$$\exists\, money' : \text{bag } COIN \bullet$$
$$size\ money' \leq FullCoinBox \wedge$$
$$money' = money \wedge$$
$$size\ money \leq FullCoinBox$$

by substituting *money* for *money'* to obtain the predicate:

$$size\ money \leq FullCoinBox$$

The predicate:

$$\exists\, paper' : \mathbb{N} \bullet$$
$$paper' \leq FullPaperTray \wedge$$
$$paper' = min\ \{FullPaperTray, paper + paperOffered?\}$$

requires a little more thought. We must show the existence of a non-negative value for *paper'*. The three numbers *FullPaperTray*, *paper* and *paperOffered?* are all non-negative and thus the minimum is defined. Moreover, this minimum value must be less than or equal to *FullPaperTray* and so the predicate is true. We can thus simplify the schema to obtain:

┌─ *PreLoadPaper* ─────────────────────────────
│ *paper* : $\mathbb{N}$
│ *requiredCopies* : $\mathbb{N}$
│ *money* : bag *COIN*
│ *credit* : $\mathbb{N}$
│ *paperOffered?* : $\mathbb{N}$
├───
│ *paper* $\leq$ *FullPaperTray*
│ *requiredCopies* > 0
│ *size money* $\leq$ *FullCoinBox*
└───

which is the state invariant together with the constraint on *paperOffered?*. This operation is not total; nonetheless, we will not worry about the possibility of negative values for *paperOffered?*. We will assume that factors outside the scope of this specification conspire to ensure that *paperOffered?* is never negative.

Set number of copies

This operation is very simple: a number is input and used to define the value of a state observation.

```
┌─ NumberOfCopies ──────────────────────────────────────
│ ΔCopier
│ copies? : ℕ
├──────────────────────────────────
│ paper' = paper
│ money' = money
│ credit' = credit
│ requiredCopies' = copies?
└──────────────────────────────────────────────────────
```

Note that the value of *requiredCopies'* is constrained to be greater than zero by the state invariant which is implicitly part of this schema. No other state observations change.

The precondition investigation for this operation is quite straightforward and left as an exercise.

Exercise 11.1 * Establish the precondition for the *NumberOfCopies* schema above.   □

Insert money

In the operation for inserting money we do not model the insertion of individual coins but a complete bag of coins. There is the possibility that coins will be rejected because they are defective or the copier coin box is full. We model the possibility of rejection only, not the cause; we do this by specifying that there exists some bag, possibly empty, of accepted coins. Because we do not specify a precise value for the output and the next state, the insert money operation is non-deterministic. There is no requirement in Z that operations should be deterministic. Whatever money is accepted is added to the copier coin box and credited for printing.

```
┌─ InsertMoney ─────────────────────────────────────────
│ ΔCopier
│ m? : bag COIN
│ reject! : bag COIN
├──────────────────────────────────
│ paper' = paper
│ requiredCopies' = requiredCopies
│ ∃ accept : bag COIN •
│         m? = accept ⊎ reject! ∧
│         money' = money ⊎ accept ∧
│         credit' = credit + value accept
└──────────────────────────────────────────────────────
```

Notice that the value of *money'* is constrained by the state invariant in order to ensure that the copier never holds more coins than *FullCoinBox*. Notice also that any residual credit is not lost.

We would expect the precondition investigation for this operation to reveal that there is an upper limit to the amount of money that can be inserted. The lower limit is of course zero.

Print

The operation for printing copies was considered in detail in §11.2 where we decided that the number of copies printed should be the minimum of the required number of copies, the number of sheets of copy paper available and the number of copies paid for. It was also decided that any refunds due should be paid out as part of the print operation.

We must now consider that the copier may not be able to give an exact refund because the required coins may not be available. In this case the refund consists of whatever coins are present in the copier with a value that is as close as possible to the refund due but which does not exceed it. In order to balance the accounts we have:

$$refund! \uplus money' = money$$

which also ensures that the refund must consist of coins that are present in the copier. To specify that the refund is as close as possible to the refund due we specify that a closer refund does not exist. If the refund is smaller than it should be then the user is left with a residual credit.

$$credit' + (value\ refund!) + Price * copies! = credit$$

In the after-state, the number of required copies is set to the number of copies requested but not printed, with the proviso that the number is not zero. This allows the user to insert more money or load more paper to complete the required copies without having to calculate the number of copies remaining. The print operation is thus:

```
┌─ Print ─────────────────────────────────────────────────
│ ΔCopier
│ copies! : ℕ
│ refund! : bag COIN
├─────────────────────────────────────────────────────────
│ copies! = min {paper, requiredCopies, copiesBought credit}
│ requiredCopies' = max {requiredCopies − copies!, 1}
│ refund! ⊎ money' = money
│ ∃ refundDue : ℕ •
│     refundDue = credit − Price * copies! ∧
│     value refund! ≤ refundDue ∧
│     ¬ ∃ coins, money'' : bag COIN •
│         coins ⊎ money'' = money ∧
│         value coins ≤ refundDue ∧
│         value coins > value refund!
│ credit' + (value refund!) + Price * copies! = credit
│ paper' = paper − copies!
└─────────────────────────────────────────────────────────
```

11.4   Reduction and enlargement

We now wish to extend the specification developed so far to model the enlargement and reduction facility. We must specify operations to load an original, set the scaling ratio and modify the print operation. This part of the specification is more challenging than that presented so far and can be omitted on a first reading.

In order to model an enlargement and reduction facility it is necessary to model original documents and copies of them. We are interested only in the graphical information present in a document and this can be modelled as a 2-dimensional grid of small dots of various colours. Each point on the 2-dimensional grid will have x and y coordinates and therefore the grid can be modelled by a subset of $\mathbb{N} \times \mathbb{N}$. We must associate a single dot of a certain colour with each point; this can be done using a function:

$$image : (\mathbb{N} \times \mathbb{N}) \nrightarrow COLOUR$$

where $COLOUR$ is a suitable given set. We will not worry about the size of the dot, but assume that the dots are sufficiently small and close together to provide the required resolution.

For a given resolution, the size of the graphical image can be modelled by the number of points.

```
A4Points == 1 .. 560 × 1 .. 900
A3Points == 1 .. 900 × 1 .. 1120
```

Every point in a document or copy must be associated with a dot of some colour, possibly white, and we therefore have the total function:

$$A4Image == A4Points \rightarrow COLOUR$$

We know that *white* must be a member of $COLOUR$; there are a few other values and so we can give a free type definition.

$$COLOUR ::= white \mid black \mid red \mid blue \mid yellow$$

A blank sheet of A4 paper would be modelled as an image in which every point within the boundary of the A4 sheet is white.

$$\mid\ BlankA4 : A4Points \rightarrow \{white\}$$

The process of transferring an image from one document to another is such that the image transferred overlays any existing image, with the proviso that only non-white dots are transferred. The function override operation could be used to overlay one image over another, while the range subtraction operation is convenient for removing the white dots.

$$copyPaperImage \oplus (originalImage \rhd \{white\})$$

If the original image is bigger than the copy paper it must be clipped. To clip an image to a given size we must specify that the domain of the image lies within a certain set of points. To clip to the A4 borders, for example, we have:

$$A4Points \lhd image$$

An image is enlarged by moving the dots further apart and reduced by moving them closer together; the colour is unaffected. The scaling ratio will be expressed as a percentage between $MinScale$ and $MaxScale$.

$$MinScale == 50$$
$$MaxScale == 200$$

The *scale* function enlarges or reduces an image by a given percentage. It does this by repositioning the dots that make up the image. For example:

$$scale(\{(10, 30) \mapsto red, (20, 40) \mapsto blue\}, 150) =$$
$$\{(15, 45) \mapsto red, (30, 60) \mapsto blue\}$$

The definition of *scale* is:

$$
\begin{array}{l}
scale : ((\mathsf{N} \times \mathsf{N}) \rightarrow COLOUR) \times \mathsf{N} \rightarrow ((\mathsf{N} \times \mathsf{N}) \rightarrow COLOUR) \\
\hline
\forall i : (\mathsf{N} \times \mathsf{N}) \rightarrow COLOUR;\ n : \mathsf{N} \bullet \\
\quad scale(i, n) = \\
\qquad \{x, y : \mathsf{N} \mid (x, y) \in \mathrm{dom}\ i \bullet \\
\qquad\qquad (x * n\ \mathrm{div}\ 100, y * n\ \mathrm{div}\ 100) \mapsto i(x, y)\}
\end{array}
$$

Every point to be scaled is multiplied by the scale factor and divided by 100. Note that the arithmetic expressions do not require parentheses since $*$ and div have the same precedence and function application associates to the left. The expression $i(x, y)$ is the colour of the image at the point (x, y).

The state

We noted earlier that the original image is not an input to the print operation and must be represented in the state. The same is true for the scaling ratio. We therefore add two components to the state definition to give:

$$
\begin{array}{l}
\_\_\ CopierScale _____ \\
paper : \mathbb{N} \\
requiredCopies : \mathbb{N} \\
money : \mathbb{N} \\
credit : \mathbb{N} \\
original : A3Points \nrightarrow COLOUR \\
ratio : MinScale \,..\, MaxScale \\
_____ \\
paper \leq FullPaperTray \\
requiredCopies > 0 \\
size\ money \leq FullCoinBox
\end{array}
$$

where the maximum size image that can be loaded is A3. The original is a partial function and so the image can be smaller than A3. Notice that we have not modified any other components and this suggests that the definition of *CopierScale* could be achieved more concisely using schema conjunction.

$$CopierScale \mathrel{\widehat{=}} Copier \wedge Scale$$

where *Scale* is:

$$
\begin{array}{l}
\_\_\ Scale _____ \\
original : A3Points \nrightarrow COLOUR \\
ratio : MinScale \,..\, MaxScale \\
_____
\end{array}
$$

We will continue to make use of schema operations in this way in order to reuse the previously defined schemas.

Initial state

The initial state is one in which the scaling ratio is 100%. The original document is not specified.

$$
\begin{array}{l}
\_\_\ InitScale _____ \\
Scale' \\
_____ \\
ratio' = 100
\end{array}
$$

We have:

$$InitCopierScale \mathrel{\widehat{=}} InitCopier \wedge InitScale$$

Operations

The *LoadPaper*, *NumberOfCopies* and *InsertMoney* operations remain unchanged apart from the need to add the new state components. We can do this by defining:

$$LoadPaperScale \mathrel{\widehat=} LoadPaper \land \Xi Scale$$

where $\Xi Scale$ indicates that the state components associated with scaling do not change when paper is loaded. (Recall that $\Xi Scale$ is the name of the schema that includes $Scale'$ and $Scale$ and specifies that the components of $Scale$ and $Scale'$ are pairwise equal.) The other operations are:

$$NumberOfCopiesScale \mathrel{\widehat=} NumberOfCopies \land \Xi Scale$$
$$InsertMoneyScale \mathrel{\widehat=} InsertMoney \land \Xi Scale$$

We require new operations, however, to load an original image and set the scaling ratio.

Loading the original

The only part of the state that changes as a result of the *LoadOriginal* operation is the value of the *original* observation.

```
┌─ LoadOrig ──────────────────────────────────
│ ΔScale
│ original? : A3Points ⇸ COLOUR
├─────────────────────────────────────────────
│ original' = original?
│ ratio' = ratio
└─────────────────────────────────────────────
```

We can thus define:

$$LoadOriginal \mathrel{\widehat=} \Xi Copier \land LoadOrig$$

Selecting the scaling ratio

Again, most of the state is unaffected by the *SelectScale* operation.

```
┌─ SelectScale ───────────────────────────────
│ ΔScale
│ r? : MinScale .. MaxScale
├─────────────────────────────────────────────
│ original' = original
│ ratio' = r?
└─────────────────────────────────────────────
```

We can thus define:

$$SetRatio \mathrel{\widehat=} \Xi Copier \land SelectScale$$

Print

The print operation outputs a number of suitably scaled copies of the original; we output a bag of images. We have already defined an operation that specifies the number of copies produced; hence, the following schema makes use of this number *copyCount*.

$$
\begin{array}{|l}
\hline
\_\,PrintImage\,\rule{4cm}{0.4pt} \\
\Delta\,CopierScale \\
copies!\,:\,\text{bag}\ A4Image \\
copyCount\,:\,\mathbb{N} \\
\hline
copies!\,= \\
\qquad \{(BlankA4 \oplus (A4Points \lhd scale(original, ratio))) \mapsto copyCount\} \\
\hline
\end{array}
$$

The variable *copyCount* is the number of copies that should be printed. This variable is intended to take the value of the variable *copies*! in the schema *Print* given earlier where we have:

$$copies! = min\ \{paper, requiredCopies, copiesBought\ credit\}$$

Schema renaming can be used to rename *copies*! as *copyCount*. The other aspects of the print operation are also defined in the *Print* schema given earlier. We can thus define the complete schema for the print operation as:

$$PrintScale \mathrel{\widehat{=}} (Print[copyCount/copies!] \wedge PrintImage) \setminus (copyCount)$$

Notice that we no longer wish to output the number of copies, so *copyCount* is not decorated with a '!' and also hidden.

Exercise 11.2 ** Extend the specification given above to include two sizes of copy paper, A4 and A3. An operation is required to select the copy paper and some means must be provided to load A3 paper. There are two subcases of the print operation to consider, depending on the size of the copy paper. Make as much use as possible of schema operations.   □

Chapter 12

Specification and Formal Methods

12.1 Introduction

In this chapter we place the topic of this book, formal specification, in the wider context of formal methods and the development of systems in general. We describe the aims of formal methods and give a very brief insight into the way in which formal specifications in Z can be incorporated into a formal method. We conclude with a short guide to further study.

The development of complex software and hardware systems is an expensive and error-prone business. Consequently, a lot of effort has been directed at establishing efficient methods for the development of such systems. The general study of methods is known as methodology. Although methods are undoubtedly important, it is generally accepted that there is no method that can be regarded as the 'holy grail' or 'silver bullet' of systems development. Most people will agree that different methods are appropriate in different circumstances and there is by no means universal agreement on the best method for a given set of circumstances.

Having said this, however, an important theme in practically all methods is the separation of concerns, that is, the breaking down of a complex problem into several less complex problems; a well-established separation is that between 'what' and 'how', specification and implementation. This distinction is of course relative to a particular stage in the development process. A drawing, for example, may be a specification which is implemented as a prototype and that prototype may then serve as a specification for a final finished product (recall the discussion in §1.3 and §1.7).

In this book we have shown how formal specifications can be produced but we have said very little about how they might be used. In Chapter 1 we argued that formal specifications are superior as far as precision is concerned. One of the most important advantages of the precision inherent in a formal specification is the possibility of establishing a very high degree of confidence in the fidelity of an implementation, that is, that an implementation behaves precisely as the specification dictates.

Testing is the usual process by which confidence in an implementation is established. A number of test cases are selected and the output of the system for each case is compared to that given in the specification, typically an informal specification. Unfortunately, it is not possible to test any but the most trivial systems fully because of the enormous number of test cases that would have to be examined. This is certainly true of state-based systems, which include computer-based systems.

With a state-based system it is not possible to extrapolate from a few successful test cases because its behaviour in similar states may be radically different. We do not have the same kind of problem with non-state-based engineered artefacts. For example, once we know a bridge can support a given weight, there is little point in testing it with smaller weights.

12.2   Verification

Verification provides an alternative to testing which solves the problem of untested cases. To verify an implementation is to demonstrate that it will perform as specified in all cases even though there may be too many cases to test individually. We will explain how an implementation is verified by considering a very simple example.

Recall the partial function:

$$onHire : EQUIP \nrightarrow CUSTOMER$$

used in the specification of the sports equipment hiring example of Chapter 8. We chose a function because mathematically it captures exactly the required structure between the sets $EQUIP$ and $CUSTOMER$. This is not a good choice, however, for writing a computer program to implement the equipment hiring system. A common technique for representing functions of this kind in a computer program is to use two 'parallel' arrays, one to store elements of $EQUIP$, the other elements of $CUSTOMER$. The association is maintained by storing each element of a pair at corresponding positions in the arrays. So for example, if $helmet7$ is stored at the ith element of the equipment array then the customer hiring $helmet7$ is stored at the ith element of the customer array. In this way, each of the sets $EQUIP$ and $CUSTOMER$ is effectively represented by a sequence.

To exploit the array data structure, we thus produce a second specification of the same system but in this specification we do not employ a function; we use instead two sequences since these are similar to arrays.

> *equipment* : seq $EQUIP$
> *customer* : seq $CUSTOMER$

The different model for the state means that operations are defined differently, so in the first specification a simple operation to record an item of equipment hired to a customer would contain the predicate:

$$onHire' = onHire \cup \{item? \mapsto customer?\}$$

whereas in the second specification the same operation would contain the predicates:

> $equipment' = equipment \frown \langle item? \rangle$
> $customer' = customer \frown \langle customer? \rangle$

Notice that in this second specification, the various items of equipment and customers are ordered but this order is not present in the definition of *onHire*. In the sense of modelling the behaviour of the equipment hiring system, the first specification is superior since it contains no extraneous information. Recall the discussion in §1.4 on the simplicity of the model.

Both specifications are intended to describe the same system but how can we ensure that this is so? In fact, what precisely do we mean when we say that the two specifications describe the same system? The attempt to answer these questions in formal terms will lead us to establish the criteria by which the two specifications should be compared.

In the discussion that follows, we will call the specification based on a function simply 'the specification' and the second specification which employs sequences 'the implementation' because it is directed at specifying how the hiring system might be implemented. There is a potentially confusing use of the word 'specification' here. A formal specification is of course a specification in the sense that it specifies something. A description, formal or informal, of the requirements for a system is often also called a specification. The meaning will be clear, however, from the context.

Consider the state space of each specification. Let us suppose that in the initial state, no equipment is on hire. In the specification the corresponding state is the empty function; in the implementation, it is two empty sequences. If two items of equipment are on hire then in the specification this is modelled by a state in which the function *onHire* contains two pairs. In the implementation, we have a choice of states because it is possible to use many different sequences to represent a single set. In general, the implementation has a larger state space than the specification. We would, however, expect each state in the implementation to correspond to at most one state in the specification. This is because the specification states typically carry no excess information. If two states differ in the specification then they represent different functions.

In contrast, if two states differ in the implementation they need not represent different functions. Figure 12.1 illustrates the relationships between the states in the state space of the implementation and states in the state space of the specification. States in both these state spaces are related to the states they represent in the application.

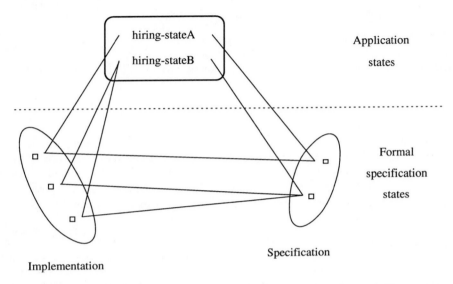

Figure 12.1: The correspondence of states between an implementation, a specification and the application

We can formally specify the relationships between the formal states illustrated in Figure 12.1 by using a schema that includes as components the components of both formal states. For every element in the function *onHire* there should be corresponding elements in the two sequences and vice versa; we thus have the schema:

$$
\begin{array}{l}
\_\,StateCorrespondence\,\underline{\hspace{5cm}} \\
onHire : EQUIP \leftrightarrow CUSTOMER \\
equipment : \text{seq}\, EQUIP \\
customer : \text{seq}\, CUSTOMER \\
\rule{6cm}{0.4pt} \\
\forall\, e : EQUIP;\ c : CUSTOMER \bullet \\
\quad onHire\ e = c \Leftrightarrow \exists\, i : \mathbb{N} \bullet equipment\ i = e \wedge customer\ i = c
\end{array}
$$

Notice that we have allowed the sequence representation to contain repeated entries.

Let us now consider how we might specify the conditions under which an operation defined in the implementation is essentially the same as an operation defined in the specification. Consider the operation of hiring an item of available equipment to a customer. We discussed earlier how this operation would be defined in the specification and in the implementation; call these operations $HireItem_{spec}$ and $HireItem_{imp}$ respectively. Let us take some arbitrary state in the state space of the specification for which the precondition of $HireItem_{spec}$ is true. We would expect the corresponding state in the implementation also to satisfy the precondition of $HireItem_{imp}$. If the $HireItem_{imp}$ operation is performed in this state we would expect any after-state to correspond to some after-state in the specification state space resulting from the performance of $HireItem_{spec}$. The relationships can best be understood by referring to the diagram in Figure 12.2.

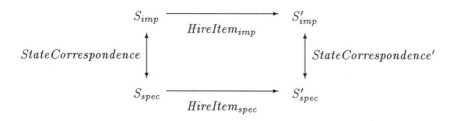

Figure 12.2: The correspondence between operations in the specification and the implementation

We can use the diagram of Figure 12.2 to give a process-style description of what it means for two operations to be equivalent. We consider the change of state due to the hiring of an item of equipment by a customer. We will assume, as is typical, that the implementation executes on a computer but that the specification does not. At some point in a process, the state of the equipment hiring system is represented by S_{spec} in the specification. Since the specification does not execute we cannot tangibly perform the $HireItem_{spec}$ operation and so we look to the implementation. The program is in the state S_{imp} which is one of the many possible states corresponding to S_{spec}. The program executes the operation to hire an item of equipment by performing $HireItem_{imp}$ and the resulting state is S'_{imp}. This state corresponds to S'_{spec}, an after-state of the operation $HireItem_{spec}$.

The *StateCorrespondence* schema provides the link between the two formal specifications and together with the formal definitions of the operations $HireItem_{spec}$ and $HireItem_{imp}$ it is possible to prove that the process illustrated in the diagram in Figure 12.2 is achievable. If we can show this for every operation of the system then we have verified the implementation with respect to the specification. In short, the implementation behaves precisely as the specification dictates that it should.

The advantage of verification over testing is that with verification we need consider only each operation on a case-by-case basis and there are likely to be considerably fewer operations than states in a typical system. We should point out that in practice, the verification of large systems is not an easy task, in terms of both the amount and complexity of the mathematics involved. Software tools are becoming available for supporting this work. The simplest are syntax checkers and type checkers which can be used to ensure a specification does not contain basic errors. These tools are completely automated and require no human intervention.

The process of performing a proof, however, is not something that can be completely automated. The task seems to be inherently creative in a way that cannot be captured within a systematic procedure. As a result, software tools are available to assist with the process of finding a proof and if the proof is expressed as a sequence of very basic steps, a software tool can check the proof. In all, this means that a human must perform the essential work in a proof.

Formal methods provide a formal language and a verification system and as such are powerful techniques. As with many techniques, however, their effectiveness in practice depends upon the judgement and skill with which they are applied. Activities other than specification and verification are, of course, required in the development of complex systems. Very large projects, for example, raise particular problems of work organization. There is an established class of structured methods that are part of software engineering and many advocates of formal methods see particular roles for specification and verification with these structured methods.

12.3   Further study

We have been selective in our coverage of the Z notation in this book. You may find more complete treatments in more advanced books, such as [6, 23, 16]. A number of large case studies of the use of Z are described in [11].

A significant omission from this book is a treatment of formal proof. Indeed, some would argue that we misrepresent formal specification by omitting serious study of formal proof. In contrast to the presentation we have given, which focused on semantics, a formal treatment of proof requires a deductive system. The development of formal systems for Z is a relatively recent activity. A preliminary proposal is given in [4]. Applications of logic in computer science are discussed in [7, 2, 18, 3]. These include computer architecture, verification of programs, logic programming, treatment of temporal aspects of systems, and deductive databases.

There are many textbooks on discrete mathematics, such as [10], and these contain a wealth of material on sets, relations and functions. There are many concepts we have omitted which may help in the presentation of a specification, and in reasoning about what has been specified. These include equivalence relations and partial orders, for example.

One important difference between the theory of sets we have presented and that given in typical discrete mathematics text books relates to types. Z is based on a typed logic and sets are typed. Most discrete mathematics books consider untyped set theory. As it will be liable to the difficulties we outlined in § 4.4, such set theory is often referred to as naive set theory. The presentation and study of naive set theory survives, in spite of the technical difficulties, because of its intuitive simplicity.

Z is a model-based[1] formal specification language. That is to say, a specification is constructed from sets, with the aid of logic. VDM-SL[13, 1, 21] is another model-based specification language. Algebraic specification [21] is an alternative approach in which the specification is not based on a model. An algebraic specification defines a system simply in terms of relationships between the operations involved. A good collection of case studies using a range of approaches to specification is [8].

---

[1] Here we use the term 'model' in the sense of set-theoretic semantics.

Bibliography

[1] D. Andrews and D. Ince, *Practical formal methods with VDM*, McGraw-Hill, 1991.

[2] R. C. Backhouse, *Program construction and verification*, Prentice-Hall, 1986.

[3] M. Ben-Ari, *Mathematical logic for computer science*, Prentice-Hall, 1993.

[4] S. M. Brien and J. E. Nicholls, *Z base standard version 1.0*, Technical Monograph PRG-107, Programming Research Group, University of Oxford, 1992.

[5] B. Cohen, W. T. Harwood and M. I. Jackson, *The specification of complex systems*, Addison-Wesley, 1986.

[6] A. Diller, *Z: an introduction to formal methods* (2nd edition), Wiley, 1994.

[7] J. H. Gallier, *Logic for computer science: foundations of automatic theorem proving*, Harper and Row, 1986.

[8] N. Gehani and A. D. McGettrick, *Software specification techniques*, Addison-Wesley, 1986.

[9] A. W. Goodman, *Modern calculus with analytical geometry, volume 1*, MacMillan, 1967.

[10] R. P. Grimaldi, *Discrete and combinatorial mathematics: an applied introduction* (2nd edition), Addison-Wesley, 1989.

[11] I. Hayes (Ed.), *Specification case studies*, 2nd edition, Prentice-Hall, 1993.

[12] D. C. Ince, *An introduction to discrete mathematics and formal system specification*, Oxford University Press, 1988.

[13] C. B. Jones, *Systematic software development using VDM* (2nd Edition), Prentice-Hall, 1990.

[14] D. Lightfoot, *Formal specification using Z*, Macmillan Press, 1991.

[15] M. A. McMorran and J. E. Nicholls, *Z user manual*, Technical Report TR 12.274, IBM (Hursley Park), 1989.

[16] B. Potter, J. Sinclair and D. Till, *An introduction to formal specification and Z*, Prentice-Hall, 1991.

[17] B. Ratcliffe, *Introducing specification using Z: a practical case study approach*, McGraw-Hill, 1994.

[18] V. Sperschneider and G. Antoniou, *Logic: a foundation for computer science*, Addison-Wesley, 1991.

[19] J. M. Spivey, *Understanding Z: A Specification language and its formal semantics*, Cambridge University Press, 1988.

[20] J. M. Spivey, *The Z notation: a reference manual*, 2nd edition, Prentice-Hall, 1992.

[21] J. G. Turner and T. L. McCluskey, *The construction of formal specifications: an introduction to the model-based and algebraic approaches*, McGraw-Hill, 1994.

[22] J. C. P. Woodcock and M. Loomes, *Software engineering mathematics*, Pitman 1989 (Reprinting).

[23] J. B. Wordsworth, *Software development with Z*, Addison-Wesley, 1992.

Appendix A

Solutions to the exercises

Chapter 1

1.1. A simple model is:

$$pop_{t+1} = pop_t - (catchRate * pop_t) + (birthRate * pop_{t-1})$$
$$catchRate \leq 1$$
$$catchRate \geq 0$$
$$birthRate \geq 0$$

If we have a quota, this is an additional constraint and so we might have:

$$pop_{t+1} = pop_t - caught + (birthRate * pop_{t-1})$$
$$caught = min\{catchRate * pop_t, quota\}$$

1.2. Use a single variable to count the number of empty spaces. This count is increased and decreased as cars come and go. The barrier remains closed if this variable has a value of 500.

1.3. Use a single variable to represent the bank balance. This balance is increased and decreased as payments and withdrawals are made. No withdrawal is allowed if the balance would be negative.

Chapter 2

2.1. In Figure 2.2 the number of ordinary cars in the car park exceeds the capacity of the car park. In Figure 2.3 the number of ordinary cars is less than zero. In Figure 2.4 one of the elements of the 'set' of passes in use is not a valid pass.

2.2. The argument given in this exercise is put forward to suggest that some of what we have defined is unnecessary. However, we cannot afford to rely on how the operations are used to ensure the integrity of the model. Moreover, such an argument makes no allowance for errors in the system, such as a fault in the car park apparatus.

2.3. *carParkCapacity* denotes the capacity of the car park. This is not a state observation, and so it is not a quantity where it makes sense to talk of a value before an operation and a value after an operation. We would thus not expect the specification to include the variable *carParkCapacity'*.

2.4.

$$
\begin{array}{|l}
carParkCapacity : \mathbb{Z} \\
\hline
carParkCapacity \geq 0 \\
carParkCapacity \leq 500
\end{array}
$$

2.5. In each state in the state space, the number of ordinary cars in the car park is between zero and *carParkCapacity*. In each such state one of the subcase properties is satisfied, and an after-state is defined. Thus the operation is total.

2.6. The operation to enquire how many ordinary spaces remain may simply output the number of ordinary spaces, say *n!*, that remain. Since there is always some number of spaces remaining, there are no subcases to this operation. This operation does not result in a change of state. The operation may be specified:

$$
\begin{array}{|l}
\underline{SpacesRemaining} \\
\Xi CarPark \\
n! : \mathbb{Z} \\
r! : REPORT \\
\hline
n! = carParkCapacity - ordinaryCars \\
r! = success
\end{array}
$$

2.8. An operation to enquire whether a pass is in use must have the pass as input. The answer to the question depends on whether the pass is in use, and so there will be two subcases. There is no change of state. We shall require an output which states whether or not the pass is in use. We shall not use the report output for this purpose. In particular we shall not make use of the schema *PassInUse*. This is because we do not wish to make reports serve two purposes. We shall, instead, have a type for the values of this new output:

$$
STATUS ::= passBeingUsed \\
\mid passNotBeingUsed
$$

We have been careful here to ensure that this type has no values in common with the type *REPORT*. The operation may then be specified as follows:

```
┌─ PassBeingUsed ──────────────────────────────────────
│ Ξ CarPark
│ p? : PASS
│ s! : STATUS
│ r! : REPORT
├──────────────────────────────────────────────────────
│ p? ∈ passesInUse
│ s! = passBeingUsed
│ r! = success
└──────────────────────────────────────────────────────
```

```
┌─ PassNotBeingUsed ───────────────────────────────────
│ Ξ CarPark
│ p? : PASS
│ s! : STATUS
│ r! : REPORT
├──────────────────────────────────────────────────────
│ p? ∉ passesInUse
│ s! = passNotBeingUsed
│ r! = success
└──────────────────────────────────────────────────────
```

The complete operation is then:

$$EnquireAboutPass \mathrel{\widehat{=}} PassBeingUsed \lor PassNotBeingUsed$$

2.9. An operation to output the set of passes in use must have a set of passes as output. Since there is always some set of passes in use, this operation does not have any subcases. This operation does not result in a change of state. The key to this exercise is to note that the output is a set of passes, and so will have type $\mathbb{P}\ PASS$. The operation may be specified:

```
┌─ PassesInUse ────────────────────────────────────────
│ Ξ CarPark
│ p! : ℙ PASS
│ r! : REPORT
├──────────────────────────────────────────────────────
│ p! = passesInUse
│ r! = success
└──────────────────────────────────────────────────────
```

2.10. In each state in the state space, the pass input is either in the set of passes in use or it is not. In each of these cases an after-state is defined. Hence, the operation is total.

Chapter 3

3.1. The complete description of the blocks scene of Figure 3.1 requires the addition of the following statements to those given in the text:

block a is on the floor	block b is on top of block a
block b is above block a	block f is on top of block b
block f is above block b	block f is above block a
block g is on top of block f	block g is above block f
block g is above block b	block g is above block a
block g is clear	block c is on the floor
block c is clear	

3.2. The complete description of the blocks scene of Figure 3.1 may now be given as:

if block x is on top of block y then block x is above block y
if block x is above block y and block y is above block z
then block x is above block z

block a is on the floor	block b is on top of block a
block f is on top of block b	block g is on top of block f
block g is clear	block c is on the floor
block c is clear	block d is on the floor
block e is on top of block d	block e is clear

3.3.

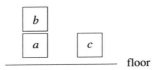

We see that in this scene block b is clear. This is justified from the description as follows. We interpret 'a block is clear unless it has something on top of it' to mean 'either a block is clear or it has something on top of it'. Since block b does not have anything on top of it, it must be clear. Block c is on the floor and clear.

3.4.

i. $\neg\,(\neg\,R \wedge P \vee Q) \Rightarrow R$

ii. $\neg\,P \Rightarrow ((P \Rightarrow Q) \Rightarrow R) \wedge S$

3.5.

   i. $(P \Rightarrow Q) \Leftrightarrow ((\neg Q) \Rightarrow (\neg P))$

   ii. $(P \vee (Q \wedge (\neg R))) \vee (Q \wedge P)$

3.6. The truth table for the predicate $(P \Rightarrow Q) \wedge (Q \Rightarrow P)$ is:

P	Q	$P \Rightarrow Q$	$Q \Rightarrow P$	$(P \Rightarrow Q) \wedge (Q \Rightarrow P)$
T	T	T	T	T
T	F	F	T	F
F	T	T	F	F
F	F	T	T	T

This demonstrates that $(P \Rightarrow Q) \wedge (Q \Rightarrow P)$ has the same truth-value properties as $P \Leftrightarrow Q$, which is what we would have expected. That this is the case lends weight to the assertion that we have selected the appropriate truth table for implication.

3.7. Often sentences such as these may be interpreted in a variety of ways, and the appropriate logical representation depends on which reading you choose. Furthermore, the analysis depends on what constituents are identified.

Let us consider 'He is a millionaire, but never gives to charity', with the constituents 'he is a millionaire' and 'never gives to charity'. Following the procedure for constructing a truth table illustrated in the text, you will see that conjunction is appropriate.

There are several ways to interpret 'This car is available with a petrol or a diesel engine'. If this statement is made by a salesman in a car showroom, it is about a model of car in general and would mean that the model range includes both petrol and diesel engines. In this case the connective is a conjunction. On the other hand, the statement could be about the particular car a customer is going to purchase, in which case the statement should be interpreted to say that the particular car will have a petrol engine, or a diesel engine, but not both. In this case the connective is the negation of equivalence again. Examples such as this emphasize the superiority of logic over English for giving precise descriptions.

3.8.

P	Q	$P \vee Q$	$\neg P$	$(P \vee Q) \wedge \neg P$	$(P \vee Q) \wedge \neg P \Rightarrow Q$
T	T	T	F	F	T
T	F	T	F	F	T
F	T	T	T	T	T
F	F	F	T	F	T

3.9. We note:

$$P \Rightarrow (Q \Rightarrow R) \Leftrightarrow P \wedge Q \Rightarrow R \Leftrightarrow Q \wedge P \Rightarrow R \Leftrightarrow Q \Rightarrow (P \Rightarrow R)$$

It would, of course, be possible to demonstrate this logical equivalence using truth tables.

3.10.

   i. $(onFloor \; b) \Rightarrow \neg (b \; onTopOf \; a)$

   ii. $(onFloor \; a) \wedge \neg (onFloor \; b)$

3.11.

$$\forall x, y : BLOCK \bullet (x \; onTopOf \; y) \Rightarrow (x \; above \; y)$$
$$\forall x, y, z : BLOCK \bullet (x \; above \; y) \wedge (y \; above \; z) \Rightarrow (x \; above \; z)$$

3.12.   The statement 'every block is either clear or has a unique block on top of it' includes an implicit 'but not both'. So as the example on page 57 suggests we may use the negation of equivalence:

$$\neg (\forall x : BLOCK \bullet clear \; x \Leftrightarrow \exists_1 \; y : BLOCK \bullet y \; onTopOf \; x)$$

3.13. The predicate:

$$\exists_1 \; y : BLOCK \bullet \forall x : BLOCK \bullet (\neg \; clear \; x \Rightarrow y \; onTopOf \; x)$$

states that there is just one block that is on top of any block that is not clear. A scene for which this is true may have at most one tower, and if there is a tower it must have height 2. Since the predicate begins with a $\exists_1$ there must actually be one block in the scene. Thus, for example, the blocks scene given as the solution to Exercise 3.3 is a suitable answer to this question. In addition, a scene with just one clear block would be a suitable answer since an implication is true whenever the antecedent is false.

3.14. In:

$$\exists x : \mathsf{N} \bullet (x \geq y \wedge \forall x : \mathsf{N} \bullet (\exists y : \mathsf{N} \bullet x > y) \wedge x > y)$$

the first occurrence of x is a binding occurrence, and it binds the second occurrence of x. The third occurrence of x is a different binding occurrence, and it binds the remaining occurrences of x. The first and fourth occurrences of y are free. The second occurrence of y is a binding occurrence which binds the third occurrence.

3.15. The formula:

$$\exists z : \mathbb{Z} \bullet z \geq 0 \wedge x = y + z$$

expresses the property that x is less than or equal to y. This property may also be expressed $x \leq y$, $x < y + 1$, and so on.

3.16. The predicate:

$$(\forall x : X \bullet P) \Rightarrow (\exists x : X \bullet P)$$

is true if whenever $\forall x : X \bullet P$ is true, $\exists x : X \bullet P$ must also be true. Superficially, then, it might appear as if this predicate is true. However, there is a catch. $\forall x : X \bullet P$ is true if there are no possible values of x, that is, X is an empty set. Under these circumstances $\exists x : X \bullet P$ is not true, since it requires the existence of something to satisfy P.

3.17. Consider the predicates:

$$\forall x : \mathbb{Z} \bullet (x = 0 \vee \neg (x = 0))$$
$$(\forall x : \mathbb{Z} \bullet x = 0) \vee (\forall x : \mathbb{Z} \bullet \neg x = 0)$$

The first is true, the second false.

Chapter 4

4.1.

$$\begin{array}{|l}
\hline
clear\_ : \mathbb{P}\, BLOCK \\
\hline
\forall x : BLOCK \bullet \\
\quad onFloor\ x \Leftrightarrow x \in \{a, c, d\}
\end{array}$$

4.2. $5 \mathbin{..} 5 = \{5\}$

4.3. $5 \mathbin{..} 4 = \varnothing$

4.4.

   i. $\{x : \mathbb{Z} \mid x * x \in 1 \mathbin{..} 100 \bullet x\}$

   ii. $\{b : BLOCK \mid \neg\, floor\ b\}$

4.5. It is the set of prime numbers. In practice, there is a largest known prime, and so the membership of this set beyond that number is not known. This limitation is practical, rather than theoretical, of course.

4.6. The set of squares of the odd numbers in the set $1 \mathbin{..} 100$ is:

$$\{x : 1 \mathbin{..} 100 \mid \neg\, even\ x \bullet x * x\}$$

4.7.

   i. $\mathbb{P}\varnothing = \varnothing$

   ii. $\mathbb{P}\{\{a\}, \{a, b\}\} = \{\varnothing, \{\{a\}\}, \{\{a, b\}\}, \{\{a\}, \{a, b\}\}\}$

4.8. By the definition:

$$\varnothing \subseteq S \Leftrightarrow (\forall\, x : T \bullet x \in \varnothing \Rightarrow x \in S)$$

for some type T. Now $x \in \varnothing$ is false for all possible values of x, and so the implication is true.

4.9.

   i. $\{2, 4, 6, 8\} \cup \{4, 6, 7\} = \{2, 4, 6, 7, 8\}$

   ii. $\{2, 4, 6, 8\} \cup \varnothing = \{2, 4, 6, 8\}$

4.10. No. For example, $\#(\{1, 2, 3\} \cup \{2\}) = \#\{1, 2, 3\}$

4.11.

   i. $\{2, 4, 6, 8\} \cap \{3, 5, 7\} = \varnothing$

   ii. $\{2, 4, 6, 8\} \cap \{4, 6, 7\} = \{4, 6\}$

   iii. $\{2, 4, 6, 8\} \cap \varnothing = \varnothing$

4.12.

   i. $\{2, 4, 6, 8\} \setminus \{4, 6, 7\} = \{2, 8\}$

   ii. $\{2, 4, 6, 8\} \setminus \varnothing = \{2, 4, 6, 8\}$

   iii. $\{2, 4, 6, 8\} \setminus \{6\} = \{2, 4, 8\}$

   iv. $\varnothing \setminus \{5\} = \varnothing$

4.13. No. For example, $\#(\{1, 2, 3\} \setminus \{4\}) = \#\{1, 2, 3\}$

4.14.   The key to the modification is to observe that the count for a set is equal to the sum obtained by adding 1 for every element in the set. This gives:

$$sum\,\varnothing = 0$$
$$sum\{x\} = 1$$
$$sum(X \cup Y) = sumX + sumY - sum(X \cap Y)$$

where $sum\{x\} = x$ has been replaced with $sum\{x\} = 1$, since we no longer need to know the size of the element, but simply that it is present.

4.15.

$$
\begin{array}{|l}
\hline
permitLimit : \mathbb{Z} \\
\hline
permitLimit \geq 0 \\
\end{array}
$$

4.16. It would not be sufficient, in this example. The set $registered'$ is not completely specified by these alternative predicates and $permits'$ is not defined. The important distinction between:

$$registered' = registered \cup \{c?\}$$

and:

$$c? \in registered'$$

is that the latter does not require that all the members of $registered$ are also in $registered'$. This is required for the integrity of the model in this example, and so we must use the former definition of $registered'$.

This example serves to emphasize the role of the two variables $registered$ and $registered'$: $registered$ denotes the value of the set of cars registered before the operation is performed; $registered'$ denotes the value of the set of cars registered after the operation has been performed. In this specification, the value of $registered'$ must be completely defined. You must not assume that part of its value is inherited from $registered$, which is simply another variable which happens to have a similar name.

4.17. Although we can infer that $c? \notin permits'$, without the additional predicate $permits' = permits \setminus \{c?\}$ we cannot infer what elements are in the set $permits'$. Thus we cannot simplify $DeregisterPlusPermit$ in the manner suggested.

4.18. For any state in the state space and any input $c?$, either $c? \notin registered$, $c? \in registered \setminus permits$, or $c? \in permits$. In each case suitable after-state and output are defined. Thus this operation is total.

4.19. If we can no longer deregister a car that also holds a permit, then we have to reconsider the schema $DeregisterPlusPermit$. If $c?$ holds a permit, then there is to be no change of state. The replacement schema is:

$$
\begin{array}{|l}
\hline
\_\,HoldsPermit\,\rule{4cm}{0.4pt} \\
\Xi RegistrationDB \\
c? : CAR \\
r! : REPORT \\
\hline
c? \in permits \\
r! = holdsPermit \\
\hline
\end{array}
$$

and the new operation for deregistering cars is:

$$Deregister \cong DeregisterOK \land Success \lor NotRegistered \lor HoldsPermit$$

4.20.

Consider an arbitrary state of the state space and an arbitrary input $c?$. In the state, either $c?$ holds a permit or it does not. If it does, one schema used to define the operation applies and suitable after-state and output are defined. If $c?$ does not hold a permit, either it is registered or it is not. A further schema deals with not being registered. If $c?$ is registered, either there are permits left to issue or there are not, and each of these cases is addressed by a schema. In each of the last three instances a suitable after-state and output are defined. Thus the operation is total.

4.21.

```
┌─ NumberPermitsLeft ──────────────────────────────
│ Ξ RegistrationDB
│ n! : ℕ
│ r! : REPORT
├──────────────────────────────────────────────────
│ n! = permitLimit − #permits
│ r! = success
└──────────────────────────────────────────────────
```

4.22.   Consider an arbitrary state of the state space and an arbitrary input $c?$. In the state, either $c?$ holds a permit or it does not. If it does, one schema used to define the operation applies and suitable after-state and output are defined. If $c?$ does not hold a permit, then either $c?$ is registered or it is not. Each of these cases is assessed by a schema in which suitable after-state and output are defined. Thus this operation is total.

4.23.

```
┌─ PermitHolder ───────────────────────────────────
│ Ξ RegistrationDB
│ c? : CAR
│ s! : STATUS
├──────────────────────────────────────────────────
│ c? ∈ permits
│ o! = permitHolder
└──────────────────────────────────────────────────
```

```
┌─ Unregistered ───────────────────────────────────
│ Ξ RegistrationDB
│ c? : CAR
│ s! : STATUS
├──────────────────────────────────────────────────
│ c? ∉ registered
│ s! = unregistered
└──────────────────────────────────────────────────
```

This schema is similar to *NotRegistered*, although for this example there would be no great gains from attempting to capitalize on this.

The full operation for enquiring about the status of a car is:

$$Enquire \mathrel{\widehat{=}} (RegisteredOnly \vee PermitHolder \vee Unregistered) \wedge Success$$

This operation is total.

4.24. You must introduce another state component, an integer, to record the total fees paid. The actual fees are unspecified, and they should be global constants in the specification.

4.25. Clearly we can model the stock of the bookshop as a set. However, the bookshop may have several copies of a particular book in stock, so in this example it is important to select the correct basic type.

Chapter 5

5.1.

$$\{prolog \mapsto jones, prolog \mapsto bottaci, smalltalk80 \mapsto bottaci,$$
$$modula2 \mapsto grubb, occam \mapsto rabhi\}$$

5.2. The relation *programmingSemesters* is depicted on the right of Figure 5.3.

5.3. The type was $\mathbb{F}\ T$ rather than $\mathbb{P}\ T$ since the comprehension involved the cardinality of sets of this type. The cardinality function can only be applied to finite sets.

5.4.

$$\{x, y : \mathbb{F}\ A \mid \#x < \#y \bullet x \mapsto y\}$$

This relation is many to many.

5.5. The type of a relation on a set A is $A \leftrightarrow A$.

5.6.

$$
\begin{array}{|l}
\_above\_ : BLOCK \leftrightarrow BLOCK \\
\hline
\forall x, y : BLOCK \bullet \\
\quad x\ above\ y \\
\qquad \Leftrightarrow x \mapsto y \in \{b \mapsto a, f \mapsto b, f \mapsto a, g \mapsto f, g \mapsto b, g \mapsto a, e \mapsto d\}
\end{array}
$$

5.7. The proper subset relation may be defined in terms of the subset relation:

$$\boxed{\begin{array}{l} =\![X]\!=\!\!=\!\!=\!\!=\!\!=\!\!=\!\!=\!\!=\!\!=\!\!=\!\!=\!\!=\!\!=\!\!=\!\!=\!\!=\!\!=\!\!=\!\!=\!\!= \\ \quad \_ \subset \_ : \mathbb{P}\,X \leftrightarrow \mathbb{P}\,X \\ \hline \forall\, S, T : \mathbb{P}\,X \bullet \\ \qquad S \subset T \Leftrightarrow S \subseteq T \wedge S \neq T \end{array}}$$

This schema defines a unique value for $\subset$ for each type T.

5.8. The generic definition of $\neq$ is:

$$\boxed{\begin{array}{l} =\![T]\!=\!\!=\!\!=\!\!=\!\!=\!\!=\!\!=\!\!=\!\!=\!\!=\!\!=\!\!=\!\!=\!\!=\!\!=\!\!=\!\!=\!\!=\!\!=\!\!= \\ \quad \_ \neq \_ : T \leftrightarrow T \\ \hline \forall\, x, y : T \bullet x \neq y \Leftrightarrow \neg\,(x = y) \end{array}}$$

5.9. If $R = \{1 \mapsto two, 2 \mapsto three, 4 \mapsto five, 5 \mapsto five\}$, $\operatorname{dom} R = \{1, 2, 4, 5\}$ and $\operatorname{ran} R = \{two, three, five\}$.

5.10.   The predicate $p1 \in \operatorname{ran} teachesProgramming$ expresses the property that $p1$ is taught by someone. The predicate $p2 \notin \operatorname{ran} teachesProgramming$ expresses the property that $p2$ is not taught by anyone.

5.11. If $R : A \leftrightarrow B$, $\operatorname{dom} R$ has the type $\mathbb{P}\,A$. $\operatorname{ran} R$ has the type $\mathbb{P}\,B$. Thus, $\operatorname{dom} R \cup \operatorname{ran} R$ is only well defined for a relation R on a set A.

5.12.

$$square \, \mathbin{\substack{\circ\\\circ}} \, plus5 = \{x : \mathbb{Z} \bullet x \mapsto x^2 + 5\}$$
$$plus5 \, \mathbin{\substack{\circ\\\circ}} \, square = \{x : \mathbb{Z} \bullet x \mapsto (x + 5)^2\}$$

5.13.

$$propertiesOfNumbers(\!|\{3, 37\}|\!) = \{small, odd, prime, large\}$$

5.14.

i. $propertiesOfNumbers^{\sim}(\!|\{small, prime\}|\!) = \{3, 6, 37\}$

ii. $propertiesOfNumbers \, \mathbin{\substack{\circ\\\circ}} \, propertiesOfNumbers^{\sim}$
$\quad = \{3 \mapsto 3, 3 \mapsto 6, 6 \mapsto 3, 6 \mapsto 6, 37 \mapsto 3, 37 \mapsto 37\}$

5.15. An example of the required relation is:

$$shareQues \cup \{paper3 \mapsto paper6, paper6 \mapsto paper3\}$$

5.16.

$$square \, \mathbin{\substack{\circ\\\circ}} \, square = \{x : \mathbb{Z} \bullet x \mapsto x * x * x * x\}$$

5.17. Consider $R_1, R_2 : \{a, b\} \leftrightarrow \{1\}$, with $R_1 = \{a \mapsto 1\}$ and $R_2 = \{b \mapsto 1\}$. $\operatorname{ran} R_1 = \{1\}$, $\operatorname{ran} R_2 = \{1\}$, so that $(\operatorname{ran} R_1) \cap (\operatorname{ran} R_2) = \{1\}$. However, $R_1 \cap R_2 = \varnothing$ and so $\operatorname{ran}(R_1 \cap R_2) = \varnothing$.

5.18. Let $R : \{a, b\} \leftrightarrow \{1\}$ be $R = \{a \mapsto 1, b \mapsto 1\}$. Let $S = \{a\}$ and $T = \{b\}$. Then $R(\!|S|\!) = \{1\}$, $R(\!|T|\!) = \{1\}$, and so $R(\!|S|\!) \cap R(\!|T|\!) = \{1\}$. However, $S \cap T = \varnothing$, and so $R(\!|S \cap T|\!) = \varnothing$.

5.19.

$$\{a : ACTIVITY;\ g : GROUP \mid (g, slot2) \mapsto a \in schedule \bullet a \mapsto g\}$$

5.20.   We need to state that every group does every activity during some session:

$$\forall g : GROUP;\ a : ACTIVITY \bullet \exists s : SLOT \bullet (g, s) \mapsto a \in schedule$$

5.21.

$$
\begin{aligned}
A \times (B \times C) = &\{1 \mapsto (a, four), 1 \mapsto (b, four), 1 \mapsto (c, four), 2 \mapsto (a, four),\\
&\quad 2 \mapsto (b, four), 2 \mapsto (c, four)\}\\
(A \times B) \times C = &\{(1, a) \mapsto four, (1, b) \mapsto four, (1, c) \mapsto four, (2, a) \mapsto four,\\
&\quad (2, b) \mapsto four, (2, c) \mapsto four\}\\
A \times B \times C = &\{(1, a, four), (1, b, four), (1, c, four), (2, a, four),\\
&\quad (2, b, four), (2, c, four), \}
\end{aligned}
$$

5.22. $(a, (b, c)) \in (A \times B) \times C$ is ill-typed, and therefore meaningless.

5.23.   The type is $LANGUAGE \leftrightarrow \mathbb{P}\, STAFF$.

5.24.

```
┌─ PrerequisitesOfSet ──────────────────────
│ Ξ PrerequisitesDB
│ msIn? : ℙ MODULE
│ msOut! : ℙ MODULE
├───────────────────────────────────────────
│ msOut! = prerequisites~(|msIn?|)
└
```

5.25.   The modules for which a given module is a prerequisite are the second elements of pairs for which the given module is the first element. Given the state relation *prerequisites* this operation maps naturally onto the relational image operator.

```
┌─ Offspring ───────────────────────────────
│ Ξ PrerequisitesDB
│ m? : MODULE
│ ms! : ℙ MODULE
├───────────────────────────────────────────
│ ms! = prerequisites(|{m?}|)
└
```

5.26. For descendants we again require the transitive closure.

Descendants _____
$\Xi PrerequisitesDB$
$m? : MODULE$
$ms! : \mathbb{P} \, MODULE$

$ms! = prerequisites^{+} (\!|\{m?\}|\!)$

5.27. You will need to introduce a second state component and a new state invariant. There will need to be additional operations to state what modules are being offered. All of the operations of the existing system will have additional subcases.

Chapter 6

6.1. The constants are:

$PASS$	a given set
$REPORT$	a free type definition
$CarPark$	the name of the schema describing the state
$PassDeparture$	the name of a schema describing an operation
$\mathbb{Z}$	a basic type
$<$	a relation

6.2. We know that $''$ can be added to any name to produce a new name. x is a legal name and hence x' is legal, in which case x'' is legal and so on.

6.3. The *OrdinaryEntry* operation will involve a state change when a car enters the car park.

6.4. The following table shows the values of the schema property for various cases.

small	profitable	small $\Rightarrow$ profitable
T	T	T
T	F	F
F	T	T
F	F	T

The property forbids investment only if the company is a small company and not profitable.

6.5. The action to buy shares of company $c?$ will be possible if the share price is less than or equal to all share prices, that is, 0 since $price? : \mathbb{N}$.

6.6.

$$SellAndBuyCompany \;\widehat{=}\; SellCompany \;\fatsemi\; BuyCompany[c?/d?]$$

6.7.

```
┌─ SellAndBuyCompany ──────────────────────────────────────
│ ΔPortfolio
│ c?, d? : COMPANY
├──────────────────────────────────────────────────────────
│ c? ∈ portfolio
│ ∃ portfolio″ : ℙ COMPANY; portfolioSize″ : ℤ •
│     d? ∉ portfolio″ ∧
│     portfolio″ = portfolio \ {c?} ∧
│     portfolio′ = portfolio″ ∪ {d?}
└──────────────────────────────────────────────────────────
```

6.8.

```
┌─ SellAndBuyCompany ──────────────────────────────────────
│ ΔPortfolio
│ c?, d? : COMPANY
├──────────────────────────────────────────────────────────
│ c? ∈ portfolio
│ d? ∉ portfolio \ {c?}
│ portfolio′ = (portfolio \ {c?}) ∪ {d?}
└──────────────────────────────────────────────────────────
```

Chapter 7

7.1. The definition states that every element in X must map to just one y. The partial function $\{1 \mapsto 1\}$ violates the definition.

7.2.

   i. Relation

  ii. Total function

 iii. Non-total function since some people have no cars

7.3. To take one example, $half\ 3 = 1$ but $double^\sim\ 3$ is not defined because 3 is not in dom $double^\sim$.

7.4. The total surjections.

7.5. Use a total injection:

$$marriedTo : MEN \rightarrowtail WOMEN$$

7.6. The total injections.

7.7.

  i. Total function

 ii. Bijection

iii. Partial injection

 iv. Relation, not a function

7.8. Assume the domain of a function is finite. Then since each element of the finite domain is related to at most one element from the target, the number of maplets can be no bigger than the size of the domain, that is, finite. The following infinite relation has a finite domain:

$$\{x : \mathbb{Z} \mid 1 \mapsto x\}$$

7.9. $\mathbb{Z} \nrightarrow \mathbb{Z}$ contains the functions $\{1 \mapsto 1\}$, $\{2 \mapsto 2\}$, and so on.

7.10. The inverse of a bijection is a bijection.

7.11. The inverse of a total injection is a partial injective surjection.

7.12. We know that:

$$f \in X \nrightarrow Y \Rightarrow \forall x : X; \ y_1, y_2 : Y \bullet f \ x = y_1 \wedge f \ x = y_2 \Rightarrow y_1 = y_2$$

similarly for g:

$$g \in Y \nrightarrow Z \Rightarrow \forall y : Y; \ z_1, z_2 : Z \bullet g \ y = z_1 \wedge g \ y = z_2 \Rightarrow z_1 = z_2$$

Assume:

$$(f \,\S\, g) \ x = z_1 \wedge (f \,\S\, g) \ x = z_2$$

Taking each conjunct:

$$(f \,\S\, g) \ x = z_1 \Rightarrow \exists y_1 : Y \bullet f \ x = y_1 \wedge g \ y_1 = z_1$$
$$(f \,\S\, g) \ x = z_2 \Rightarrow \exists y_2 : Y \bullet f \ x = y_2 \wedge g \ y_2 = z_2$$

If $f \ x = y_1 \wedge f \ x = y_2$ then $y_1 = y_2$ from the definition of a function; similarly g is a function and so $z_1 = z_2$.

7.13. Let $f == \{a \mapsto a, b \mapsto b, c \mapsto c\}$ and let $g == \{a \mapsto b\}$. Then:

$$f \oplus g = \{a \mapsto a, b \mapsto b, c \mapsto c\} \setminus \{a \mapsto a\} \cup g$$

but:

$$(f \setminus g) \cup g = \{a \mapsto a, b \mapsto b, c \mapsto c\} \cup g$$

which is not a function.

7.14. If *catalogue* is a surjection then we cannot add any new books to the catalogue.

7.15. We can insist that *catalogue* is not a surjection:

$$catalogue : BOOK \rightarrowtail CLASSNUMBER$$
$$catalogue \notin BOOK \twoheadrightarrow CLASSNUMBER$$

7.16. This is not possible in general but in this case we know that any book that is borrowed is not recorded as on loan. This means that *catalogue book?* $\notin$ dom *onLoan* and so $\oplus$ will not remove any elements from *onLoan*.

Chapter 8

8.1.

$$
\begin{array}{l}
\hline
\textit{HireFailInformative} \\
\hline
\Xi SportsHire \\
c? : CUSTOMER \\
e? : \mathbb{P}\,EQUIP \\
missing! : \mathbb{P}\,EQUIP \\
\hline
e? \not\subseteq free \\
missing! = e? \setminus free \\
\hline
\end{array}
$$

Chapter 9

9.1.

   i. $\langle margaret, dorrie, fran, janet \rangle$

  ii. $\langle niah, vicki, niah, jane \rangle$

 iii. $\langle 6, 5, 4, 3, 2, 1, 0 \rangle$

9.2. The third element of the sequence is missing.

9.3.

    ran s

9.4.

$\langle \rangle$

9.5.

$$
\begin{array}{l}
\boxed{\begin{array}{l}
[X] \\
\hline
last : \mathrm{seq}_1\ X\ \to\ X \\
front : \mathrm{seq}_1\ X\ \to\ \mathrm{seq}\ X \\
\hline
\forall\, s : \mathrm{seq}_1\ X\ \bullet \\
\qquad last\ s = s(\#s)\ \wedge \\
\qquad front\ s = \{\#s\} \lhd s
\end{array}}
\end{array}
$$

9.6.

$$
\begin{array}{l}
\boxed{\begin{array}{l}
[X] \\
\hline
last : \mathrm{seq}_1\ X\ \to\ X \\
front : \mathrm{seq}_1\ X\ \to\ \mathrm{seq}\ X \\
\hline
\forall\, s : \mathrm{seq}_1\ X\ \bullet \\
\qquad last\ s = head(rev\ s)\ \wedge \\
\qquad front\ s = tail(rev\ s)
\end{array}}
\end{array}
$$

9.7.   We require the notion of a subsequence. If s is a sequence then t is a subsequence of s if $t \subseteq s$ and t is a sequence. The union of a sequence s with a subsequence of s is a sequence and the intersection of a sequence s and a subsequence of s is a sequence.

9.8.

s

9.9.   If the ith element is 'beyond' the end of the sequence, no element is removed.

$$
\begin{array}{l}
\boxed{\begin{array}{l}
[X] \\
\hline
subseqTo : (\mathrm{seq}\ X \times \mathbb{N}_1)\ \nrightarrow \mathrm{seq}\ X \\
\hline
\forall\, s : \mathrm{seq}\ X;\ i : \mathbb{N}_1\ \bullet \\
\qquad subseqTo\ (s, i) = \{x : \mathbb{N}_1 \mid x \in \mathrm{dom}\ s \wedge x < i \bullet x \mapsto s\ x\}
\end{array}}
\end{array}
$$

9.10.

$$
\begin{array}{l}
\boxed{\begin{array}{l}
[X] \\
\hline
subseqToFrom : (\mathrm{seq}\ X \times \mathbb{N}_1)\ \nrightarrow \mathrm{seq}\ X \\
\hline
\forall\, s : \mathrm{seq}\ X;\ i : \mathbb{N}_1\ \bullet \\
\qquad subseqToFrom\ (s, i) = \\
\qquad\qquad subseqTo(s, i) \frown rev(subseqTo(rev\ s, \#s - i + 1))
\end{array}}
\end{array}
$$

9.11. Yes, we specify that a passenger joins the passport queue but that no passenger leaves the customs queue. If the passenger who joins the queue is in the customs queue then we violate that state invariant because that passenger ends up in both queues. The state invariant also states that each sequence is an injection and so a passenger cannot join the passport queue if he or she is already there.

Chapter 10

10.1.

    i. $\langle\!\langle beans, beans, beans, pasta, cheese, cheese \rangle\!\rangle$

    ii. $\langle\!\langle 0, 1, 1, 2, 2, 2, 3, 3, 3, 3, 4, 4, 4, 4, 4 \rangle\!\rangle$

10.2.

    i. $\{ milk \mapsto 2, bun \mapsto 2, apple \mapsto 1 \}$

    ii. $\{ 3 \mapsto 3, 0 \mapsto 2, 4 \mapsto 2, 2 \mapsto 3, 1 \mapsto 2 \}$

10.3.

    i. $\{ x : \mathbb{N} \mid x \leq 2 \bullet x \mapsto x + 1 \}$

    ii. $\{ x : \mathbb{N} \mid x \leq 4 \bullet x \mapsto 5 - x \}$

10.4. The values of $minOrderLevel?$ and $maxOrderLevel?$ are constrained.

Chapter 11

11.1.

$$
\begin{array}{|l}
\hline
\textit{PreNumberOfCopies} \underline{\hspace{5cm}} \\
\textit{Copier} \\
copies? : \mathbb{N} \\
\hline
\end{array}
$$

Index of symbols

Index

Notes

Notes

Notes

Notes